GA ARCHITECT

現代建築界で活躍している建築家の全貌を、気鋭の批評家書き下ろしの作家論、現地取材の写真、建築事務所の全面的な協力を得た詳細な図面、簡明な作品解説により立体的に編集した大型サイズの作品集。巻末には作品リスト、文献リストを収録。変貌を続ける現代建築家の肖像を現時点で正確に把握、記録することを試み、現代建築家全集の最新決定版を意図しました。各巻は建築家それぞれの個性を最大限に表現できるよう多彩な構成をとっています。

This is a series of monographs in which each issue is dedicated to an architect and is a complete chronological account of the architect's work to date. GA ARCHITECT is presented in a large format full of arresting photographs most of which are taken soley for the purpose of illustrating the articles and are heretofore unpublished. Each volume features texts by foremost architectural critics, historians or fellow designers, and the architect's own account of the works.

Japanese and English text
Size: 300×307mm
2–5, 9–11, 14号は絶版。
Vols. 2–5, 9–11 and 14 are out of print.

15 磯崎新
ARATA ISOZAKI 3 1991-2000

論文・作品解説：磯崎新
作品：ティーム・ディズニー・ビルディング／豊の国情報ライブラリー／京都コンサートホール／奈良町現代美術館・図書館／なら100年会館／ラ・コルーニャ人間科学館／バス・ミュージアム／静岡県コンベンション・アーツセンター〈グランシップ〉／静岡県舞台芸術センター／海市計画／オハイオ21世紀科学工業センター／秋吉台国際芸術村／他

Text: Arata Isozaki
Works: Team Disney Building; Toyo-nokuni Libraries for Cultural Resources; Kyoto Concert Hall; Nara Centennial Hall; DOMUS Interactive Museum about Humans; Buss Museum of Art; Shizuoka Convention & Arts Centr "Granship"; Shizuoka Performing Arts Center; Akiyoshi International Art Village; and others

264 total pages, 96 in color
並製：¥ 6,648／上製：¥ 9,333

16 安藤忠雄
TADAO ANDO 3 1994-2000

論文：W・J・R・カーティス
作品解説：安藤忠雄
作品：兵庫県立看護大学／大阪府立近つ飛鳥博物館／京都府立陶板名画の庭／兵庫県立木の殿堂／サントリーミュージアム／アイキャナー／リー邸／六甲の集合住宅Ⅲ／FABRICA（ベネトン・アートスクール）／淡路夢舞台／直島コンテンポラリーアートミュージアム・アネックス／ユネスコ瞑想空間／TOTOセミナーハウス／南岳山光明寺／他

Text: William J.R. Curtis/ Tadao Ando
Works: College of Nursing, Art and Science, Hyogo; Chikatsu-Asuka Historical Museum + Plaza; Garden of Fine Art, Kyoto; Museum of Wood; Suntory Museum; Eychaner /Lee House; Rokko Hausing III; FABRICA (Benetton Communication Research Center); Awaji-Yumebutai; Naoshima Contemporary Art Museum, Annex; Komyo-ji Temple; and others

276 total pages, 48 in color
¥ 6,648

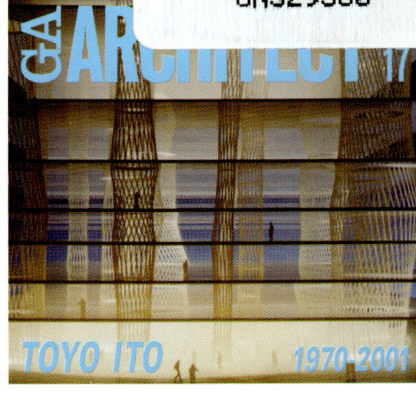

17 伊東豊雄
TOYO ITO 1970-2001

論文：原広司　作品解説：伊東豊雄
作品：アルミの家／中野本町の家／PMTビル―名古屋／笠間の家／シルバーハット／東京遊牧少女の包／横浜風の塔／中目黒Tビル／八代市立博物館・未来の森ミュージアム／養護老人ホーム八代市立保寿寮／八代市広域消防署／長岡リリックホール／大館樹海ドームパーク／大田区休養村とうぶ／大社文化プレイス／せんだいメディアテーク／他

Text: Hiroshi Hara/ Toyo Ito
Works: Aluminium House; White U; PMT Building; House in Kasama; Silver Hut; Exhibition Project for Pao, a Dwelling for Tokyo Nomad Women; Tower of Winds; T Building in Nakameguro; Yatsushiro Municipal Museum; Old People's Home in Yatsushiro; Yatsu-shiro Fire Station; T Hall in Taisha; Sendai Mediatheque; and others

217 total pages, 90 in color
¥ 5,700

TADAO ANDO DETAILS
安藤忠雄ディテール集

平面や断面、パースが重ね合わされ、スケールの異なるディテールが挿入された三次元性を持つ独自の図法。その図面には、あらゆる事象を捉えながら結晶化させた建築理念が投影され、建築を創造することの意志が凝縮されています。住吉の長屋から現在まで、主要作品を網羅するこのディテール集の中に、時代に流されず、建築の本質を求めて止まないもう一つの安藤空間が展開します。

Overlayered plans, sections and perspectives, with various details in different scales, Ando's drawing has unique three dimensional character. The drawings represent not only the literal information of details, but also his philosophy of architecture. From "Row house in Sumiyoshi" to recent projects, these two volumes contain Ando's architectural details of major projects and embody the spirits of Ando, who is the evangelist of the essence of architecture.

Japanese and English text
Size: 300×307mm

1 EDITED BY YUKIO FUTAGAWA
CRITICISM BY PETER EISENMAN
企画・編集：二川幸夫
論文：ピーター・アイゼンマン

List of Works
Row House in Sumiyoshi (Azuma House)/Wall House (Matsum oto House)/Glass Block House (Ishihara House)/Rokko Housing I/Koshino House/Festival/BIGI Atelier/Town house in Kujo (Izutsu House)/Iwasa House/TIME'S I/II/Church on the Water/and others

168 total pages
¥ 4,806

2 EDITED BY YUKIO FUTAGAWA
CRITICISM BY FRANCESCO DAL CO
企画・編集：二川幸夫
論文：フランチェスコ・ダル・コ

List of Works
Tea House in Oyodo/Karaza Theater/Rokko Housing II/Galleria[akka]/Collezione/Naoshima Contemporary Art Museum and Annex/Museum of Literature, Himeji and Annex/Otemae Art Center/Matsutani House Addition/and others

148 total pages
¥ 4,714

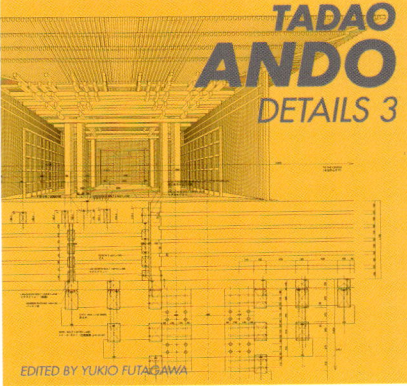

3 EDITED BY YUKIO FUTAGAWA
TEXT BY TADAO ANDO
企画・編集：二川幸夫
文：安藤忠雄

List of works
Pulitzer Foundation for the Arts/Sayamaike Historical Museum, Osaka/The International Library of Children's Literature/Modern Art Museum of Fort Worth/Church of the Light, Sunday School/Komyo-ji Temple/Shiba Ryotaro Memorial Museum/4 × 4 House/and others

148 total pages
¥ 4,714

表記価格には消費税は含まれておりません。

GA DOCUMENT
Global Architecture

GA DOCUMENT presents the finest in international design, focusing on architecture that expresses our times and striving to record the history of contemporary architecture. Striking black-and-white and vibrant color photographs presented in a generous format make for a dynamic re-presentation of spaces, materials and textures. International scholars and critics provide insightful texts to further inform the reader of the most up-to-date ideas and events in the profession.

Vols. 1, 16, 18, 20, 23, 25, 28, 29, 32, 36, 47, 54 are out of print.

多様に広がり、変化を見せる世界の現代建築の動向をデザインの問題を中心に取り上げ、現代建築の完全な記録をめざしつつ、時代の流れに柔軟に対応した独自の視点から作品をセレクションし、新鮮な情報を世界に向けて発信する唯一のグローバルな建築専門誌。掲載する作品をすべて現地取材、撮影することで大型誌面にダイナミックに表現し、その空間、ディテールやテクスチャーを的確に再現する。

Size: 300 × 297 mm

1, 16, 18, 20, 23, 25, 28, 29, 32, 36, 47, 54号は絶版。(17, 19, 21, 73号は在庫僅少)

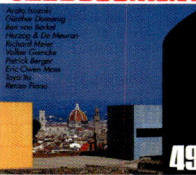
GA DOCUMENT 49
作品：磯崎新、フィレンツェ・ビエンナーレ'96：Time and Fashion／ギュンター・ドメニク＆ヘルマン・アイゼンコックル、カール・フランツェンス大学学部棟他／ベン・ファン・ベルケル、トウェンテ国立美術館増改築／ヘルツォーク＆ド・ムーロン、風刺漫画美術館／フォルカー・ギーンケ、植物園の温室／エリック・オーエン・モス、サミター／伊東豊雄、長岡Lホール／他
Works: A. Isozaki *Biennale di Firenze '96: Time and Fashion*; G. Domenig and H. Eisenköck, *Karl Franzens University RESOWI Faculty, extension of the Library*; B. V. Berkel *National Museum Twenthe, extension and conversion*; Herzog & De Meuron *Caricature and Cartoon Museum*; V. Giencke *Glasshouses at the Botanical Gardens*; E. O. Moss *Samitaur*; Toyo Ito *Nagaoka L Hall*; and others
120 pages, 48 in color ¥2,903

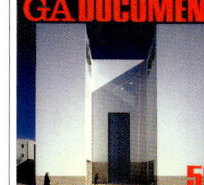
GA DOCUMENT 50
インタヴュー・作品・プロジェクト：トッド・ウィリアムズ＆ビリー・ツィン　作品：アルヴァロ・シザ、マルコ・ドゥ・カナヴェーゼスの教会、アダルベルト・ディアス、アヴェイロ大学機械工学科棟／J・マヌエル・ガリェゴ、コルーニャの美術館／磯崎新、岡山西警察署／エンリケ・ノルテン、テレビ局の複合施設／リカルド・レゴレッタ、メキシコシティ芸術都市／他
Interview, Works & Projects: T. Williams & B. Tsien *The NSI, Phoenix Art Museum, Cranbrook Athletic Complex*; and others　Works: A. Siza *Church of Marco De Canavezes*; A. Dias *University of Aveiro, Department of Mechanical Engineering*; J. M. Gallego *Museum of Fine Art, La Coruña*; A. Isozaki *Okayama-Nishi Police Station*; E. Norten *Televisa Mixed Use Building*; R. Legorreta *The City of the Arts*; and others
120 pages, 48 in color ¥2,848

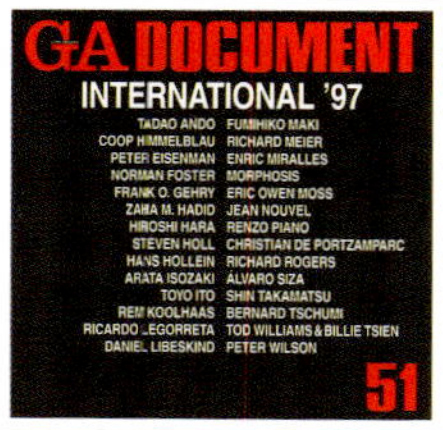

GA DOCUMENT 51
特集：GA INTERNATIONAL '97 第6回＜現代世界の建築家＞展
Special Feature: "GA INTERNATIONAL '97" Exhibition at GA Gallery
Tadao Ando, Coop Himmelblau, Peter Eisenman, Norman Foster, Frank O. Gehry, Zaha M. Hadid, Hiroshi Hara, Steven Holl, Hans Hollein, Arata Isozaki, Toyo Ito, Rem Koolhaas, Daniel Libeskind, Ricardo Legorretta, Fumihiko Maki, Richard Meier, Enric Miralles, Morphosis, Jean Nouvel, Eric Owen Moss, Renzo Piano, Christian de Portzamparc, Richard Rogers, Álvaro Siza, Shin Takamatsu, Bernard Tschumi, Peter Wilson, Tod Williams & Billie Tsien
120 pages, 24 in color ¥2,848

GA DOCUMENT 52
作品：E・O・モス、オフィス・コンプレックス／A・プレドック、アリゾナ・サイエンス・センター／槇文彦、風の丘葬祭場／ボレス＋ウィルソン、ロッテルダムの埠頭広場、他／H・ホライン、ロワー・オーストリア展示場、他／原広司＋アトリエ・ファイ、京都駅ビル／N・フォスター、ビルバオ市地下鉄駅／P・シメトフ、エヴルーの図書館／R・ボフィル、オリンピック・プール
Works: E.O. Moss *Pittard Sullivan*; A. Predock *Arizona Science Center*; F. Maki *Kaze-no-Oka Crematorium*; Bolles + Wilson *Quay Building, Light Forum, Albeda College*; H. Hollein *Lower Austrian Exhibition Hall, Light Forum*; Hiroshi Hara+Atelier Φ *Kyoto Station Building*; N. Foster *Bilbao Metro*; P. Chemetov & B. Huidobro *Library in Evreux*; R. Bofill *Olympic Swimming Pool*
120 pages, 48 in color ¥2,848

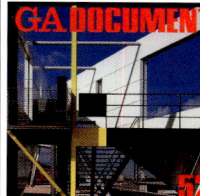
GA DOCUMENT 53
作品：OMA、ユトレヒト大学・エデュカトリアム／S・ホール、シアトル大学・聖イグナティウス礼拝堂／N・フォスター、コメルツバンク本社屋、他／R・ロジャース、テームズ・ヴァレー大学・LRC／W・P・ブルーダー、リッデル・アドヴァタイジング＆デザイン／B・チュミ、ル・フレノワ国立現代芸術スタジオ／C・ド・ポルザンパルク、ナシオナル通りのハウジング／他
Works: OMA *Educatorium, Utrecht University*; S. Holl *Chapel of St. Ignatius*; N. Foster *Commerzbank Headquarters, American Air Museum in Britain*; R. Rogers *L.R.C. Thames Valley University*; C. de Portzamparc *Paris, Rue Nationale*; F. Soler *Suite Sans Fin, Rue Emile Durkheim*; Studios Architecture *North Charleston Campus, Silicon Graphics Computer System*
120 pages, 54 in color ¥2,848

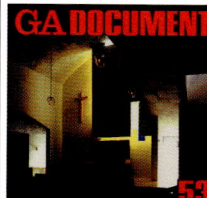
GA DOCUMENT 55
作品：R・マイヤー、ゲッティ・センター／R・ピアノ、バイエラー財団美術館／磯崎新、群馬県立近代美術館現代美術棟／安藤忠雄、綾部工業団地交流プラザ／TOTOセミナーハウス／MZRC、フランス・スタジアム／メカノ、デルフト工科大学図書館／原広司、宮城県図書館／R・レゴレッタ、サン・アントニオ中央図書館
Works: R. Meier *Getty Center*; R. Piano *Beyeler Foundation Museum*; A. Isozaki *Museum of Modern Art, Gunma-Contemporary Art Wing*; T. Ando *Ayabe Community Center*; T. Ando *TOTO Seminar House*; MZRC *Stade de France*; Mecanoo *Library of the Delft University of Technology*; H. Hara *Miyagi Prefectural Library*; and others
132 pages, 54 in color ¥2,848

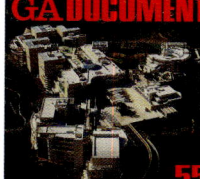
GA DOCUMENT 56
作品：S・ホール、ヘルシンキ現代美術館／S・フェーン、氷河博物館／S・フェーン、アウクルト・センター／コープ・ヒンメルブラウ、UFAシネマ・センター／P・アンドルー、シャルル・ドゴール空港2・ホールF／S・カラトラヴァ、アラメダ橋と地下鉄駅／S・カラトラヴァ、貿易センター／S・カラトラヴァ、カンポ・ボランティン歩道橋
Works: S. Holl *Kiasma, Museum of Contemporary Art*; S. Fehn *Glacier Museum*; S. Fehn *The Aukrust Centre*; Coop Himmelblau *UFA Cinema Center*; P. Andreu *CDG 2—Hall F*; S. Calatrava *Alameda Bridge and Underground Station*; S. Calatrava *Alameda Bridge and Underground Station*; and others
120 pages, 42 in color ¥2,848

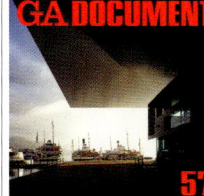
GA DOCUMENT 57
作品：ジャン・ヌヴェル、ルツェルン・コンサートホール／アルヴァロ・シザ、アリカンテ大学管理・教室棟／アーキテクチュア・スタジオ、ヨーロッパ連合議事堂／磯崎新、秋吉台国際芸術村　静岡県コンベンションアーツセンター「グランシップ」　なら100年会館
論文：「パノプティコンからアーキペラゴへ」磯崎新
Works: J. Nouvel *Lucerne Culture and Convention Centr*; Á. Siza *Rectory of The University of Alicante*; Architecuture Studio *European Parliament*; A. Isozaki *Akiyoshidai International Art Village, Shizuoka Convention & Arts Center "Granship", Nara Centennial Hall*
Essay: "From Panopticon to Archipelago" by Arata Isozaki
132 pages, 54 in color ¥2,848

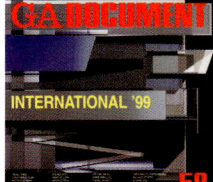
GA DOCUMENT 58
特集：GA INTERNATIONAL '99 第7回＜現代世界の建築家＞展
Special Feature: "GA INTERNATIONAL '99" Exhibition at GA Gallery
Tadao Ando, Coop Himmelblau, Peter Eisenman, Norman Foster, Frank O. Gehry, Zaha M. Hadid, Hiroshi Hara, Steven Holl, Hans Hollein, Arata Isozaki, Toyo Ito, Ricardo Legorreta, Fumihiko Maki, Mecanoo, Richard Meier, Enric Miralles, Rafael Moneo, Morphosis, Eric Owen Moss, Dominique Perrault, Renzo Piano, Christian de Portzamparc, Richard Rogers, Álvaro Siza, Bernard Tschumi, Tod Williams/ Billie Tsien
108 pages, 24 in color ¥2,848

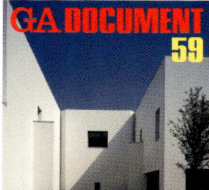
GA DOCUMENT 59
作品：アルヴァロ・シザ、ポルト現代美術館／黒川紀章、ヴァン・ゴッホ美術館新館／ダニエル・リベスキンド、フェリックス・ヌッスバウム美術館　ユダヤ美術館／妹島和世＋西沢立衛、飯田市小笠原資料館／ノーマン・フォスター、ドイツ新議事堂、ライヒスターク／フレデリック・ボレル、ペルポール通りの集合住宅
Works: Á. Siza *Contemporary Art Museum of Oporto*; K. Kurokawa *New Wing of Van Gogh Museum*; D. Libeskind *Felix Nussbaum Haus, Berlin Museum with the Jewish Museum*; K.Sejima+R. Nishizawa *O-Museum*; N. Foster *New German Parliament, Reichstag*; F. Borel *Housing Building, Rue Pelleport*
120 pages, 54 in color ¥2,848

GA DOCUMENT 60
フォーカス・オン・アーキテクト①：E・ミラージェス　作品：B・チュミ、建築学校　アルフレッド・ラーナー・ホール／H・ホライン、ドナウ・シティの小学校／S・ホール、クランブルック科学研究所／Ch・d・ポルザンパルク、ポルト・マイヨーの会議場増築／UNスタジオ、ヘット・ヴァルクホフ美術館／モーフォシス、ヒポ・アルプ・アドリア・センター
Focus on Architect 1: E. Miralles B. Tagliabue Works: B. Tschumi *School of Architecture, Alfred Lerner Hall at Columbia University*; H. Hollein *Bilingual Elementary School*; S. Holl *Cranbrook Institute of Science*; Ch. de Porzamparc *Extention of the Paris des Congrès*; UN Studio *Museum Het Valkhof*; Morphosis, *Hypo Alpe-Adria-Center*
132 pages, 54 in color ¥2,848

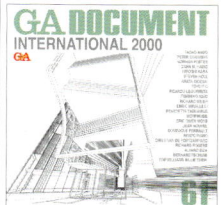
GA DOCUMENT 61
特集：GA INTERNATIONAL 2000 第8回＜現代世界の建築家＞展
Special Feature: "GA INTERNATIONAL 2000" Exhibition at GA Gallery
Tadao Ando, Peter Eisenman, Norman Foster, Zaha M. Hadid, Hiroshi Hara, Steven Holl, Arata Isozaki, Toyo Ito, Ricardo Legorreta, Fumihiko Maki, Richard Meier, Enric Miralles Benedetta Tagliabue, Morphosis, Eric Owen Moss, Jean Nouvel, Dominique Perrault, Renzo Piano, Christian de Portzamparc, Richard Rogers, Álvaro Siza, Bernard Tschumi, Tod Williams Billie Tsien
108 pages, 48 in color ¥2,848

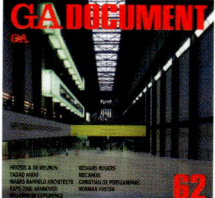
GA DOCUMENT 62
作品：ヘルツォーク＆ド・ムーロン、テート・モダン／安藤忠雄、FABRICA（ベネトン・アートスクール）、淡路夢舞台／エキスポ2000ハノーバー／ミレニアム・エクスペリエンス／R・ロジャース、ウッドストリートのオフィス／メカノ、ナショナル・ヘリテイジ／ミュージアム／C・ド・ポルザンパルク、グラス市裁判所／N・フォスター、カナリー・ウォーフ駅／他
Works: Herzog & de Meuron *Tate Modern*; T. Ando *FABRICA*; T. Ando *Awaji-Yumebutai*; Marks Barfield Architects *Millennium Wheel*; EXPO 2000 Hannover; *Millennium Experience*; R. Rogers, *88 Wood Street, London EC2*; Mecanoo *National Heritage Museum*; Ch. de Portzamparc *Grasse Courts of Justice*; N. Foster *Canary Wharf Station*
132 pages, 66 in color ¥2,848

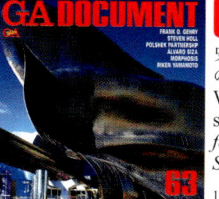
GA DOCUMENT 63
作品：F・O・ゲーリー、E・M・P、コンデ・ナスト、ヴォンツ分子科学センター／S・ホール、サルファティ通りのオフィス／ポルシェック・パートナーシップ、アメリカ自然史博物館ローズ・センター／A・シザ、サンチャゴ大学情報科学学部／モーフォシス、ロングビーチの小学校、ダイヤモンド・ランチ・ハイスクール／山本理顕、公立はこだて未来大学、埼玉県立大学
Works: F. O. Gehry *E. M. P., Condé Nast, Vontz Center*; S. Holl *Sarphatistraat Offices*; Polshek Partnership *Rose Center, American Museum of Natural History*; A. Siza *Faculty of Information Science*; Morphosis *Intenational Elementary School, Diamond Ranch High School*; R. Yamamoto *Future University of Hakodate, Saitama Prefectural University*
120 pages, 60 in color ¥2,848

表記価格には消費税は含まれておりません。

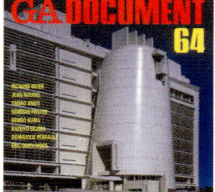
GA DOCUMENT 64
作品：R・マイヤー，イスリップ連邦裁判所，フェニックス連邦裁判所／J・ヌヴェル，ナント裁判所／安藤忠雄，南岳山光明寺／フォスター，スタンフォード大学医療科学研究センター／隈研吾，馬頭町広重美術館／妹島和世，hhstyle.com／D・ペロー，オリンピック・ヴェロドローム／スイミング・プール／E・O・モス，ステルス，ビルディング1/2，アンブレラ
Works: R. Meier *United States Courthouse & Federal Building, Sandra Day O'Connor United States Courthouse*; J. Nouvel *Palais de Justice de Nantés*; T. Ando *Komyoji, Temple*; N. Foster *Center for Clinical Science Reseach, Stanford University*; K. Kuma *Bato Machi Hiroshige Museum*; K. Sejima *hhstyle.com*; and others
120 pages, 54 in color　　¥2,848

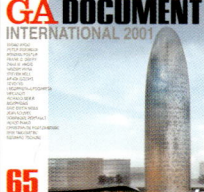
GA DOCUMENT 65
特集：GA INTERNATIONAL 2001 第9回〈現代世界の建築家〉展
Special Feature: "GA INTERNATIONAL 2001" Exhibition at GA Gallery
Tadao Ando, Peter Eisenman, Norman Foster, Frank O. Gehry, Zaha M. Hadid, Hiroshi Hara, Steven Holl, Arata Isozaki, Toyo Ito, Legorreta+Legorreta, Mecanoo, Richard Meier, Morphosis, Eric Owen Moss, Jean Nouvel, Dominique Perrault, Renzo Piano, Christian de Portzamparc, Shin Takamatsu, Bernard Tschumi
108 pages, 48 in color　　¥2,848

GA DOCUMENT 66
作品：F・O・ゲーリー，パリザー・プラッツ3／DGバンク／S・ホール，ベルヴュー・アート・ミュージアム／伊東豊雄，せんだいメディアテーク／ボレス・ウィルソン，ルクソール・シアター／R・ピアノ，KPNテレコム・オフィス・タワー，メゾン・エルメス／原広司，札幌ドーム／N・フォスター，グレート・コート／T・ウィリアムズ B・ツィン，ウィリアムズ屋内プール／他
Works: F. O. Gehry *Pariser Platz 3 / DG Bank Building*; S. Holl *Bellevue Art Museum*; T. Ito *Sendai Mediatheque*; Bolles-Wilson *Luxor Theater Rotterdam*; R. Piano *KPN Telecom Office Tower, Maison Hermès*; H. Hara *Sapporo Dome*; N. Foster *Great Court, British Museum*; T. Williams B. Tsien *Williams Natatorium*; and others
120 pages, 60 in color　　¥2,848

GA DOCUMENT 67
作品：R・ロジャース，ロイズ・レジスター・オブ・シッピング，アシュフォード・アウトレット・センター／UNスタジオ，NMRセンター，ゴミ処理場／安藤忠雄，大阪府立狭山池博物館／メカノ，天使聖母マリア教会，カナダブレイン・カルチャー・センター／B・チュミ，コンサート＆エギジビション・ホール"ゼニス"／J・ヌヴェル，メゾン・コニャック・ジェイ／他
Works: R. Rogers *Lloyd's Register of Shipping, Ashford Designer Retail Outlet Centre*; UN STUDIO *NMR Facilities*; T. Ando *Osaka Prefectural Sayamaike Historical Museum*; MECANOO *R.C. Chapel St. Mary of the Angels*; B. Tschumi *Concert Hall and Exhibition Complex (Zenith)*; J. Nouvel *Rueil Malmaison Fondation Cognacq-Jay*; and others
108 pages, 54 in color　　¥2,848

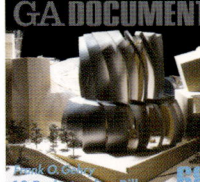
GA DOCUMENT 68　Frank O. Gehry　13 Projects after Bilbao
レイ＆マリア・スタータ・センター／マルケス・ド・リスカルのホテル／コーコラン・アート・ギャラリー／オー・オキーフ・ミュージアム／ル・クロス・ジョーダン／ウィニック・インスティテュート／アート・センター／デザイン・カレッジ／アスター・プレイス・ホテル／他
Ray and Maria Stata Center; Hotel at Marques de Riscal; Venice Gateway; Corcoran Gallery of Art; Ohr-O'Keefe Museum; Le Clos Jordan; Winnick Institute; Redevelopment of Lincoln Center; Art Center College of Design; Astor Place Hotel; and others
108 pages, 42 in color　　¥2,848

GA DOCUMENT 69
作品：伊東豊雄，ブルージュ・パビリオン／G・ヘン，トランスペアレント・ファクトリー・ドレスデン／D・ペロー，メディアテーク・ヴェニシュー／H・ホライン，オーストリア大使館，ゲネラリ・メディア・タワー／J・ヌヴェル，コープ・ヒンメルブラウ／M・ウェドホーン／W・ホルツバウアー，ガソメター・アパートメント／N・フォスター，ミレニアム・ブリッジ／他
Works: T. Ito *Brugge Pavilion*; G. Henn *Transparent Factory Dresden*; D. Perrault *Médiathèque, Vénissieux*; H. Hollein *Austrian Embassy Berlin/ Generali Media Tower*; J. Nouvel/ COOP Himmelblau/ M. Wehdorn/W. Holzbauer *Apartment Housing Gasometer*; and others
108 pages, 60 in color　　¥2,848

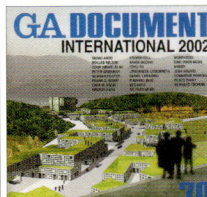
GA DOCUMENT 70
特集：GA INTERNATIONAL 2002 第10回〈現代世界の建築家〉展
Special Feature: "GA INTERNATIONAL 2002" Exhibition at GA Gallery
Tadao Ando, Bolles-Wilson, Coop Himmelblau, Peter Eisenman, Norman Foster, Frank O. Gehry, Zaha M. Hadid, Hiroshi Hara, Steven Holl, Arata Isozaki, Toyo Ito, Legorreta+Legorreta, Daniel Libeskind, Fumihiko Maki, Mecanoo, Richard Meier, Morphosis, Eric Owen Moss, MVRDV, Jean Nouvel, Dominique Perrault, Renzo Piano, Bernard Tschumi
108 pages, 54 in color　　¥2,848

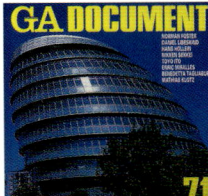
GA DOCUMENT 71
作品：N・フォスター，大ロンドン市庁舎／D・リベスキンド，帝国戦争博物館北館／H・ホライン，ヴァルカニア，ヨーロッパ火山公園／日建設計 安田幸一，ポーラ美術館／伊東豊雄，サーペンタイン・ギャラリー・パヴィリオン2002／E・ミラージェス B・タグリアブエ，色の公園，ディアゴナル・マル公園／M・クロッツ，アルタミラ・スクール
Works: N.Foster *City Hall, Greater London Authority Headquarters*; D. Libeskind *Imperial War Museum-North*; H. Hollein *Vulcania, European Volcano Park*; Nikken Sekkei/K. Yasuda *Pola Museum of Art*; T. Ito *Serpentine Gallery Pavilion 2002*; E. Miralles B. Tagliabue *Parc dels Colors, Parc de Diagonal Mar*; M. Klotz *Altamira School*; and others
108 pages, 60 in color　　¥2,848

GA DOCUMENT 72
スイス博覧会　作品：F・O・ゲーリー，ピーター・B・ルイス・ビルディング／Z・ハディド，ベルギーゼル・スキージャンプ台／D・ペロー，市庁舎＋ホテル／磯崎新，セラミックパークMINO／J・ヌヴェル＋大林組，電通本社ビル／S・カラトラヴァ，YSIOSワイナリー／R・モネオ，天使聖母マリア大聖堂／他
EXPO.02, Switzerland　Works: F. O. Gehry *Peter B. Lewis Building*; Z. Hadid *Bergisel Ski Jump*; D. Perrault *Town Hall/Hybrid Hotel in Innsbruck*; A. Isozaki *Ceramics Park Mino*; J. Nouvel + Obayashi Corporation *Dentsu Headquarters*; S. Calatrava *Ysios Winery, City of Arts and Sciences*; R. Moneo *Our Lady of the Angeles Cathedral*; and others
120 pages, 60 in color　　¥2,848

GA DOCUMENT 73
特集：GA INTERNATIONAL 2003 第11回〈現代世界の建築家〉展
Special Feature: "GA INTERNATIONAL 2003" Exhibition at GA Gallery
Tadao Ando, Coop Himmelblau, Peter Eisenman, Norman Foster, Frank O. Gehry, Zaha Hadid, Hiroshi Hara, Steven Holl, Arata Isozaki, Toyo Ito, Fumihiko Maki, Richard Meier, Morphosis, Eric Owen Moss, Jean Nouvel, Dominique Perrault, Renzo Piano, Richard Rogers, Bernard Tschumi
108 pages, 60 in color　　¥2,848

GA DOCUMENT 74
作品：Z・ハディド，ローゼンタール現代美術センター／R・マイヤー，クリスタル・カテドラル・ポシビリティ・シンキング国際センター／安藤忠雄，フォートワース現代美術館／スティーヴン・ホール，シモンズ・ホール／F・O・ゲーリー，リチャード・B・フィッシャー・パフォーミング・アーツ・センター／レンゾ・ピアノ，"音楽公園"オーディトリアム／他
Works: Z. Hadid *Rosenthal Center for Contemporary Art*; R. Meier *International Center for Possibility Thinking, Crystal Cathedral*; T. Ando *Modern Art Museum of Fort Worth*; S. Holl *Simmons Hall*; F. O. Gehry *Richard B. Fisher Center for the Performing Arts*; Renzo Piano *"Parco della Musica" Auditorium*; and others
108 pages, 60 in color　　¥2,848

GA DOCUMENT 75
作品：F・O・ゲーリー，ウォルト・ディズニー・コンサートホール／W・ブルダー，ネバダ美術館／槇文彦，福井県立図書館・文書館／I・M・ペイ，ドイツ歴史博物館増築棟／B・チュミ，フロリダ国際大学建築学部棟／フューチャー・システムズ，セルフリッジズ・バーミンガム／O・ニーマイヤー，サーペンタイン・ギャラリー・パヴィリオン2003／他
Works: F. O. Gehry *Walt Disney Concert Hall*; W. Bruder *Nevada Museum of Art*; F. Maki *Fukui Prefectural Library & Archives*; I. M. Pei *Exhibition Hall for German Historical Museum*; B. Tschumi *Paul L. Cejas School of Architecture Building*; F. Systems *Selfridges Birmingham*; O. Niemeyer *Serpentine Gallery Pavilion 2003*; and others
108 pages, 66 in color　　¥2,848

GA DOCUMENT 76
作品：OMA，イリノイ工科大学マコーミック・キャンパス・センター／マーフィ/ヤーン，イリノイ工科大学学生寮／スティーヴン・ホール，ロイジウム・ビジター・センター
Works: OMA *Illinois Institute of Technology, McCormick Tribune Campus Center*; Murphy/Jahn *Illinois Institute of Technology, State Street Village*; Steven Holl *Loisium Visitors' Center*
84 pages, 70 in color　　¥2,848

GA DOCUMENT 77　SPECIAL ISSUE: Arata Isozaki
論文：「発起」磯崎新　作品：山口情報芸術センター／セラミックパークMINO　プロジェクト：フィレンツェ新駅／中央美術学院現代美術館／ブラーネス・プロジェクト／上海文化公園「海上芸園」／カタール国立図書館／カタール・エデュケーション・シティマスタープラン／他
Essay: *"The Road Not Taken"* by Arata Isozaki; Works: *Ceramics Park MINO*; Projects: *Central Academy of Fine Arts, Museum of Contemporary Art, Blanes Project, Culture Theme Park Shanghai, Hai Shang Yi Yuan, Qatar National Library*; and others
168 pages, 84 in color　　¥4,200

GA DOCUMENT 78
作品：エンリック・ミラージェス ベネデッタ・タグリアブエ，ヴィゴ大学／ホセ・クルス・オバーリェ，アドルフォ・イバニェス大学／ジャン・ヌヴェル，ガリア＝ローマ期美術館／マンシーリャ＋トゥノン，マドリッド歴史資料センター／メイヤー・エン・ファン・スフォーテン，INGグループ本社屋／他
Works: Enric Miralles Benedetta Tagliabue *University of Vigo*; José Cruz Ovalle *University of Adolfo Ibañez*; Jean Nouvel *Gallo-Roman Museum*; Mansilla + Tuñón *Madrid Regional Documentary Center*; René van Zuuk *Arcam, Architectural Center Amsterdam*; and others
108 pages, 60 in color　　¥2,848

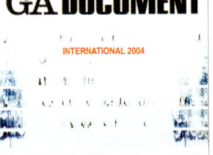
GA DOCUMENT 79
特集：GA INTERNATIONAL 2004 第12回〈現代世界の建築家〉展
Special Feature: "GA INTERNATIONAL 2004" Exhibition at GA Gallery
Tadao Ando, Coop Himmelblau, Norman Foster, Frank O. Gehry, Zaha Hadid, Hiroshi Hara, Steven Holl, Arata Isozaki, Toyo Ito, Morphosis, Jean Nouvel, OMA, Dominique Perrault, Renzo Piano, Richard Rogers, Kazuyo Sejima + Ryue Nishizawa/SANAA, Bernard Tschumi
100 pages, 56 in color　　¥2,848

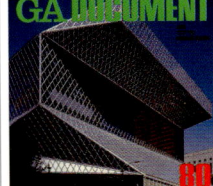
GA DOCUMENT 80
作品：OMA，シアトル中央図書館／伊東豊雄，まつもと市民芸術館／ノーマン・フォスター，30セント・メリー・アクス，アルビオン河岸再開発，キャピタル・シティ・アカデミー
Works: OMA *Seattle Central Library*; Toyo Ito *Matsumoto Performing Arts Centre*; Norman Foster *30 ST Mary Axe, Albion Riverside Development, Capital City Academy*
108 pages, 72 in color　　¥2,848

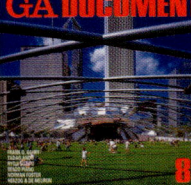
GA DOCUMENT 81
作品：フランク・O・ゲーリー，マサチューセッツ工科大学レイ＆マリア・スタータ・センター，ジェイ・プリッツカー・パヴィリオン／安藤忠雄，地中美術館／鈴木了二，物質試行47 金刀比羅宮プロジェクト／レンゾ・ピアノ，ピオ神父巡礼教会／ノーマン・フォスター，マクラーレン・テクノロジー・センター／ヘルツォーク＆ド・ムーロン，フォーラム2004ビルディング＆プラザ
Works: Frank O. Gehry *Jay Pritzker Pavilion*; Tadao Ando *Chichu Art Museum*; Ryoji Suzuki *Experience in Material No. 47, Project Konpira*; Renzo Piano *Padre Pio Pilgrimage Church*; Norman Foster *McLaren Technology Centre*; and others
120 pages, 78 in color　　¥2,848

表記価格には消費税は含まれておりません。

GA JAPAN
ENVIRONMENTAL DESIGN

日本の新しい優れた現代建築のエッセンスを主に国内に向けて発信する隔月刊の建築デザイン専門誌。建築思想、技術思想を照射しつつ、建築のデザインに迫る本格的建築総合誌です。

Japanese Text Only／Size: 300 × 228mm

71
新 現代建築を考える ○と×「金沢21世紀美術館」
批評座談会：妹島和世・西沢立衛・伊東豊雄・二川幸夫
特集：GA JAPAN 2004——建築家14組の最新計画案を紹介
青木淳／安藤忠雄／石山修武／磯崎新／伊東豊雄／北川原温／隈研吾／小嶋一浩＋赤松佳珠子／妹島和世／高松伸／原広司／古市徹雄／槇文彦／山本理顕

作品：SANAA／金沢21世紀美術館　原広司／韮崎東ヶ丘病院　西沢大良／砥用町林業総合センター　竹中工務店／第二吉本ビルディング　北川原温／豊島学院高校・昭和鉄道高校 新2号館

新連載：白と黒／小嶋一浩　連載：建築・設備のフロンティア／髙間三郎
GA広場：「複雑でありながら整理された部分と全体」つくばエクスプレス 柏の葉キャンパス駅／渡辺誠，「軽やかなクリスタルの中で繰り広げられる世界」オペラ『ヴォツェック』の舞台デザイン／安藤忠雄，「衛生と収集」／塚本由晴，「HPシェルがつくるランドスケープ」とりりん／原田真宏・原田麻魚，「構造家の思考法：徐光」，IKADA乗りの視線，他

176 pages, 96 in color　¥2,333

GA JAPAN 2004　第13回＜現代日本の建築家＞展

2004年11月3日（水）—12月26日（日）

日本を代表する14組の建築家の最新プロジェクトを模型やドローイング等で紹介します。

火曜日—日曜日：12:00—6:30 pm　月曜休館（但し祝日は開館）
入場料：500円（前売券・団体10名以上：400円）

GAgallery ジーエー・ギャラリー
東京都渋谷区千駄ヶ谷3-12-14　tel.(03)3403-1581　http://www.ga-ada.co.jp

表記価格に消費税は含まれておりません。

66
［総括と展望］
座談会：[建築 2003／2004] 塚本由晴・日埜直彦・二川由夫
特集：建築の内と外
青木淳／伊東豊雄／入江経一／隈研吾／妹島和世＋西沢立衛／原広司／槇文彦／山本理顕

作品：妹島和世＋西沢立衛／ディオール表参道　内藤廣／みなと未来線 馬車道駅　磯崎新／山口情報芸術センター　佐藤総合計画／神奈川県立近代美術館 葉山　竹山聖／大阪府立北野高校　六稜会館　岸和郎／京都・小野
記事：「地下空間利用に対する問題提起」
連載：建築・設備のフロンティア／髙間三郎，モダン・シアター・ストーリー／本杉省三，東京・小説／隈研吾

176 pages, 72 in color　¥2,333

67
特集：建築の光——6人の日本人建築家が考えていること
安藤忠雄／磯崎新／伊東豊雄／隈研吾／原広司／槇文彦

作品：伊東豊雄／みなとみらい線 元町・中華街駅　北川原温／佐世保新みなとターミナル　渡辺誠＋西部交通建築事務所／九州新幹線「新水俣駅」　隈研吾／安養寺木造阿弥陀如来坐像収蔵施設
記事：現場レポート 2004
金沢21世紀美術館／妹島和世＋西沢立衛・佐々木睦朗，まつもと市民芸術館／伊東豊雄建築設計事務所，トッズ表参道／伊東豊雄建築設計事務所・竹中工務店
連載：モダン・シアター・ストーリー／本杉省三，建築・設備のフロンティア／髙間三郎
GA広場：「リバーシブルなフィルター」LANVIN BOUTIQUE GINZA／中村拓志，構造家の思考法：新谷眞人，IKADA乗りの視線，「3Dワンルームを実現した16mmの鉄板」梅林の家／妹島和世・佐々木睦朗，他

168 pages, 72 in color　¥2,333

68
対談：「機能主義でもポストモダンでもなく」磯崎新・小嶋一浩
「ユニット＝一住戸という構築的方法を越えられるか」山本理顕・隈研吾

作品：小嶋一浩＋赤松佳珠子／ブリッジ・アーツ＆サイエンス・カレッジ　隈研吾／東京農業大学「食と農」の博物館・進化生物学研究所，東雲キャナルコートCODAN 3街区　飯田善彦／名古屋大学野依センター 野依記念物質科学研究館・野依記念学術交流館　古市徹雄／浄土宗麟鳳山九品寺本堂　山口隆／ダイナミックツール本社ビル　岸和郎／住田歯科診療医院

連載：モダン・シアター・ストーリー／本杉省三，建築・設備のフロンティア／髙間三郎
GA広場：「建築に姿を与えるガラス・スクリーン」東京大学法学系教育棟・横浜アイランドタワー／槇文彦，「[箱]の設計思想の展開」なおず幼稚園／難波和彦，「25m²に3部屋を現実化する」船橋アパートメント／西沢立衛，「計画学的価値観に載らない住宅」門前仲町の住宅，中野の住宅，巣鴨の住宅，天沼の住宅／佐藤光彦，他

168 pages, 72 in color　¥2,333

69
新 現代建築を考える ○と×「まつもと市民芸術館」
批評座談会：伊東豊雄・原広司・二川由夫

作品：伊東豊雄／まつもと市民芸術館　谷口吉生／広島市環境局中工場　安藤忠雄／野間自由幼稚園，加子母村ふれあいコミュニティセンター　内藤廣／最上川ふるさと公園センターハウス　隈研吾／村井正誠記念美術館，分とく山　鵜飼哲矢／イームズコレクターの家　椎名英三／直方の海

連載：建築・設備のフロンティア／髙間三郎，モダン・シアター・ストーリー エピローグ／本杉省三
GA広場：「小さな水平面を積み上げる」iz house／藤本壮介＋佐藤淳，「スペックではなく現象を操作する」／マティアス・シューラー，「フラグメンタルに散りばめられた床」TiO／小泉雅生，「建築マテリアルが人の心にまで浸透する」は CARACOLA／安部良，「HAPTICなものづくり」原研哉，「2004ミラノ・サローネ・レポート」，他

176 pages, 88 in color　¥2,333

70
新 現代建築を考える ○と×「物質試行47 金刀比羅宮プロジェクト」
批評座談会：鈴木了二・高松伸・二川幸夫

特集：[建築と水Ⅰ]安藤忠雄／菊竹清訓／隈研吾／鈴木了二／高橋晶一／古市徹雄
座談会：[新たなる自由の獲得に向けて] ゲント市文化フォーラム・プロジェクト（指名設計競技応募案）／伊東豊雄＋アンドレア・ブランジ設計共同体
作品：鈴木了二／物質試行47 金刀比羅宮プロジェクト　安藤忠雄／地中美術館　石山修武／富士ヶ嶺 観音堂　北川原温／サンタリア聖教会＋ヴィラ・エステリオ　坂倉建築研究所／所沢市民体育館

連載：建築・設備のフロンティア／髙間三郎
GA広場：「ビバリーヒルズにオープン、コールハース、2つ目のプラダ」／二川由夫，「ガラスブロック構造を現実化する」クリスタル・ブリック／山下保博＋佐藤淳，「距離感と密度感の決定因」芦屋小学校複合施設現場レポート／小泉雅生，他

176 pages, 80 in color　¥2,333

GA 素材空間

20世紀の建築は、様々な素材の登場により、新しい建築様式が生まれました。21世紀を迎えるにあたって、建築デザインを素材面から考えてみようと、この雑誌では、ほかの産業で開発されている材料も含めて、建築に応用できる素材の発見と、現在、一般的に使用されている建築材料についても、研究・改良されていく様子をリポートしていきます。

Japanese Text Only, Size: 300×228 mm

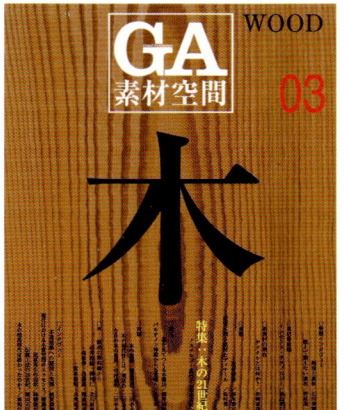

03 木の21世紀
ノスタルジー素材から未来素材へ

木――創造の最前線から：8人の建築家、構造家の話―石井和紘・岡村仁・北川原温・高松伸・内藤廣・難波和彦・宮本佳明・六角鬼丈
対談：木の素養―藤森照信×二川幸夫／木の現代性とは―隈研吾×二川由夫／今日の木の世界―中村義明×二川幸夫
論文：森を見てつくる木構法　網野禎昭／パルテノン神殿から五重塔へ―花里利一
インタヴュー：木造建築への疑問と実践　納賀雄嗣／現代における木質空間のエッセンス　齋藤裕／民家再生から見えてきたこと　降幡廣信／伝統工法の21世紀　稲山正弘／木の暗黒時代は終わったのか？　林知行
巻頭インタヴュー：地球と素材　石田秀輝／燃えて燃えない素材　菅原進一
技術最前線：インセクト・テクノロジー　長島孝行
新素材の現在：「DUCTAL」とは何か？　松岡康訓
連載：記憶に残る素材とディテール 第3回　松村秀一／素材探訪 第2回　杉本賢司

144 total pages, 40 in color　¥2,476

Global Architecture

従来の、建築家から発信されるフォーマルなプレゼンテーションを集めただけの作品集から脱却した、わかる建築書=PLOT（プロット）。
建築の設計は、完成されるまで紆余曲折のスタディが成されています。
一人の建築家の背景と、プロセスの発展を追い、何故この建築が完成したのかを、完成作品と現在進行中のプロジェクトと共に、詳細に編集しました。

Japanese Text Only, Size: 300×228mm

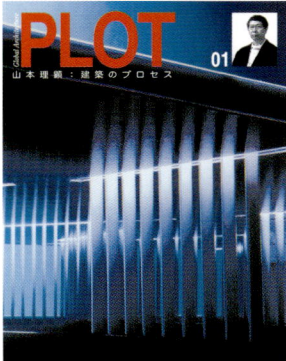

01 山本理顕

作品
岡山の住宅、岩出山町立岩出山中学校、埼玉県立大学、広島市西消防署、公立はこだて未来大学、横浜市営住宅「三ツ境ハイツ」他

プロジェクト
東雲集合住宅A街区、北京建外SOHO、岡山の住宅2、和歌山市立大学（仮称）設計競技案、公園レストハウス

184 total pages, 56 in color　¥2,333

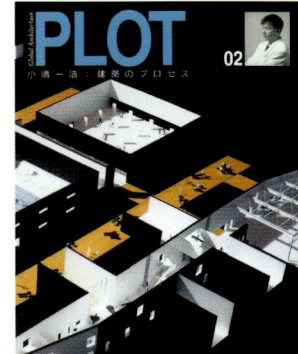

02 小嶋一浩

作品
ビッグハート出雲、スペースブロック上新庄、吉備高原小学校、宮城県迫桜高校

プロジェクト
ハノイモデル、東京大学先端科学技術研究センター（IV-1）、北京建外SOHO/SOHO別荘、カタールエデュケーションシティ／ブリッジ・アーツ＆サイエンス・カレッジ、氷室ハウス 他

200 total pages, 64 in color　¥2,333

03 伊東豊雄

掲載作品
横浜市営地下鉄M駅インテリア・デザイン、桜上水K邸、ブルージュ・パヴィリオン、フローニンゲン・アルミニウム・ハウジング、コニャック・ジェイ病院、マーラー4 ブロック5,、松本市市民会館（仮称）、北京CCTVプロジェクト、リラクゼーションパーク イントレヴィエハ、オスロ・ウェストバーネン・プロジェクト、トッズ表参道ビル 他

184 total pages, 64 in color　¥2,333

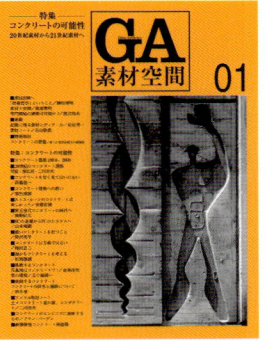

01 コンクリートの可能性
――20世紀素材から21世紀素材へ

対談：原広司×二川幸夫
コンクリート建築1900-2000：20世紀を代表する104作品
論文・インタヴュー：柳田博明／岡部憲明／渡辺邦夫／高橋靗一／菊竹清訓／安藤忠雄／樫野紀元／山本理顕／黒川紀章／梅沢良三／松岡康信／金森洋史／五十嵐純一／坂牛卓／二川由夫／アラン・バーデン
連載：石山修武　松村秀一

160 total pages, 16 in color　¥2,476

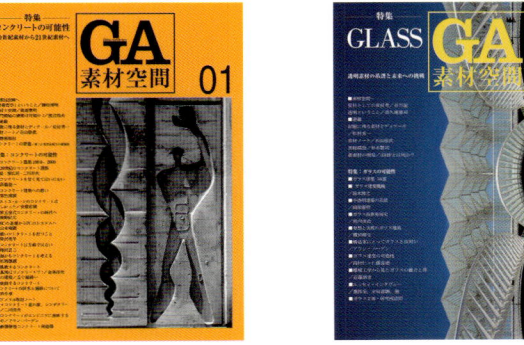

02 GLASS
ガラスの可能性

ガラス建築選集：19～20世紀を代表する72作品
ガラスの空間：最近作10篇
論文・インタヴュー：谷川渥／鈴木了二／桑久庵憲司／伊藤節郎／大西博＋杉崎健一／仁藤喜徳＋岡村仁／アラン・バーデン／林昌二／コリン・ヤーカー／鈴木博之／横田暉生／葉祥栄／岡部憲明／赤坂喜顕／池内清治／近藤靖史
連載：松村秀一　杉本賢司

160 total pages, 16 in color　¥2,476

GA JAPAN 別冊①

20世紀の現代建築を検証する ○と×

鉄・ガラス・コンクリートの出現から、ミース・コルビュジエ・ライトの巨匠時代を経て、現代日本建築にいたるまで。建築家・磯崎新と建築史家・鈴木博之による20世紀の横断。

磯崎 新
鈴木博之

第1章：新古典主義からモダニズムの誕生へ
第2章：技術とその意味
第3章：一つで歴史に残る家
第4章：前衛か、体制か
第5章：大戦前後
第6章：南北米・欧、それぞれの展開
第7章：最後の巨匠、そして日本

Japanese Text Only, Size: 300×228 mm
198 total pages, 72 in color　¥2,800

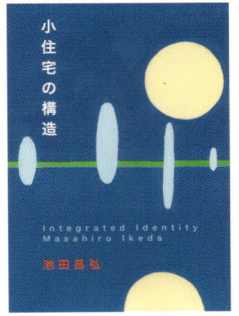

Japanese Text Only, Size: 210×148mm

小住宅の構造　池田昌弘

構造家として建築デザインをバックアップするだけでなく、建築家のコラボレーターとして、構造、意匠といったセクションの枠組みを外し、それらの境界を自由に横断することで、そこにあるすべての才能を統合する「インテグリスト」=池田昌弘。建築家と共同で進めた小住宅の設計プロセスとその思想を、インタヴューと、写真／ドローイング／模型／CGなどの豊富なヴィジュアルで紹介します。

掲載作品：Ta house／Y house／O house／s house／S/N／八王子の家／腰越のメガホンハウス／屋根の家／amb-flux／Beaver House／Conoid／BLOC／町屋project、C House、Thea-ory House、nkm／RECO-house／ペンギンハウス／Lucky Drops／ナチュラルイルミナンス／ナチュラルスラット／ナチュラルエリップス／ナチュラルウェッジ／ナチュラルストラータ／Y House

208 total pages　¥2,200

日本の現代建築を考えるⅡ
○と×

磯崎新：静岡県コンベンションアーツセンター・グランシップ、なら100年会館、秋吉台国際芸術村、横 文彦：ヒルサイドテラス 山本理顕：埼玉県立大学 伊東豊雄：大社文化プレイス、せんだいメディアテーク 小嶋一浩：ビッグハート出雲、黒川紀章：大阪府立国際会議場 日建設計：さいたまスーパーアリーナ 安藤忠雄：南岳山光明寺 小嶋一浩＋三貂満真：宮城県迫桜高等学校 原 広司：札幌ドーム 石山修武：世田谷村 高橋銑一：群馬県立館林美術館

312 total pages　¥1,900

MA MODERN ARCHITECTURE
1851-1919

第1章：ガラス、鉄、鋼、そしてコンクリート 1775-1915　第2章：シカゴ派の建築―都市と郊外 1830-1915　第3章：アール・ヌーヴォーの構造と象徴主義 1851-1914　第4章：オットー・ワグナーとワグナー派 1894-1912　第5章：工業生産と文化の危機 1851-1910

224 total pages, 48 in colors　¥2,300

MA MODERN ARCHITECTURE
1920-1945

第6章：北ヨーロッパの風土建築としての煉瓦造近代建築 1914-1935　第7章：古典主義の伝統とヨーロッパのアヴァンギャルド 1912-1937　第8章：ヨーロッパの芸術と建築における千年王国的な衝撃 1913-1922　第9章：地方都市と共同都市計画：建築とアメリカの運命 1913-1945　第10章：インターナショナル・モダニズムと国民的自覚 1919-1939

288 total pages, 48 in colors　¥2,300

反回想Ⅰ
磯崎 新

GA JAPANで好評を博した同名タイトルの連載をもとに、新たな原稿を加えて単行本化しました。1960年代から80年代初頭までの氏の作品を振り返り、その背景と時代を浮彫にします。作品集「GA ARCHITECT ARATA ISOZAKI」の裏読本的内容。

320 total pages　¥2,380

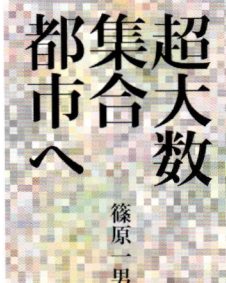

超大数集合都市へ
篠原一男

アフリカ・ヨーロッパ・南北アメリカ・日本という地域軸と、古代から現代までの2000年を超える時間軸を、縦横に織り上げることによって論じられる「都市」。

160 total pages　¥1,900

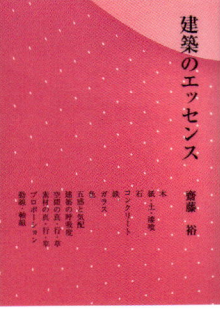

建築のエッセンス
齋藤 裕

木や漆喰、コンクリートなどの材料から空間の構成法まで、時代や風土を越えてエッセンスを抽出し、再解釈することで現代の建築家が忘れかけている建築の本質にせまります。

320 total pages　¥2,476

表記価格に消費税は含まれておりません。

A.D.A. EDITA Tokyo

GA DOCUMENT 82
Publisher: *Yukio Futagawa*
Editor: *Yoshio Futagawa*

Published in October 2004
©A.D.A. EDITA Tokyo Co., Ltd.
3-12-14 Sendagaya, Shibuya-ku,
Tokyo, 151-0051 Japan
Tel. 03-3403-1581
Fax.03-3497-0649
e-mail: info@ga-ada.co.jp
www.ga-ada.co.jp

Logotype Design: *Gan Hosoya*

Printed in Japan by
Dai Nippon Printing Co., Ltd.

All rights reserved.

Copyright of Photographs:
©*GA photographers*
All images are provided by Steven Holl Architects except as noted.

GA DOCUMENT 82
発行：二川幸夫
編集：二川由夫

2004年10月22日発行
エーディーエー・エディタ・トーキョー
東京都渋谷区千駄ヶ谷3-12-14
電話(03)3403-1581(代)
ファクス(03)3497-0649
e-mail: info@ga-ada.co.jp
www.ga-ada.co.jp

ロゴタイプ・デザイン：細谷巖

印刷・製本：大日本印刷株式会社

禁無断転載

ISBN4-87140-182-0 C1352

取次店
トーハン・日販・大阪屋
栗田出版販売・誠光堂
西村書店・中央社・太洋社

Cover page: Natural History Museum of Los Angeles County
Title pages: Toolenburg-Zuid Living in the 21st Century

Copyediting: Takashi Yanai (pp.8-27)
和訳：菊池泰子

目次 / Contents

「探求の手段」スティーヴン・ホール	8	"Vehicle of Research" Steven Holl
Xky エクスクレイパー，市庁舎タワー　ヴオサーリ，フィンランド	28	Xky Xcraper, Town Center Towers　Vuosaari, Finland
ネルソン・アトキンズ美術館　カンザス・シティ，ミズーリ州	34	Nelson Atkins Museum of Art　Kansas City, Missouri, U.S.A.
人類史博物館　ブルゴス，スペイン	42	Museum of Human Evolution　Burgos, Spain
リヨン交流美術館　リヨン，フランス	50	Musée des Confluences　Lyon, France
コーネル大学建築学部　イサカ，ニューヨーク州	58	Cornell University Department of Architecture　Ithaca, New York, U.S.A.
トーレンブルフ＝ゾイド，21世紀の住宅　スキポール，オランダ	64	Toolenburg-Zuid Living in the 21st Century　Schipol, The Netherlands
ピノー財団　パリ，フランス	72	Pinault Foundation　Paris, France
ロサンジェルス郡美術館　ロサンジェルス，カリフォルニア州	80	Los Angeles County Museum of Art (LACMA)　Los Angeles, California, U.S.A.

Global Architecture

スイス大使館公邸 ワシントンD.C.	86	New Residence at Swiss Embassy Wasington D.C., U.S.A.
ニュータウン：グリーン・アーバン・ラボラトリー 柳沙半島，南寧，中国	92	New Town: Green Urban Laboratory Liusha Peninsula, Nanning, China
WTC 跡地プロジェクト ニューヨーク，ニューヨーク州	100	Projects for WTC Site New York, New York, U.S.A.
ロサンジェルス自然歴史博物館 ロサンジェルス，カリフォルニア州	110	Natural History Museum of Los Angeles County Los Angeles, California, U.S.A.
欧州・地中海文明美術館 マルセイユ，フランス	118	Musée des Civilisations de l'Europe et de la Méditeranée Marseille, France
ルクセンブルク新国立図書館 ルクセンブルク	126	New National Library of Luxembourg Luxembourg
ロンバルディア地方行政府センター ミラノ，イタリア	134	Lombardia Regional Government Center Milan, Italy

SPECIAL ISSUE

Vehicles of Research
Interview with Steven Holl
探求の手段
スティーヴン・ホール・インタヴュー

Steven Holl　スティーヴン・ホール

GA INTERVIEW

GA: Competitions have been very important to your career and practice. What is the particular attraction of the competition for you?

Steven Holl: What are competitions in general for an architect? I think back to 1975 or 1976 when I began to practice and didn't have any work. A lot of young architects do competitions to try to get work. In my mind I wasn't doing competitions to get a job, to me competitions were vehicles for research and experiment. I saw the competition as a sort of frame in which you could test ideas; you could make explorations that maintained the highest ideal.

GA: Would you say the competition then was a way of discovering your style?

SH: When I put out my little manifesto, Anchoring in 1989 I was thinking about the pluralism that existed in architecture at the time: the many different approaches that currently coexisted. There's an emptiness in that kind of pluralism, a kind of alphabet soup of approaches to architecture. I was against creating a personal style as a way to mark myself among these many different architectures. But at the same time I was suspicious of general theory or ideology. A general theory doesn't apply to a different culture or a different site or a different circumstance. This dilemma led me to appreciate the competition as a probe for what I called, in 1989, an "approach based on limited concept". Limited concept is about how the singularity of a site or situation or program could yield infinitely different architectural possibilities depending on those particularities. And therefore the competition was a perfect vehicle for me in thinking about how to develop a theory of limited concept.

GA: You say that winning the job wasn't the goal for you. But is that really the case?

SH: Competitions were, and still remain for me, primarily about ideas. When I look back at the second competition I made for the housing competition for Manila in 1975, in collaboration with James Tanner, there was really no architecture. Our proposal was about the absence of architecture, the possibility that if you clearly laid out the spaces of the city, if you gave permanent tenure to people on the land, they would build their own houses on these plots. Even though the competition documents called for low-cost housing, we violated the brief. From my very first competitions I went contrary to the rules and instead tried to drive the design in a particular way. I always took the risk of being disqualified for the test of an idea—or a new strategy.

GA: What are some particular discoveries that you've made in competition?

SH: The Porta Vittoria competition of 1986 was very important for me as a design experiment and discovery. This project became a central piece in an exhibition at the Walker Art Center entitled Phenomena of Relations within the City and was my first study of a phenomenological way of envisioning new urban plans. We were paid $30,000 and four of us worked on this for six months with great enthusiasm. We felt that the city of Milan would never build anything and they never have. The site is still a train yard. But the competition was a great opportunity and a very important part of my development.

Then we won a competition, for a Ameika Gedenk Bibliothek in Berlin. Thirteen avant-garde of my generation were invited and participated in it. There was Thom

---

GA：これまでのキャリアと仕事をみますと、コンペティションがとても重要な位置を占めていますね。その特別な魅力とは、何でしょうか？

スティーヴン・ホール：一人の建築家にとって、コンペの普遍的な意味とは何かということですか？　事務所を開いたばかりで、仕事は一つもなかった1975年から76年ごろに戻って考えると、若手の建築家の多くが、仕事を手に入れるためにコンペをしていましたね。ぼくの心のなかでは仕事をとるためにコンペをしているつもりはありませんでした。ぼくにとって、コンペは研究と実験のための手段でした。アイディアをテストすることが出来、最高の理想を保ったまま追求していける、一種の枠組みとしてコンペをみていたんです。

GA：ということは、コンペは自分のスタイルを発見する方法だということですか？

Steven Holl：1989年に、自分のささやかなマニフェスト、『アンカリング』を出したとき、ぼくは当時の建築界に広がっていた多元論について考えていました。さまざまな建築手法が広く共存していたんです。このような多元主義的な方法、アルファベット文字に切り抜いたパスタを入れたスープのような、建築のアプローチにはどこか虚しさがあります。多種多様な建築の海のなかで自分を目立たせる方法として個性的なスタイルをつくることには反対でした。けれど同時に、いわゆる一般的な理論やイデオロギーも疑わしく感じていました。一般的な理論では、異なる文化や立地条件に対応できませんから。このジレンマから、1989年に"限定されたコンセプトに基づいたアプローチ"と名付けた方法を精密に研究するための場として、コンペの価値を意識するようになったんです。"限定されたコンセプト"は、敷地や状況、プログラムの固有性から、それぞれの特色に依存した、無限に異なる建築の可能性をどのように生み出し得るかを問うものです。ですから、コンペは、ぼくにとって、"限定されたコンセプト"理論をどのように展開させるかを考えるための手段としてパーフェクトだったのです。

GA：仕事を獲得することが目的ではなかったということですが、ほんとうにそうですか？

SH：コンペは、ぼくにとって、今も変わりなく、何よりもまずアイディアに関わるものなのです。2番目のコンペのときに戻りますが、1975年、マニラのハウジングのコンペにジェイムズ・タナーと組んで参加しました。ところが、そこには現実には建築は存在していないことに気付きました。ぼくたちの案は建築の不在、「もし都市の空間を分かりやすく並べ、人々に土地の永久的な所有権を与えれば、ここに彼らは自分たちの家を建てるだろう」という可能性をめぐるものになりました。コンペの要綱はローコスト・ハウジングを求めていましたが、ぼくたちはそれを破ったのです。ごく最初のコンペから、ぼくは規則とは反する方向に進み、代わりに、普通とは違う方法でデザインを進めようと試みていたんですね。アイディア、あるいは新しい戦略をテストするために、失格になる危険をいつも犯していた。

GA：コンペで見つけた特別な発見には、たとえばどんなものがありますか？

SH：1986年のポルタ・ヴィットリアのコンペは、デザインの実験と発見という点で、ぼくにはとても重要なものでした。このプロジェクトは、ウォーカー・アート・センターでの"都市のなかの関係がつくりだす現象"と題する展覧会の中心的な展示となり、新しい都市計画を構想するための現象学的方法に関するぼくの最初のスタディになったものです。3万ドルをもらい、6ヶ月のあいだ、4人で夢中になってこのプロジェクトに打ち込みました。ミラノ市は決して何も建てず、何も手にしないだろうことは感じてい

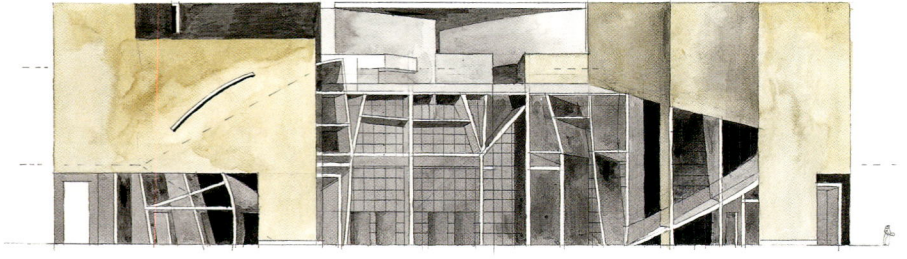

Palazzo del Cinema, Venice, Italy, 1990-91

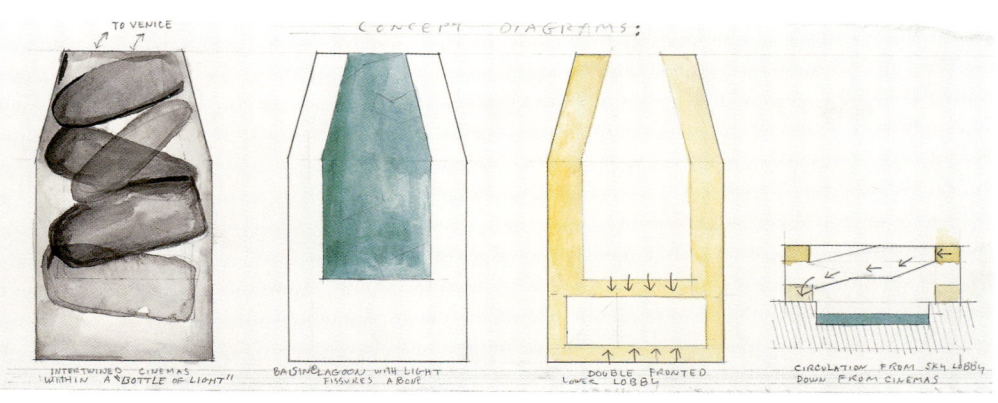
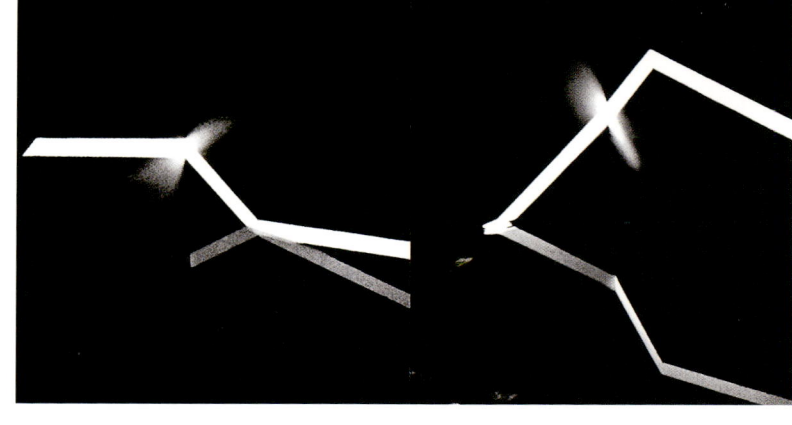
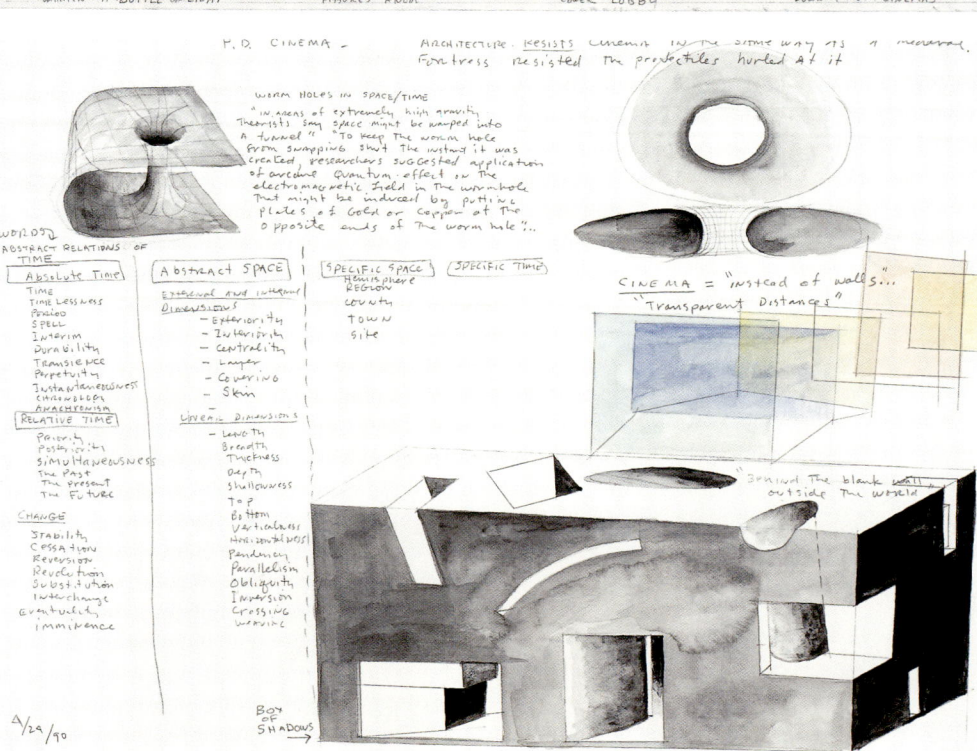

Palazzo del Cinema

An invited competition for the rebuilding of the Venice Film Festival building on the Lido in Venice.

The connection of the Lido site to Venice by water is emphasized by a grand arrival of space on the lagoon. Filled with diaphanous light from gaps between the cinemas above, this space would also be a place for the Lido community.

Time in its various abstractions links architecture and cinema. The project involves three interpretations of time and space:

1) Collapsed and extended time within cinema is expressed in the warp and extended weave of the building, analogous to cinema's ability to compress (20 years into 1 minute) or extend (4 seconds into 20 minutes) time.

2) Diaphanous time is reflected in sunlight dropping through fissure space between the cinemas into the lagoon basin below. Ripples of water and reflected sunlight animate the grand public grotto.

3) Absolute time is measured in a projected beam of sunlight that moves across the "cubic pantheon" in the lobby.

The projection of light in space, light in reflection, and light in shade and shadow are seen as programs to be achieved parallel to solving functional aspects.

パラッツォ・デル・チネマ
ヴェネチアのリドにあるヴェネチア映画祭のための建物の建て替えコンペ。

リドの大地とヴェネチアの水による結びつきは、干潟に面した空間に船を乗り付けることで強調される。上を覆う映画館の狭間から漏れ落ちる透けるような陽光に満たされるこの空間は、同時にリドのコミュニティのための場でもある。

時間をいろいろな形で抽象化するという点で、建築と映画には通じるところがあるのだが、このプロジェクトでは、空間の中の時間と光について3つの解釈がとられている。

1) 映画では時間が縮んだり伸びたりするが、それが建築のゆがみや引き延ばしという形で表現される。それは時間を圧縮したり（20年を1分に）、伸ばしたり（4秒を20分に）することの可能な映画のアナロジーである。

2) 希薄な時間は映画館の隙間から干潟の水面に落ちる陽光に反映される。小波とそれに反射する光が、広い岩屋に生命を吹き込む。

3) 絶対的時間は、ロビーの「キュービック・パンテオン」に射し込む光の移動によって計られる。空間に鋭く射し込む光、反射光、影の中を舞う微妙な光は、機能的な側面を解決する事と平行して考えるべきモノとみなした。

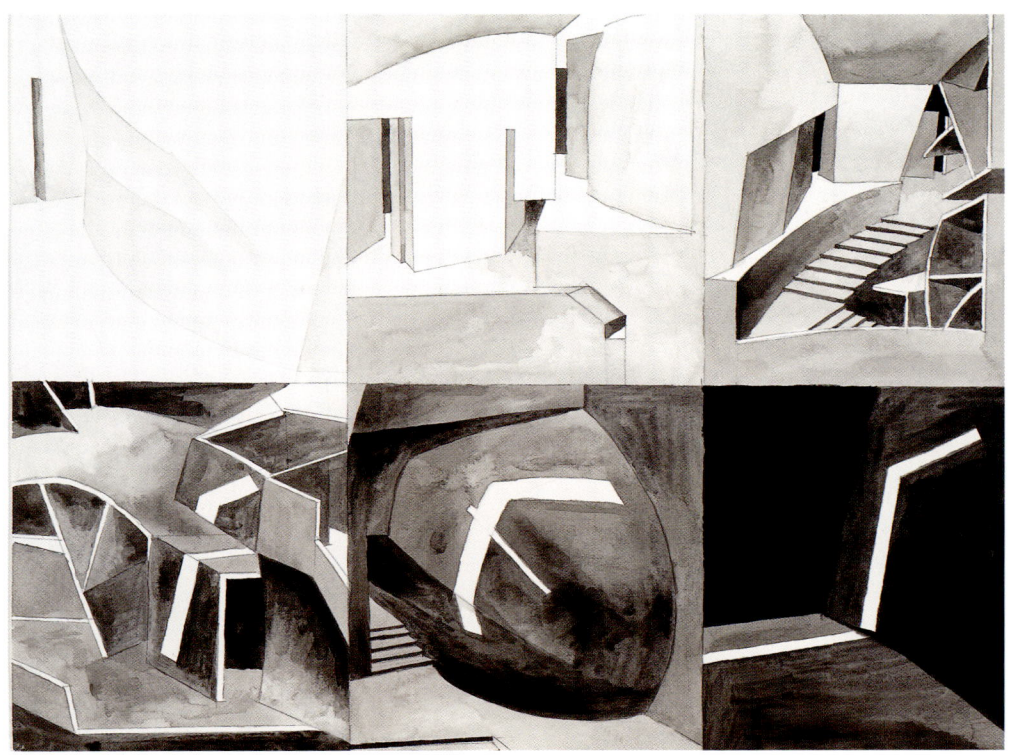

Palazzo del Cinema, Venice, Italy, 1990-91

Mayne, Bernard Tschumi etc. We won unanimous first prize. I remember the telephone call from Berlin; it was 1988. We went to Berlin for design development but then the government changed and the new building senator came in, overthrew the decision and so it never proceeded. Right at that time the Berlin wall came down and I could not adequately protest the mistreatment by the senator. This troubling circumstance was the first time that I actually won a competition.

In 1990 we were invited to participate in the design for the Palazzo del Cinema; in competition with James Stirling, Aldo Rossi, Rafael Moneo, Jean Nouvel and others. I was the youngest and most unknown to be invited. I was very excited and and went to Venice to see the site; we worked for six months. We explored the relation of cinema and architecture via time and light. Cinema as the most powerful media today was to be contained in the "vessel" of architecture. Time can be collapsed or expanded in cinema; we devised accordion-like cinemas which interlocked with the vessel hanging over a lagoon arrival space. It was an intense dialogue, where cinema "burned holes" in the architecture.

Then in 1992 we were invited to the competition for the Museum of Contemporary Art in Helsinki, which had 416 entries. We actually won this competition, which seemed a complete fluke. I was honored just to be on the invited list with Alvaro Siza, Kazuo Shinohara and Coop Himmelblau etc; I didn't expect to win. The whole experience was exhilarating by 1998; they realized this building just as we designed it in the competition. The Fins are very tough on a lot of fronts, but they didn't compromise the architecture.

In June of 1993, the announcement came that we had won three competitions within a week and half. Along with Helsinki we won the "Urban Arms" in Dusseldorf, and a competition for housing in Zollikerberg, Switzerland. In the end it's good that all of these did not go forward together; that would have required I triple my office instantly.

The competition for the expansion of the Nelson Atkins Museum of Art in 1999 is the largest competition we've won recently and it is currently under construction. This is a very interesting case, because as a competition the brief prescribed that the 140,000 sq. ft. addition be built on the north side of the building over the parking lot doubling the size of the existing building. We competed with Machado and Silvetti, Tadao Ando, Christian de Portzamparc; all of them followed the rules. I said that the brief was pointing the wrong direction. I envisioned that you should keep this forecourt area free and create an arrival court there instead of a new building. I felt that on this site one should engage the landscape and make the sculpture garden aspect of this institution really important. In this particular competition there were five participants who each had to present their proposed projects to the jury. The first thing I did was apologize. I told them I hope to participate, but when I saw the rules and I saw the situation, I realized that the ideal solution was in violation of the rules. There is a stone inscription at the top of the existing building that says, "The soul has more need for the ideal than for the real." I told the jury that when I was walking around the building and I read the inscription, I realized the direction in which to go. I apologized for ignoring the rule of building over the north parking lot and

ました。あの敷地は今も操車場のままです。けれど，このコンペは，素晴らしい機会でしたし，とても重要な勉強になりました。

そのあと，ベルリンのアメイカ・ゲデンク図書館のコンペに優勝したんです。同世代の前衛たち13人が招かれコンペに参加していました。トム・メインやベルナール・チュミなどね。ぼくたちの案が満場一致の第1位でした。ベルリンから電話がかかってきて，デザインを進めるためにベルリンに行きました。1988年のことです。ところが，そこで政権が交替し，建設族の議員が介入してきて決定を覆したので，先には進めなかった。ちょうどその当時，ベルリンの壁が崩壊して，議員による不正な扱いに十分な抗議をすることが出来なかったのです。この混乱状態が，ぼくが実際にコンペに勝った初めての機会でした。

1990年，パラッツォ・デル・チネマのデザインに参加するように招待されました。ジェームズ・スターリング，アルド・ロッシ，ラファエル・モネオ，ジャン・ヌヴェルなどとのコンペでした。ぼくは招かれたなかで最年少かつ最も知られていなかった。夢中になり，敷地を見にヴェニスまで行きました。6ヶ月，準備に費やしました。時間と光を媒介として映画と建築の関係をいろいろ考えたのです。現代の最も強力なメディアとしての映画を建築の"船"のなかに収める。時間は映画のなかで崩壊しあるいは膨張する。運河の船着き場の上に張り出した"船"と抱き合わされたアコーディオンに似た映画館。それは緊張した対話であり，建築のなかに広がる映画の"明るく燃え立つ空洞"なんです。

次に，1992年，ヘルシンキの現代美術館のコンペに招待されました。これには416の案がエントリーされていた。実際にこのコンペに勝ったのですが，まったく偶然の巡り合わせに思えました。アルヴァロ・シザ，篠原一男，コープ・ヒンメルブラウなどと一緒にこのコンペに招かれたことだけで名誉で，勝つことは期待していなかった。1998年まで，体験したすべてが，気持ちのよいものでした。主催者は，コンペでぼくたちがデザインした通りにこの建物を完成させたんです。仕事の最前線で関わったフィンランドの人たちはとてもタフでしたが，建築について妥協はしなかった。

1993年6月，1週間半のあいだに3つのコンペに勝ったという知らせが入りました。ヘルシンキと共に，デュッセルドルフの"アーバン・アームズ"，スイスのゾリッカーベルクのハウジング・コンペに勝ったんです。結局，これらの3つが，すべて一緒に進行することにならなくてよかったのです。そうなっていたら，すぐにも事務所を3倍の大きさにしなければならなかったでしょうからね。

1999年のネルソン・アトキンズ美術館増築のためのコンペは，最近，ぼくたちが1位になった最大のプロジェクトで，今，工事中です。これはとても面白いケースで，コンペの要綱は，140,000平方フィートの増築棟を既存建物の北側，地下駐車場の上の敷地に建て，今の建物の広さを2倍にすることを条件にしていました。マチャド＆シルヴェティ，安藤忠雄，クリスチャン・ド・ポルザンパルクが競争相手で，彼らは皆，条件に従いました。ぼくは，それは間違った方向を指しています，と言ったんです。敷地を新しい建物で埋めてしまうのではなく，来館者のためのコートをつくるべきだと思いました。この敷地はランドスケープと結びつけるべきで，この美術館の彫刻庭園的な側面をつくることがとても大切だと感じていたからです。この通常とは変わったコンペには，5人の参加者がいて，それぞれが審査員に自分の提案について説明しなければならない。最初にぼくがしたことは謝ることでした。ぼくは彼らにこう話しました。このコンペに

GA INTERVIEW

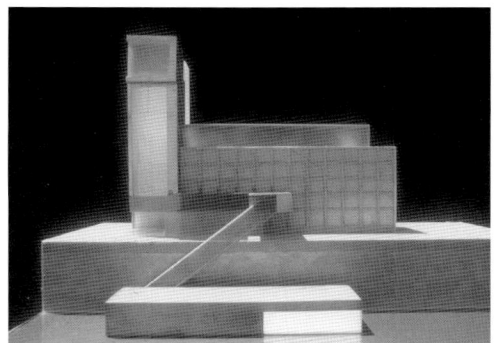 

Urban Arms, Dusseldorf: model (left) and realised building without arms (right)

asked to show them what I came up with as an alternative. I explained how this scheme would maintain the integrity of the original building and ensure that even after future additions the original building would remain monumental. Unlike the frequently expanded Metropolitan Museum in New York which has a "bag of cats" approach to additions, expanding its footprint, their museum, NAMA, would always retain the integrity of the volume of the existing building.

It was an exciting moment; in the end the jury unanimously voted for our project. Six months later the trustees unanimously supported that decision and now the project is 85% complete.

GA: You call competitions vehicles for research. Can you elaborate?
SH: Given the proper amount of time, lets say three months minimum, competitions have become a way to conduct various kinds of research that would go on in parallel. For example, when we began the competition for the Palazzo del Cinema, we had six months and I read everything that I could on cinema. I had the chance to read both of Deleuze's volumes, Cinema 1 and Cinema 2. In these works, Deleuze argues that classical prewar cinema was characterized by the movement-image but that this gives way to the time-image in the postwar era. This is the way Deleuze organizes these two books; he argues that time in its pure state rises up to the surface of the screen in all the great cinema after WWII.

What comes out of these readings for me sometimes reemerges later on. Some of the ideas that I discovered in Deleuze in 1990, reemerge in 2003 in the cinematic loop aspect of the Beijing Project that we're currently working on; in particular, the idea of making an urban sector to be "filmic" in its spatial experience. Competitions can be like ongoing postgraduate research. If you approach each competition with a certain degree of intensity they each become little learning opportunities for continuing research. Another example is the competition for the Fondation Pinault; I went back and reread Breton's Nadja and reread Baudilaire's Paris Spleen and then I began to read the works of Mallarmé, one of France's great modern poets. Mallarmé had a way of making poetry very close to music and very close to philosophy. My library contains a history of the competitions I've done. I bought the books Cinema I and Cinema II during the Palazzo del Cinema competition. In my collection on the

参加したいのですが，条件を読み，敷地の状況を見て，理想的な答えは，この条件を破ることだと気付きました。今建っている本館の頂には，石に次のような文章が刻まれています。「魂は現実よりもはるかに理想を必要とする」。建物の周りを歩き回っているときに，この銘刻文を読み，進むべき方向に気付きました。北側の駐車場の上に建てるという条件を無視したことを審査員に謝り，どのような代替案をつくったか見てくれるように頼みました。そして，この案が既存建物との一体性を保つことを説明し，将来，さらに拡張してもそのモニュメンタルな性格は残ることを断言しました。頻繁に拡張され，その足元を広げていく，込み入った増築の方法をとっているニューヨークのメトロポリタン美術館とは違い，この美術館，NAMAは，オリジナルの建物との一体感を常に保ち続けると思います。

最後に，審査員たちが，ぼくたちの案を満場一致で評決した瞬間は興奮しましたね。それから6ヶ月後，評議会も全員がこの決定を支持してくれ，今，その85％が完成しています。

GA：コンペは探求の手段だと考えているということですが，詳しくはどういうことですか？
SH：適切な時間を与えられたとして，最低3ヶ月でしょうか，コンペは平行して進む様々な種類の探求を実行する手段になります。たとえば，パラッツォ・デル・チネマのコンペを始めたときは，締め切りまでに6ヶ月あって，ぼくは映画館に役立ちそうなものは手当りしだい読みました。ドゥルーズの映画についての2巻本，『シネマ1』，『シネマ2』もこの機会に全部読みました。この本のなかで，ドゥルーズは，戦前の古典的な映画を特徴づけていたのは動きの映像化だが，これが戦後の時間の映像化に道を開いた

と主張しています。これがドゥルーズがこの本を組立てる方法になっていて，彼は，第二次大戦後の優れた映画作品にはすべて，時間がその純粋な状態で，スクリーンの表に浮かびあがっていると論じています。

こうした読書から得たことは，ときどき後からデザインのなかに再び現れます。面白いことに，1990年，ドゥルーズのなかで発見したアイディアが，ぼくたちが今進めている，2003年の北京プロジェクトの，フィルミック・ループと呼んでる環状に連続する住戸構成に使われています。その空間を映像的なものとして体験できるようにしたところなど，特にそうですね。コンペは，大学院生の継続中の研究課題のようなものかもしれない。ひとつひとつのコンペに，あるレベルの集中力で臨めば，そのひとつひとつが研究を継続して行くための小さな学習の機会になる。別な例はピノー財団のコンペです。昔に戻ってブルトンの『ナジャ』を読み直し，ボードレールの『パリの憂鬱』を読み直し，それから，フランスの偉大な現代詩人の一人，マラルメの作品を読み始めました。マラルメは，音楽に非常に近い方法，哲学に非常に近い方法で作詩しています。ぼくの蔵書は，いわば参加したコンペの歴史のようなものです。パラッツォ・デル・チネマのコンペのあいだに『シネマ1』と『シネマ2』の本を買いました。ぼくの蔵書のなかのステファヌ・マラルメの詩集には，"2001年5月，パリ，スガン島のコンペのために"という書き込みが表紙の内側にあります。資料と作品の間にはなんらかの関係がある。スガン島では，偶然性を用いること，方法としての偶然性というアイディアに惚れ込んでいました。今までに，このアイディアを一度だけ，1997年に建った，アムステルダムのヘト・オーステン社のプロジェクトで使っています。そこでは，ほんとうに，サイコロを投げて，メンガー・スポンジの建物の開口部を決めている。立体をつくりあげたとこ

Berlin AGB Library
This project is a competition entry for an addition to the Amerika Gedenk Bibliothek in Berlin and surrounding area.
The design extends the philosophical position of the open stack—the unobstructed meeting of the reader and the book—by organizing the offerings along a browsing circuit. The circuit is a public path looping the entire library. The library stacks are developed as furniture, giving different characteristics to area of the open plan. The concept of a browsing circuit is given memorable variety by these different stack arrangements.

ベルリン・アメリカ記念図書館
ベルリンのアメリカ記念図書館の増築とその周辺部のコンペ応募案。
　閲覧者と書物が直接出会うことのできる開架式書架の考え方を発展させ，本を眺めながら全体を一巡できるよう書架を配置した。このルートは，図書館全体の蔵書を提示するとともに建物を一周するための出入り自由な通路でもある。書架は家具として扱い，連続する空間の中，それぞれのエリアに相応しい性格を与える。このようにしてそれぞれ独自の本棚を設けることによってブラウジング・サーキットにはそれぞれの場所が心に留まりやすくなるような多様性が与えられる。

Interior of office　事務所内部

work of Stephane Mallarmé, a note on the inside cover reads "May 2001 for Ile Seguin Competition, Paris". There's a relationship between the material and the work. In the case of Ile Seguin I was enamored with the use of chance and the idea of chance as an operation. I've used that one other time in my life, for the project for the Het Oosten Company in Amsterdam, built 1997. There we actually used throws of dice to locate the openings in the menger sponge building. Once we had established the prism we used chance to determine where the openings were. At that point we were working with Morton Feldman, a great composer of parallel significance to John Cage. As a method of musical composition, Feldman said "I choose chance as a mode of operation".

　Our method in the competition for Ile Seguin was an exciting development which was similar to something we've done before but not exactly the same. Mallarmé, especially his wonderful poem called A Throw of the Dice, became my muse for the Ile Seguin competition project: the first chance operation located the main voids and then we hinged and flipped the island to create the university building after the first throw. The development of the project begins with these operations but then it intensifies. I started with this technique of establishing the sense or character of the space by watercolor first. Developing slots frame the voids from which you can see the river. First I made perspective drawings, then we built a fragment model and attached it to the plan; working that backwards each time until we had the basic scheme. It isn't just a chance operation; it's using a "spatial projective" technique after the chance operation that allows the whole space to come together.

ろで，開口の位置を決めるのに偶然性を利用したんです。当時ぼくたちは，ジョン・ケージと並んで重要かつ偉大な作曲家モートン・フェルドマンと仕事を進めていました。作曲の方法として，フェルドマンは「偶然性を選ぶ」と言ってました。

　スガン島のコンペで使った方法は，アムステルダムと似た方法をさらに刺激的に展開したものですが，まったく同じではない。マラルメ，特に『骰子一擲』と題する彼の素晴らしい詩が，スガン島のコンペ案のためのミューズになっています。骰子一擲というか，最初に偶然性の方法を使って，中心となるいくつかのヴォイドの位置を決め，そのあと，大学の建物を構成する。プロジェクトはこうした方法で始まりますが，次にそれを強化していきます。そのために空間の雰囲気や性格を決めていくのですが，まずそれを水彩で描き始める。ヴォイドを枠取る細い開口を練り上げていく。そこからは川が見える。最初にパースを描き，次に断片的な模型をつくり，それを平面に置いていく。基本的なスキームがまとまるまで，毎回，元に戻って作業する。単なる偶然性ではない。偶然性を用いたあと，すべてのスペースを一体化することのできる"空間の投影"というテクニックを使っています。

　ですから，この実験では，断片を内省的にデザインし，それからプランのなかにそれを投げ返します。これは，ぼくが空間構成のための反転の空間テクニックと呼んでいるもので，空間がどう見えるか，予測して決めておくのではなく，直観的な立場からそれを実際に引き出し，その模型をつくり，プランの断片をつくり，それから，プランの断片を3段階全体へ戻して織り上げます。

　最初のドローイングにはまだコンセプトが見えてこない。明晰なコンセプトが現れる前に，さまざまな可能性を試しているという感じがある。ぼくにとって，スガン島はと

GA INTERVIEW

Berlin AGB Library, Berlin, Germany, 1988 * *

GA DOCUMENT

16

Museum of Contemporary Art, KIASMA, Helsinki, Finland, 1996-98

Museum of Contemporary Art, KIASMA, Helsinki
The site for Kiasma lies in the heart of Helsinki at the foot of the Parliament building to the west, with Eliel Saarinen's Helsinki Station to the east, and Alvar Aalto's Finlandia Hall to the north. The challenging nature of this site stems from the confluence of the various city grids, from the proximity of the monuments, and from the triangular shape that potentially opens to Töölö Bay in the distance.
 The concept of Kiasma involves the building's mass intertwining with the geometry of the city and landscape which are reflected in the shape of the building. An implicit cultural line curves to link the building to Finlandia Hall while it also engages a "natural line" connecting to the back landscape and Töölö Bay. In the landscape plan, extending the bay up to the building will provide an area for future civic development along this tapering body of water, which also serves as a reflecting pool for the Finlandia Hall and new development along the south edge of the water. The horizontal light of northern latitudes is enhanced by a waterscape that would serve as an urban mirror, thereby linking the new museum to Helsinki's Töölö heart, which on a clear day, in Aalto's words, "extends to Lapland."

ヘルシンキ現代美術館
新しい現代美術館、"キアズマ"の敷地は、西に議事堂、東にエリエール・サーリネンのヘルシンキ駅、北にアルヴァ・アアルトのフィンランディア・ホールが近接するヘルシンキの中心部にある。設計意欲をかきたてられるこの敷地の性格は、さまざまな都市グリッドの合流点であることと、記念碑的建築との近さ、遠くに見えるトゥーリョ湾に向かって開放できる可能性を持った三角形の形態から生まれている。
 "キアズマ（交差）"というコンセプトによって、建物は都市と風景の持つジオメトリーと織り合わされ、それが建築形態に反映される。暗黙の内に文化性を含んだ曲線がこの建物をフィンランディア・ホールへと結び、一方で、背後の風景とトゥーリョ湾を結ぶ"自然のライン"ともかみ合っている。湾を建物まで引き延ばすという景観計画のなかで、この水の先細になった広がりに沿って将来の都市開発エリアが提供されることになろう。それはまた、フィンランディア・ホールと水路の南端に位置する計画地のリフレクティング・プールとしての役割も果たす。北緯圏の水平線近くの光が、都市の鏡となる水辺風景を強調し、新美術館をヘルシンキの、晴れた日には、アアルトの言葉を借りれば「ラップランドまで広がる」トゥーリョ湾の深奥部へとつなぐ。

**

Void Space/Hinged Space Housing
Concept: From hinged space to the silence of void space.
 Four active north-facing voids interlock with four quiet south-facing voids to bring a sense of the sacred into direct contact with everyday, domestic life. To ensure emptiness, the south voids are flooded with water; the sun makes flickering reflections across the ceilings of the north courts and apartment interiors.

ヴォイド・スペース・ヒンジド・スペース・ハウジング
コンセプト：ヒンジの作る空間からヴォイドの静寂まで。
北側に向いた，4つの活動的なヴォイドと，南向きのやはり4つではあるが静かなヴォイドをかみ合わせることで，日々の家庭生活と神聖な感覚を直接的に結びつけようとした。空間が何も無いままに護られるよう，南側のヴォイド下のスラブには水を張る。ここに反射したきらめく光は，北のヴォイドの天井やアパートの室内の天井まで届く。

So in this experiment we are designing fragments introspectively and then casting backwards into plan. This is something that I call a reverse spatial technique of making spaces: instead of having an a priori idea about what the space looks like, you actually draw it from an intuitional standpoint, make a model of it, make plan fragment, and then weave the plan fragment back into the overall—three steps.

The earliest drawings are without concept yet. They are feeling there way around the possibilities before the clarity of the concept comes forth. To me that was a very important competition. I remember when I went to Paris and spent a week studying the site and met Francois Pinault the great art collector. I went to his office and developed a good rapport with him because I could identify all the work he had in his office. There was an Ad Reinhardt, two Robert Rymans, and an Agnes Martin. I knew about the people he had collected and told him stories about visits with Agnes Martin. He was very impressed. And I remember when I started the competition, I'd heard through the rumor mill that he wanted Ando to do this project but was persuaded to hold a competition. So five people were in invited and in the end he chose Ando. But I have no regrets. We had four months to conceive the project and the research part of the work was very important. The fact that I was able to work at this level and this intensity with the thought of working with this operation connected to Mallarmé and on this incredible site on the Seine was significant for me.

GA: Are you disappointed when you don't win the competition?

SH: Of course there's some disappointment but here we expected Ando to win. In some cases I'd rather not know the outcome of the competition, just go on to the next thing and don't worry about it. I feel that a body of work that one does can't be measured only by the things that get built. It can also be measured by the aspiration; the desire, what the desire is, what the hope of architecture is. That's the measurement. So the real reason to do a competition like this is much closer to pure architectural desire than to whatever I wanted to make on a particular site or around a particular idea. It would have been great to build it, but I don't believe you have to build it to have the thing exist as a meaningful work.

Thom Mayne was asking me to list 100 built buildings that were influential for a book he's making about architecture of the 20th century. So I began to think about it and I ended up sending Thom an email saying it seems to me that there are a number of buildings that were more influential even though they were never built, such as the Maison Suspendu by Paul Nelson in 1938 or the Endless House by Friedrich Kiesler. That house is still influencing a lot of people today. Or Alberto Giacometti's "The Palace at 4 A.M.", a piece of incredible spatial work with mystery of linear potential. In fact I gave The Palace at 4 A.M. as an architectural assignment to my studio at Columbia. One time I also gave a Piranesi drawing, one of the Carceri drawings, to my students and asked them to build models of these impossible perspectives.

I believe that there's important meaning in the work even if it's not built. Once it's concretized as a scheme, there's a model, there's a hope, there's an idea that exists as a project and that's another reason why a competition, for me, becomes a place where one could do these explorations and feel hopeful. It's not always about

ても重要なコンペでした。パリに行って，敷地を研究し，著名なアート・コレクターであるフランソワ・ピノーと会うなどして，1週間を過ごしたときのことをよく覚えています。オフィスに行き，彼と共感のもてる関係を結ぶことができました。オフィスにあったコレクションのすべてが彼を語っていたからです。アド・ラインハルト，ロバート・ライマンの作品が2つ，アグネス・マーティンの作品がありました。彼のコレクションの作者をぼくは知っていて，アグネス・マーティンを訪ねたときのことを話したりしました。彼はとても感動してました。思い出すのですが，コンペの準備を始めたとき，噂を流した人から，ピノー氏は最初から安藤にこの仕事をさせたいと思っていたのだが，コンペにするように説得させられたのだと聞かされました。それで，5人が招待され，結局，彼は安藤を選んだ。でも無念さはないんですよ。4ヶ月かけてプロジェクトを考え，仕事の調査研究の部分はとても重要でしたし。マラルメと結びついた方法を用いたコンセプトをもって，この高いレベルと緊張感のなかで，そしてこのセーヌ川に浮かぶ奇跡のような敷地で仕事ができたという事実が，ぼくには大切なことでした。

GA： コンペに勝てなかったとき，失望しませんでしたか？

SH： もちろん，ある程度の失望はありますが，ここでは安藤が勝つと予期していましたからね。コンペの結果を知ることなく，次の仕事にとりかかって，コンペについては気にかけないでいたいこともあります。しかし，作品の本質は，建てられたもののみによっては測り得ないと感じています。それはまた，憧れ，欲望，どんな欲望か，建築が希望しているものは何かによって測ることもできます。それこそが基準となるものです。つまり，このようなコンペに参加するほんとうの理由は，特定の敷地に，特定のアイディアを巡ってぼくがつくりたいと思うどんなものよりも，純粋な建築的欲望に遙かに近いのです。それを建てることは素晴らしいことであるでしょうが，意義深い作品として存在するために，実際に建てられなければならないとは，ぼくは信じていないのです。

以前，トム・メインが，20世紀の建築について彼が編集中の本のために，影響を受けた100の実際に建てられた建築をあげてほしいと頼んできました。それについて考え始め，

S. Holl at meeting with staff 事務所スタッフと打ち合わせ

Void Space/Hinged Space Housing, Fukuoka, Japan, 1989-91

With study model of Beijing project　北京プロジェクトのスタディモデルと

winning, or about your competitor, or about rivalry. It's about research and a hope of making something that has a certain intensity of meaning. If you reach a certain intensity, it is potentially stronger than a less ambitious piece of work that gets built. In the unbuilt state the design most fully embodies the thought, the experiment, the idea and reading of its inception; unrestricted by time, function, physical limits.

GA: How much time do you spend at the beginning of a competition incubating ideas?

SH: How long does it take to have a creative idea? I'd say there's no way to know that. The driving idea might come on the first day, or it might take ten months. A client would ask me how long it would take to come up with an idea for a project. I have to tell them that I am not sure. I can tell a client exactly how long it can take to do working drawings, and exactly how long it would take for design development, and approximately how long construction would take, but the initial idea could come in a few hours or a few months. I've lost several jobs because of this! I've had on the other hand some very ideal clients that would give me six months to do a house. The problem with competitions is that you always have this frame of time, so I've decided that if it's shorter than six weeks I'm not even going to attempt it. I need the time to do the parallel research, to experiment, to play.

I have 33 people here from which to create a team for a competition. However, if there's not enough time to give it thought, then we're just going through the motions. The depth and the originality of the ideas and, let's say, the degree to which they embrace authenticity of the site and circumstances are, to me, the driving force. It's of

結局トムに次のようなEメールを送って終わりました。建てられなかったにもかかわらず，建てられたものよりも遙かに影響を受けた建築がたくさんあるようにぼくには思えます。たとえば，ポール・ネルソンの1938年のメゾン・サスペンデュ，フレデリック・キースラーのエンドレス・ハウスなど。こうした家は今でも多くの人に影響を与えています。あるいはアルベルト・ジャコメッティの「午前4時の宮殿」。リニアーな潜在力を備えたミステリアスな素晴らしい空間的作品です。事実，コロンビア大学のぼくのスタジオで，「午前4時の宮殿」を建築の課題にしたことがあります。一度，ピラネージの「牢獄」のドローイングの一枚を与えて，これらの現実には不可能なパースペクティヴの模型をつくるように要求したこともある。

たとえ建たなかったとしても，作品には重要な意味があると信じています。ひとたびスキームとして具体化すると，模型があり，希望があり，プロジェクトとして存在するアイディアがある。それが，ぼくにとってコンペがなぜ，これらの探求をすることが可能で，希望を感じられる場所であるかのもう一つの理由です。それは常に，勝つことや，競争相手や，対抗意識とかいうことであるわけではないのです。意味のある強度を持った何かをつくる探求や希望に関わることです。ある集中性に達すれば，強い願望の点で劣る建てられた作品よりもその潜在的な可能性は強いのです。建てられていない状態において，デザインは思考，実験性，アイディア，その発端での読みを最も完全に表現しています。時間や機能や物理的限界によって拘束されずにね。

GA：コンペのためのアイディアが形をとり始めるまでにはどのくらいの時間が必要なものですか？

SH：創造的なアイディアが生まれるまでにかかる時間ですか？　それを知るすべはない，と言うほかないでしょう。最初の日に浮かぶかもしれないし，10ヶ月かもしれない。クライアントはプロジェクトの構想はどのくらいでまとまりますか，と聞いてくる。ぼくは，分かりませんと答えるほかない。実施図面をつくるのにどのくらいかかるか，デザ

Desk of S. Holl　S・ホールの机

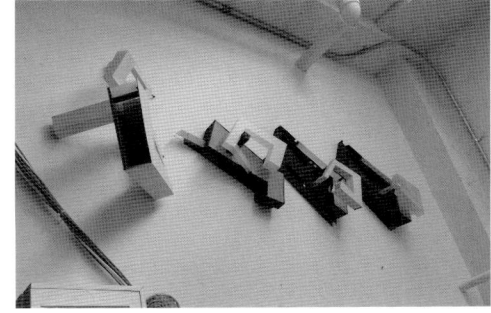

Study models スタディモデル

no use to build the building if the building has no meaning. That's a personal struggle I've had from the beginning when I first wrote Anchoring, about the balance between the experiential phenomena of the actual space and the idea which is the force that drives the design. That is a reconciliation one makes when you realize a project. The force that drives the design is a big creative question mark that comes out of a lot of research and a lot of careful moments of recollection and a kind of intuitive, magical, revelation moment, and there's no way of knowing how long that's going to take. You also probably have dry periods where it takes six months to have an original idea. I don't believe what I think Peter Eisenman once said "you only have one idea and you keep doing it over and over again." I don't believe that architects need a signature style—or even a consistency of style. I remember Emerson's admonition "consistency is the hobgoblin on little minds." Working on a competition encourages the potential to widen the mind to the possibilities of experimental areas that one might not have tried before under normal circumstances.

GA: Any projects in New York?

SH: We have a project at the Pratt School of Architecture under construction. The only built exterior in New York is StoreFront for Art and Architecture, done in collaboration with Vito Acconci in 1993.

GA: Can you tell me what 9.11 has meant for your work?

SH: I was here; you can see looking out my office window, the towers were right there. I was coming up the elevator and then the elevator man, said it "looks like an accident; a plane has hit the WTC." Then my assistant said, "There's another plane."

インの展開にどのくらいかかるか正確に答えられますし，工事にはどのくらいか，おおよその時間は答えられますが，最初のアイディアは，数時間，あるいは数ヶ月で生まれるかも知れない。このためにいくつも仕事をなくしたんですよ！ その一方で，住宅のために6ヶ月与えてくれるような理想的なクライアントにも何人か恵まれています。コンペの問題は，この時間の枠組みが常にあることで，6週間以下しか時間がないものは，やってみようとさえ思わない。平行して，研究し，実験し，遊ぶ時間が必要なんです。

ぼくのスタジオには33人いて，コンペのチームを組めます。けれど，それに思想を与えるための十分な時間がなければ，お義理なものになるだけです。アイディアの深さと独創性，いうなればサイトの本質をどこまで深く捉えるかが，ぼくにとっての推進力となります。建物に意味がなければ，それを建てることは無駄なことです。それが，現実の空間で感じられる具体的な現象と，デザインの推進力となるアイディアの間の均衡について，最初に『アンカリング』のなかで書いたそのときからずっと続いてきた個人的な闘いなんです。それが，プロジェクトを具体化するとき行われる折り合いともいうべきものです。デザインを推し進める力は，数多くの調査，数多くの細心の注意が注がれる記憶の瞬間，一種の直観的で，魔法的で，啓示的な瞬間から生まれてくる大きな創造的疑問符であり，それを得るまでにどのくらいの時間がかかるか知りようはありません。独創的なアイディアがわくのに6ヶ月もかかるような，不毛な時期もたぶんあるでしょう。ピーター・アイゼンマンの言葉だったと思うんですが，「ひとつのアイディアだけを持ち，それを繰り返し繰り返し追求し続けなさい」ということをぼくは信じていません。建築家が著名のあるスタイル，あるいはスタイルの一貫性を持つことが必要であるとも思っていません。エマーソンの忠告，「一貫性は狭量な心に宿るいたずらな小鬼」を思い

Study models スタディモデル

Model shelves　模型棚

Interior of office: reception area　事務所内部：レセプション

By the time I got here both towers had been hit and we knew that it was not an accident. The feeling was terrible. I had big 12 power binoculars and I could see from upper floors… people jumping. I sent everyone in the office home. There was a feeling of enormous anxiety. I didn't have a feeling of anger. It was much deeper and unexplainable. I got up the next morning and began to do watercolors. And for a while I did a series of black watercolors every morning. I began to make these drawings about a memorial space. A place of darkness and light that was on the Hudson River, the idea of floating a huge memorial out at the edge of the river. You would see a kind of horizon line of light; a white line projecting through a darkness of these rectangles of blackened concrete cast back from places where cracks of light would come through.

Right around this time in February Max Protecht wanted to do an exhibition about "Visions for the World Trade Center". My first project was a Floating memorial and Folded Street. I ended up working the entire year of 2002 on different projects related to the World Trade Center site. I worked on the Max Protecht show and then Herbert Muchamp had a New York Times invitational for "Visions for the World Trade Center" and then we were in the final competition for the site. Now there's a television documentary that gives the truth of the matter as it is now, Visions of Ground Zero; it tells the nasty but true story about the circumstances and the developer. So around the topic of what is a competition, this was not a legitimate competition. It was a pseudo competition. There was no intention from the land owners to execute any of the five projects. There were no real architects on the jury.

出します。コンペの作品をつくることは，通常の環境の下では前もって試せないだろう実験的な領域の可能性に心を広げる力を，勇気を与えてくれるんです。
GA： ニューヨークでのプロジェクトには何かありますか？
SH： プラット・スクール・オブ・アーキテクチュアのプロジェクトが今工事中です。ニューヨークで唯一外から見えるのは，ストアフロント・フォー・アート・アンド・アーキテクチュアの構成だけ。1993年，ヴィト・アッコンチと一緒にやったものです。
GA： 9月11日は，あなたの仕事にとってどんな意味を持っていますか？
SH： あの日ぼくはここにいました。ぼくのオフィスの窓から外が見えるけれど，真正面にタワーがあったんです。ぼくはエレベータで上がってきたところで，エレベータの運転手が言った「事故のようだ。飛行機が世界貿易センターにぶつかった」。続いてぼくのアシスタントが言った。「もう一機いる」。ここに着いたその時に，2つのタワーに衝突したのです。ぼくたちはそれが事故でないと分かった。ひどい恐怖を感じました。大きな12倍の双眼鏡を持っていて，タワーの上の階から……人々が飛び降りるのが見えた。オフィスにいた全員を家に帰しました。とてつもなく大きな不安な感じがあった。怒りはなく，もっと深く，説明しがたい感情です。翌朝，起きあがると，水彩を描き始めた。しばらくのあいだ，毎朝，黒の水彩画を描き続けた。そしてこれらのドローイングから追悼の空間をつくり始めました。ハドソン川の岸辺から，闇と光で構成された巨大なメモリアルが浮かぶように立ち上がる。水平線のように見える光が描く線があり，その白い線は，黒く塗られたコンクリートで組立てられた矩形の闇をつらぬき，光が射し込むいくつもの裂け目のある場所から立ち返る。

ちょうどこのころ，2月に，マックス・プロテッチは"世界貿易センターのための未

One of the problems with this competition is that all the energy and the amazing effort of talented architects from all over the world trying to make visions for this site are wasted by this travesty of commercial manipulative control when such a place is so important to the public. Right when this competition was being synthesized, the land should have been shifted to control by the City of New York. At that moment there was a proposal to trade the land underneath JFK and Newark Airports from the Port Authority for this site. Suddenly the City would control most of the site and the planning department could be involved with a higher degree of urban responsibility. It didn't happen; what's going on is one of the most compromised events of manipulation, cynical non-intention and mud wrestling between architects. It's just a circus. In my mind, it's not a competition.

GA: Can you give me an example of competition you feel was not compromised?

SH: The Museum of Contemporary Art in Helsinki was correctly and carefully organized. The jury met for one month before they came to a decision. And once they made their decision, our project as a work of architecture, was never tampered with. I had to reduce the size, and get it in budget. I had to get over a number of hurdles. But they never once tried to tamper with the integrity of the architecture. During the initial jury, Shinohara was the leading choice and we were second. As I understand the story, they suddenly realized in looking at his plans that it would be difficult to get the art in and out of the building and then they started to look more carefully at our building and found that it functioned better. That's something a jury realized after a long analysis of the problem. Helsinki was run as a competition where there's integrity. There's a clear intention to build what was competed. There was a proper jury with architects, city officials and the director of the museum, Tuula Arkio. She was a tireless advocate for the architecture from the moment of the jury, throughout design development and construction. My collaborating Finnish architect Juhani Pallasmaa, and Tuula Arkio made the Kiasma building a wonderful realization of a fine competition.

GA: So, the majority of your recent work has shifted outside of the United States. What is the difference between doing competitions here in the United States and in Europe or Asian countries?

SH: Where the invitations come from is also a bit about chance. Invitations seem to come from nowhere. I remember when an invitation from Arata Isozaki changed my life. I had just had a show at the Museum of Modern Art. It was November, 1988; the exhibition was opening in February on Ash Wednesday 1989. We were just putting it all together. It was exciting to be given the chance to have a show at the Museum of Modern Art; however, it completely bankrupted me, because MoMA didn't have the money to support us, to build the models, to finish the walls. I just had a four or five person office, and I was literally scraping by. I wasn't able to pay my rent. Then all of a sudden a fax comes in from Japan asking if I would be willing to design a 30-unit apartment building in Fukuoka? As if that was a question. Of course! It wasn't just an opportunity to do my first work in Japan, but it saved me from economic collapse. So that was like magic. Where did that come from? In my experience it's been a little bit like that.

来像"について，展覧会をしたいと考えたのです。ぼくの最初のプロジェクトは浮かぶような追悼の空間と折り返しながら空間を上って行く道で構成されていました。世界貿易センターの跡地に関係する異なったプロジェクトを2002年いっぱいかけてつくりました。ぼくはマックス・プロテッチでの展覧会の準備をして，次に，ハーバート・ミュシャンプによる"世界貿易センターのための未来像"を描くニューヨーク・タイムズの招待コンペがあり，次に，敷地跡のための最終コンペにぼくたちも入った。現在それがどうなっているか，真相を伝えるテレビ番組を今やっています。"グラウンド・ゼロの未来像"。その番組では，状況と開発業者についての実に不快だが真実の話を伝えている。つまり，コンペとは何かという原則から言えば，これは真正のコンペではなかった。これは擬似コンペでした。土地の所有者には，5つのプロジェクトのどの一つも実施するつもりはなかった。審査員には誠実な建築家は入っていなかった。このコンペの問題の一つは，この敷地のために理想像をつくろうとした世界中から参加した才能ある建築家のすべてのエネルギーと驚くべき努力がすべて，商業主義的な茶番劇によって失われてしまったことです。こうしたサイトが社会にとって非常に重要であるにもかかわらず。このコンペがまとめられたそのときに，この土地をニューヨーク市の管理下に転換すべきだったのです。あのとき，JFK空港とニューアーク空港の港湾局の管理下にある土地を，この敷地と交換する提案がありました。それが行われていれば，急遽，市は敷地の大半を管理することになり，高度な都市的責任を持って介入できたでしょう。しかし，そうはならなかった。何が進行しているかといえば，巧みにコントロールされた妥協の産物，建築家のあいだの，シニカルで無意味な泥仕合です。バカ騒ぎに過ぎない。ぼくの心のなかでは，これはコンペというものではありません。

GA：今までに妥協の産物でないと感じたコンペはありましたか？

SH：ヘルシンキの近代美術館は，正しく，注意深く組織されていました。審査員は，決定に至るまでに，1ヶ月間，会合を持ちました。そして，一度決定すると，この一連の建築としてのプロジェクトは，歪曲されることは全くなかったのです。大きさを縮め，予算内に納めたり，いくつものハードルを越えなければなりませんでした。しかし，主催者側は建築の全体性に対し一度も干渉してくることはなかった。最初の審査では篠原が最も有力な選択で，ぼくたちは2番手でした。しかし，ぼくの理解するところでは，審査員たちは突然，篠原のプランでは，建物の内外にアート作品を受け入れることは難しいだろうということに気付き，ぼくたちの建物をもっと丁寧に検討し始め，こちらの方が上手く機能することが分かったのです。それは，問題についての長い分析の後に審査員が気付いたものです。ヘルシンキは誠実なコンペとして運営されていました。公正な競争の結果，選ばれたものを建てようという明快な意図がありました。建築家，市の職員，美術館の館長の入った適切な審査団でした。トゥーラ・アルキオ。彼女は審査の時期から，デザインの展開，工事の段階，そのすべてを通して，疲れを知らない支援者でした。ぼくに協力してくれたフィンランドの建築家，ユハニ・パラッスマーとトゥーラ・アルキオが，キアスマの建物を，よく運営されたコンペの成果そのままに実現させてくれたのです。

GA：ところで，最近の仕事の大半が海外にシフトされています。ここ，アメリカでのコンペと，ヨーロッパやアジアの国々でのコンペには違いがありますか？

SH：どこから招待が来るかにも，多少の偶然があります。招待はどこからともなく来るように思えます。磯崎新からの招待がきたとき，ぼくの人生を変えたことを思い出しま

Makuhari Housing
The new town of Makuhari is sited on a dredged fill at the rim of Tokyo Bay. The concept interrelates two distinct types: silent heavyweight buildings and active lightweight structures.
 The silent buildings shape urban space and passage with apartments entered via inner garden courts. The concrete bearing walls have thick facades and a rhythmic sequence of openings. Slightly inflected according to sunlight they gently bend space and passage. Celebration of natural phenomena is taken up by the lightweight "activist" forms. Individuated "sounds" invade the heavyweight "silence" of the bracketing buildings.
 Inspired by Basho's The Narrow Road to the Deep North, the semi-public inner gardens and the perspectival arrangement of activist houses form an inner journey.

幕張ベイタウン・パティオス11番街
幕張の新しい町は、東京湾岸の埋め立て地に位置する。ここでのコンセプトは2つの明確なタイプを関係付けている：静かな重量感のある建物とアクティブな軽快なストラクチャである。
 静寂の建物はアーバン・スペースと、内部コートヤードからか各住戸に入るパッセージを作り出す。コンクリートによる対力壁は重厚なファサードを作りだし、そこにはリズミカルな開口部が与えられている。その空間とパッセージは陽光により緩やかに曲げられている。軽快な「活動者」のフォルムは自然現象を祝福するかのようである。個性化された「サウンド」は重量感のあるブラケット型の建物の「静寂」に押し寄せる。
 芭蕉の奥の細道にインスパイヤされ、半公共的な内部庭園と、遠近法的に配置される一連の「活動者の家」によって、内部空間に「旅路」を作りだしている。

 Another time in 1993, we had finished the Helsinki competition, and I didn't have any new work. Suddenly it's May of 1993. There are only two people left in the office and I haven't paid the rent in four months. I go to Amsterdam to teach at the Berlage Institute because I need the money, but it's still not enough money to support the office so I'm trying to schedule extra lectures. I receive a phone call from Helsinki and my office manager says "OK there's two kinds of news. Do you want to hear the good news or the bad news? I say "Give me the bad news first." She says "It's about the honorarium for Helsinki because of the drop in the Fin Mark against the dollar is only going to be $19,000. The good news is that we won the competition!" And that competition came with an honorarium of $50,000 so I immediately paid off my rent and paid off my debts and just barely got out of the hole. This is another case where something just happens and suddenly I am working in both Japan and Finland. I would go to a meeting in Japan and then fly to New York and then to Helsinki. Sometimes I wouldn't have time to come back to New York. At the time I couldn't imagine working in locations farther apart. And guess what? I have to work farther apart now. I have projects in Nanjing, Beijing, and Beirut. Architecture today is unpredictably international. We often compete against the same architects; in Rome it's Ando, Zaha, and Rem and then in China it's the same architects but on the opposite side of the earth! It's very strange, but the internet and ability to fly quickly, to connect everything together allows this new global dialogue to happen. Perhaps there's the tendency for clients to bring the architect from farther away just for the exotic nature of it.

 I really appreciated building in Japan and in Finland because you have dedicated craftsmen and builders that are difficult to find in the United States. Here it's hard to get dedicated contractors and harder to get good craftsmen. I have always had very positive experiences building in other place. On the other hand, difficulty comes when we get short listed for a project and they want to go visit my work. They have to fly all around the world: from Helsinki, to Tokyo, to Amsterdam.
GA: How is working in China?
SH: Working in China and working in Asia, for me, has been a very optimistic experience. When I worked with Isozaki for Void Space/Hinged Space Housing in Fukuoka, I went to Japan 30 times. The client and builders were really careful. Towards the end of the project, I was very exhausted from travel. As soon as we were finished we got another call for another housing block in Makuhari. The client had gone to Fukuoka and out of the five architects that worked there, they had liked our housing block the best. So then they hired me, I then flew to Japan 30 more times! The last time I flew was for the opening of Makuhari in 1996. Then the Japanese economic bubble burst. The Asian buildings were such great projects but they were hard to show any potential US client. No one who considered using me as an architect will be interested in flying to Japan to see my work. Now what's interesting about working in China is that suddenly my Japan projects are so close. When the China clients were deciding whether or not to hire us, they went to Japan to look at Fukuoka and Makuhari. Both of those projects are still looking very good. Back in 1996, who could imagine I would be building in China. I had no inkling of that pos-

す。MoMAから展覧会の開催の話があったばかりの時でした。1988年の11月です。1989年2月の聖灰水曜日がオープニングでした。すべてをまとめ上げたところだった。MoMAで展覧会を開くチャンスを与えられるなんてわくわくすることでした。ところが、それはぼくたちを完全に破産させてしまったんです。美術館にはぼくたちをサポートして、模型をつくり、壁面構成をする資金がなかった。ぼくにもなかった。4，5人の事務所を持ったばかりで、文字通りなんとかギリギリでやっていたんです。部屋代も払えない。ちょうどそのとき、日本から突然、ファックスが入ったんです。福岡に30戸のハウジングをデザインする気持ちはありませんか。まるで質問のようでした。もちろんです！ それは日本でのぼくの最初の仕事となったばかりでなく、経済的破綻からも救ってくれた。ですから、それは魔法のようなものでした。どこからきたのだろうか？ ぼくの人生にはそれに似た経験が、多少なりともあるんです。
 もう一つは、1993年、ヘルシンキのコンペ案を終えたところで、ぼくには新しい仕事は何もなかった。突然に、1993年5月。事務所に残っていたのは2人だけで、4ヶ月分の家賃がたまっていた。資金が必要だったので、アムステルダムのベルラーヘ・インスティテュートに教えに行くことにしたけれど、事務所を維持するにはそれだけでは十分ではないので、臨時のレクチャーを入れようと画策していたんです。そこへ、ヘルシンキから電話が入り、事務所のマネージャーが言った。「いい？，2種類のニュースがあるの。よいニュースと悪いニュース，どちらが聞きたい？」。ぼくは「悪いニュースを先に言ってくれ」と答えた。彼女は言った。「ヘルシンキの賞金は、フィンランドマルクの対ドル相場が落ちたために、1万9千ドルにしかならないみたい。よいニュースは、私たちがコンペに優勝したこと！」。しかも、コンペの賞金には5万ドルが付いてきたので、

すぐに家賃と負債を払い、借金はすっかりなくなった。あわやというまさにそのとき何かが起こる、というもう一つのケースだった。そして突然、日本とフィンランドの両方で仕事が始まった。日本での打合せに行き、ニューヨークに飛び、それからヘルシンキに向かう。ときどき、ニューヨークに戻る時間がなくなった。当時、ぼくには遥か離れた土地で仕事をすることが想像できなかった。どんなだと思う？ 今、さらに離れた場所で仕事をしなければならない。南京、北京、ベイルート。建築は今、予測できないほどインターナショナルなものになっています。ぼくたちは、しょっちゅう同じ人たちと競争している。ローマで安藤やザハやレムと、次には中国で。同じ顔ぶれ、しかし地球の反対側で！ とても妙な感じですが、インターネットや飛行機、すぐにもすべてを結合してしまう状況がこの新しいグローバルな対話を引き起こしている。クライアントには、もしかすると、異国風なものを求めて、はるか遠くから建築家を招く傾向があるのかもしれないね。
 日本やフィンランドで建てることの価値を、ぼくはほんとうに高く評価しています。なぜなら、アメリカにはない献身的な職人と建設会社が存在するからです。アメリカでは熱心なビルダーや、優秀な職人を探すのはすごく難しい。ですから、日本やフィンランドに建てるときは、常にとてもポジティヴな気持ちになれます。その一方、一番難しい点は、ぼくがプロジェクトの最終候補者リストに載ったとすると、クライアントはぼくの建物を見に行きたいと思うのに、世界中を飛び回らなければならないことです。ヘルシンキから、東京へ、そしてアムステルダムへ。
GA：中国での仕事はどんな様子なんでしょうか？
SH：中国で仕事すること、アジアで仕事することは、これまでずっと、ぼくにはとても

Makuhari Housing, Chiba, Japan, 1992-96 ✶✶

Model of housing complex, Beijing

楽観的になれる体験でした。磯崎と，福岡のヴォイド・スペース／ヒンジド・スペース・ハウジングの仕事をしたときは，30回日本に行きました。クライアントも建設業者も実に丁寧な仕事振りでした。終わり頃になると，旅のためにぼくはすっかり消耗していました。終わるとすぐに，幕張のもう一つのハウジングに声がかかりました。クライアントは福岡に行き，そこで仕事をした5人の建築家の建物のなかで，ぼくたちのを一番気にいったんです。そこで，彼らはぼくを雇い，ぼくはさらに30回，日本に飛ぶことになった。最後のフライトは1996年のオープニングのためでした。そして，日本のバブル経済がはじけたのです。アジアでの建物は，こうしたとても素晴らしいプロジェクトですが，その力をアメリカのクライアントに見せることは困難です。ぼくを建築家として使おうと思い，ぼくの作品を見に日本まで飛んでくる気になる人は誰もいない。ところが，今，中国で仕事をすることになって嬉しいのは，ぼくの日本でのプロジェクトが近くなったことです。中国のクライアントは，ぼくを雇おうかどうか決めかねているときは，福岡や幕張を見に日本に来ます。両方のプロジェクトとも，今も，とてもよい状態に保たれています。1966年当時，ぼくが中国で仕事するだろうなんて誰が想像しただろうか。そんな可能性を，ぼくはまったく感じていませんでした。この中国での仕事は，エキサイティングで，予想もしなかった，嬉しい出来ごとでした。ぼくの日本の建物は，8年間たってもそこにしっかりと建ち，状態もよく，人々もいまだに喜んで住んでくれています。それは新しいクライアントにぼくに対する信頼を与えてくれました。おかげで，北京のハウジングで試してみたいと思うことを通すのは前より楽になりました。クライアントが，北京のプロジェクトとある程度関係性のある，ぼくの北京以前の作品を日本で見ることが出来るからです。ぼくの作品の大半がアジアに実現するなんて想像もしていなかったので，それはちょっと妙な気分ですが，そんな風に進んでいるようです。北京のこのプロジェクトはぼくのどこにある建物よりも大きな集合体になるでしょう。映画館，ホテル，ブリッジでつながった"フィルミック"な環状の住戸棟，幼稚園。巨大な建物です。3年前にさえ，決して想像できなかった，魅力的な未知の存在です。

こうしたことには，シアトルで育った子供としての直観があったかもしれないと言えるかも知れません。父と母とぼくは，よくシータック国際空港に寄って，飛行機が離陸するのを見ていたものです。1955年当時，そこに行くのは日曜日のちょっとわくわくする体験でした。豊かな家ではなく，どこかへ飛んで行くお金があったわけでもありませんが，そこにはこの，好奇心をかきたてられるような感覚があり，飛行機が太平洋を西へ向かって離陸して行くところをよく覚えています。シアトルから日本へ向かうとき流れるノースウエスト・オリエントのテーマソングを思い出します。また，シアトルの風景もぼくには日本を思い出させます。プージェット海峡の輝く水があり，富士山はレーニア山の従兄弟のようなものです。シアトルのある種の風景は，ぼくの心をアジアに連れて行きます。ヨーロッパで，ローマとロンドンのAAスクールで教育を受けたにも拘らずヨーロッパではないのです。今，ぼくの人生のこの時点で，56歳なんですが，今，進行している，ぼくの最大の仕事はアジアにあります。今，ニューヨークから北京に向かって飛行機が離陸するとき，小さなモニタのデータを見つめていると，飛行機は機首を真上に向ける！　数時間後，画面は変わり，飛行機は今，北極点にあり，北京に向かって下降するのが分かる。まず上昇し，次に下降して行く。東と西が交替して行く。ぼくは，さまよえる旅人のように感じる。東へ行くのでも西へ行くのでもなく，上がった

sibility. This China work is an exciting, unpredictable, positive event. It also gave new clients the confidence from work that I had already built, still in good shape, now standing for eight years and people still enjoy living there. My arguments about the things I want to try to do for housing in Beijing become easier because clients can go to those sites in Japan and see earlier works that have some relationship to them. It's funny because I never imagined that the largest amount of my work would end up in Asia, but it seems it's going that way. This project in Beijing will be the largest collection of my buildings anywhere. There's going to be the cinemateque, the hotel, the bridge-connected filmic loop apartments, the kindergarten. It's a huge work. It's an interesting unknown that I would have never have imaged, even three years ago.

I could say that maybe I had an intuition about Asia as a child growing up in Seattle. My father and mother and I used to stop at the Seatack International Airport and watch the planes take off. Back then in 1955, it was an exotic thing to do on Sunday. Even though we were not wealthy and didn't have the money to fly anywhere, there was this feeling of mystery and I remember the planes taking off, heading west over the Pacific Ocean. I remember the Northwest Orient's theme song being played as they would take off from Seattle to Japan. Also the landscape of Seattle reminds me of Japan. There's the reflecting water of Puget Sound, and Mt. Fuji to me is the cousin of Mt. Rainier. The kind of landscape in Seattle puts my mind in Asia and not in Europe, even though I was educated in Europe: in Rome and at the Architectural Association in London. At this point in my life, I'm 56 years old, and my biggest ongoing new work is in Asia. Now when the plane takes off from New York to Beijing—when you watch the little screen monitor which gives statistics, the plane is headed straight up! After a few hours the screen changes and you see the plane now is at the North Pole heading down to Beijing—first going up, now going down; east and west are being replaced, I feel more like a wandering exile, not going east or west, but like a "new ghost" going up and down.

October, 2004, at Steven Holl's studio
Interview by Yoshio Futagawa
Copyediting by Takashi Yanai

り，下がったりする"新種の幽霊"といったところでしょうか。

2004年10月，スティーブン・ホールのスタジオにて
インタビュー：二川由夫
和訳：菊池泰子

Excepted as noted: photos by Yoshio F.
* provided by Steven Holl Architects
** photos by GA photographers

at conference room 会議室にて

TOWN CENTER TOWERS
XKY XCRAPER

Vuosaari, Finland
Design: 1999

Night view from sea 海からの夜景

GA PROJECT

Architects: Steven Holl Architects—Steven Holl, Solange Fabiao, principals-in-charge; Justin Korhammer, Annette Goderbauer, project team
Associate architect: Vesa Honkonen Architects
Program: housing and retail facilities

Concept:

The new center for the town of Vuosaari is a double tower forming a gateway on a raised plaza facing the horizon of the Gulf of Finland. The tilt of the earth's axis, 23.5 degrees, defines the geometry of the towers (T.23.5° and T.90°). Vuosaari, near Helsinki, the northern most metropolis on earth, is the place where the northern end of the earth's axis always points (North Star).

Public spaces of the "X" Towers at the base are earth-bound:
- a rough Finnish granite plaza at the "Gateway" opening
- sloped grass play area ramps for children
- enclosed cafe and shopping area.
- a "snow-tank" fountain

Public space at the top of the "X" Towers are skybound:
- an observation level "Polaris" cafe on T.23.5°
- an inside-outside terrace with "Diurnal Circles" stairs
- a "blind room" arrival area with computer screen exhibits dedicated to the motions of the earth and time
- a wooden sauna topped by a helicopter pad (on the T.90°)

Hinged-Space Apartments. The dwellings in the new "X" Towers aim at flexibility, change, and functionality. Large light weight wooden pivot doors in various rotations form the different rooms and private sleeping areas within each flat. During a special gathering all the "hinged-space" doors can be opened forming one continuous flat with magnificent views. During the night, "hinged-space" doors can be closed into several private bedrooms. The glazed balcony areas of the flats have "hinged-space" doors allowing them to be closed or open during summer or winter.

The pair of towers open at the base to frame a view of the distant sea horizon, over a plaza in rough red Finnish Granite. Below the shops and cafes join the building to its south and east neighbors. Tower 23.5° has an "inclinator" traversing its tilt which has a padded bench along its cabin to take visitors to the public observation and cafe terrace. This tower contains smaller apartments and floor through apartments where the two towers join. Tower 90° has two elevators, and at its upper level a sauna terrace and a heliport.

The glass curtain wall of the towers is one of highest grade "Low E" double glass with slight colored tint for shading. The sun facing elevators are green tinted white while others are yellow tinted. All rooms have operable windows and natural cross-ventilation. The night-time view of the new town-center presents a warm and glowing presence in this place of bi-polar rotation.

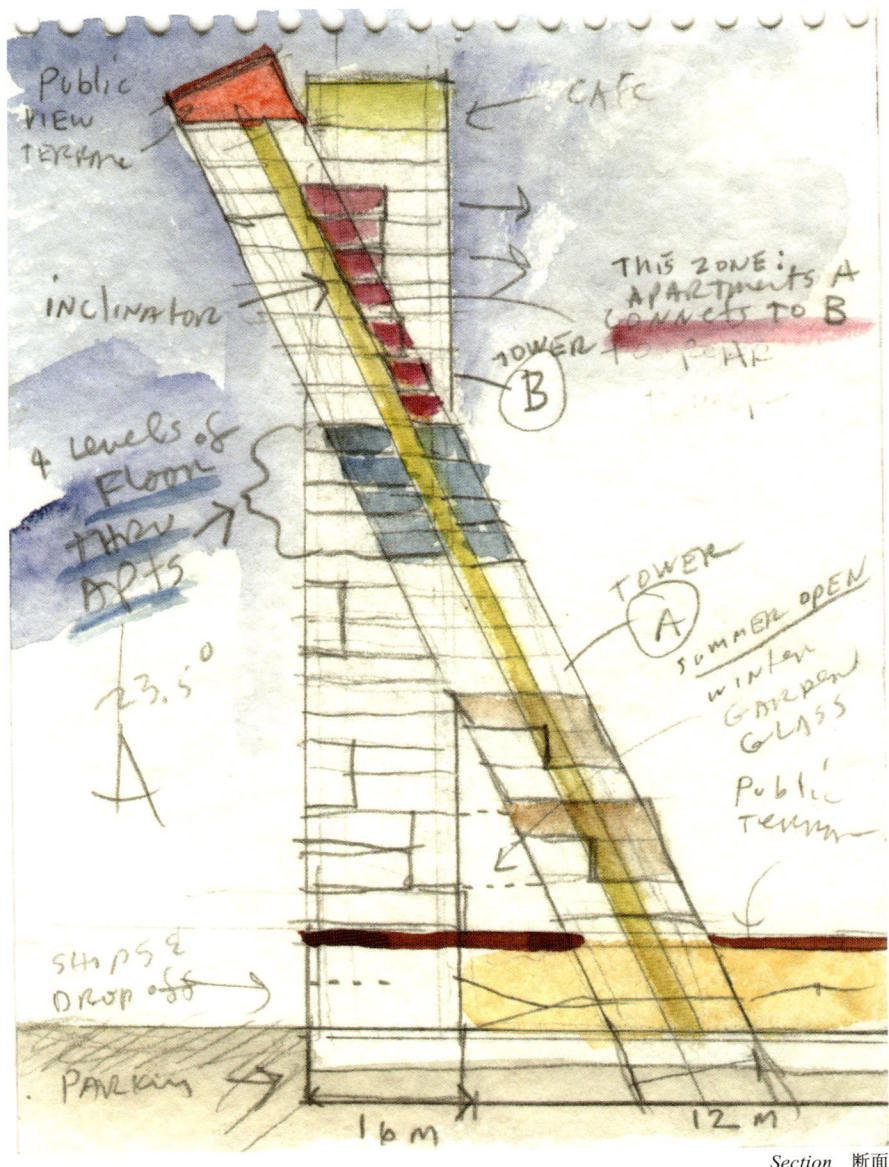

Section 断面

GA DOCUMENT

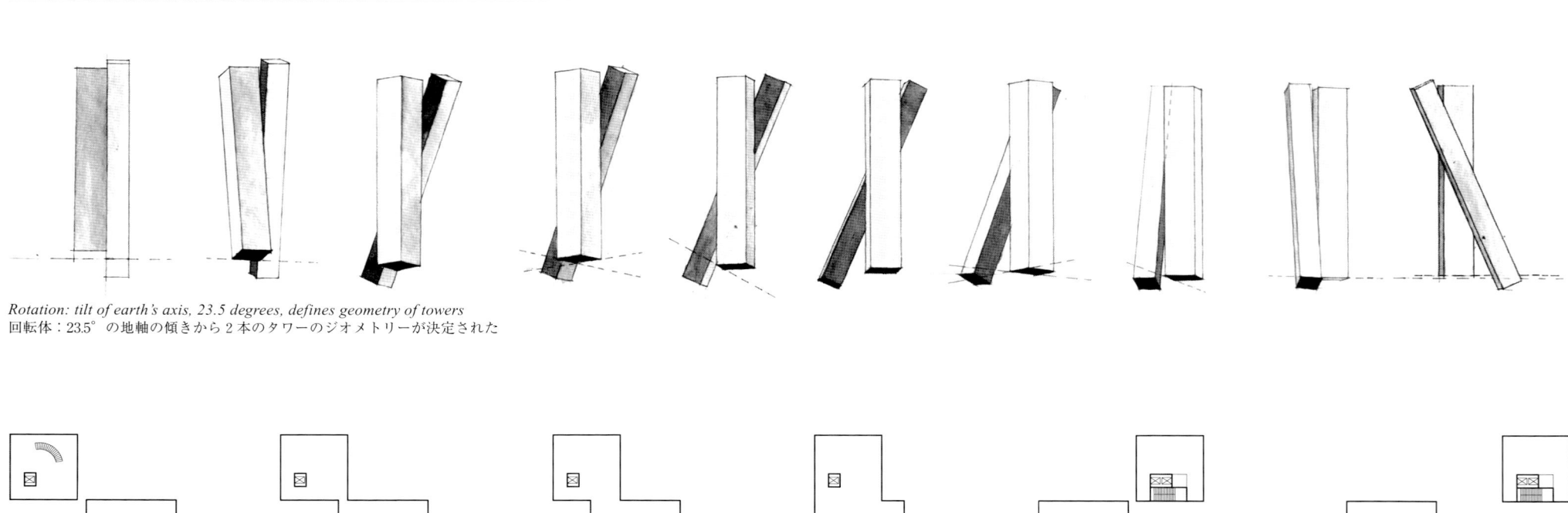

Rotation: tilt of earth's axis, 23.5 degrees, defines geometry of towers
回転体：23.5°の地軸の傾きから2本のタワーのジオメトリーが決定された

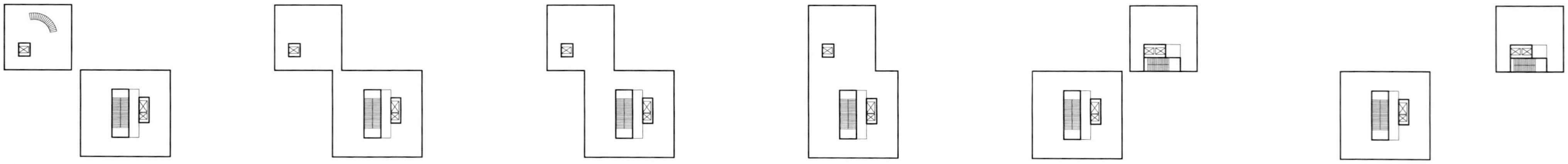

Plans

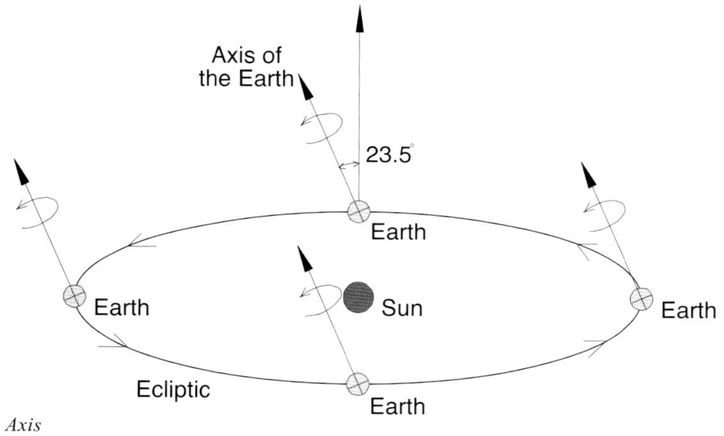

Axis

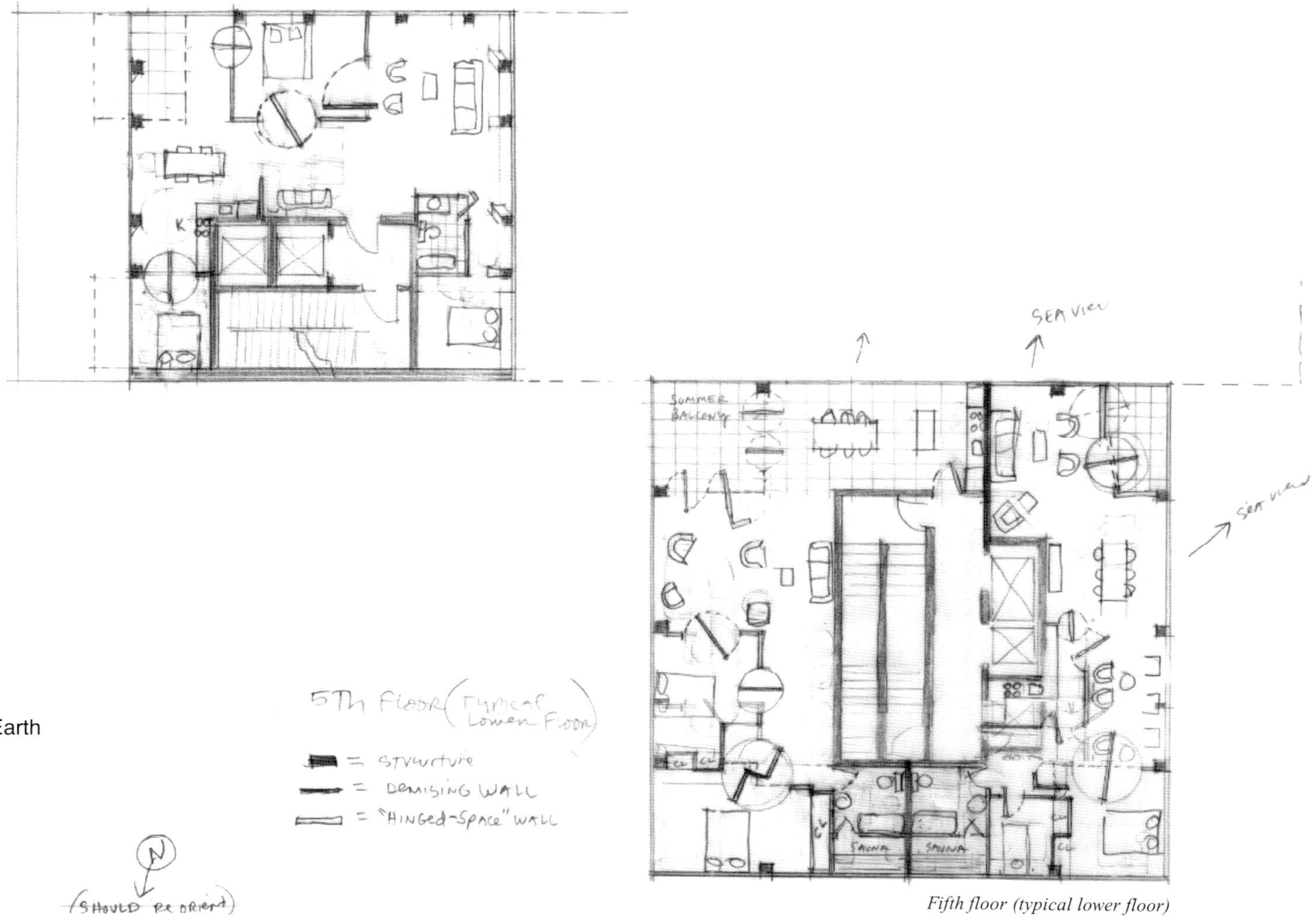

Fifth floor (typical lower floor)

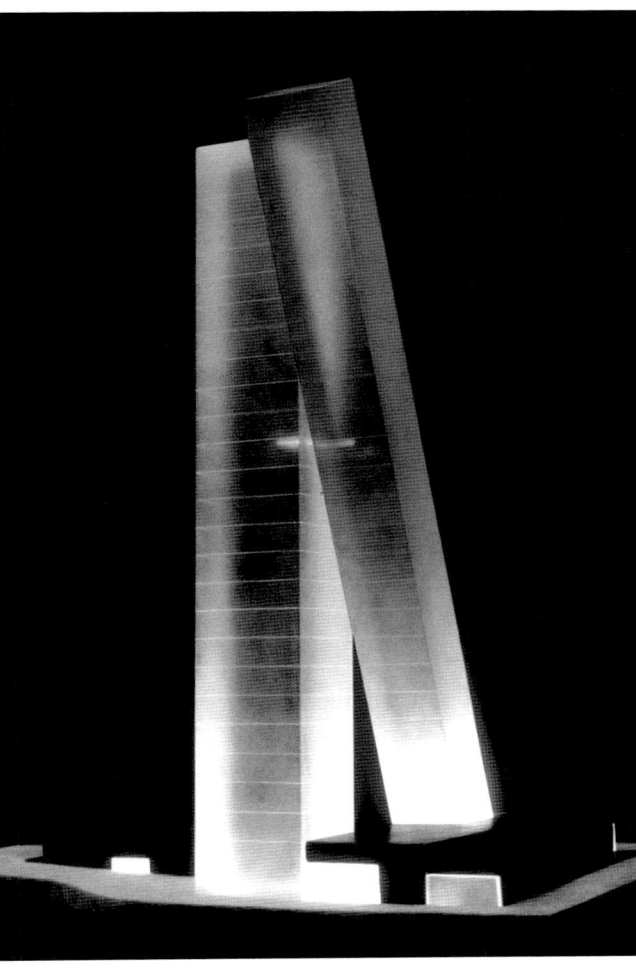

ヴオサーリの新しいタウン・センターは，フィンランド湾の水平線を前にして，高く持ち上げられた広場の上にゲートウェイをかたちづくる対のタワーである。23.5°の地軸の傾きから，2本のタワーのジオメトリーが決定された（タワー23.5°とタワー90°）。地球上で最北に位置する大都市ヘルシンキに近いヴオサーリでは，地軸の北端が常に北極星を指している。

"X"タワーの基部を構成する公共空間は大地と結ばれる
—フィンランド産の肌理の粗い花崗岩を敷き詰めた"ゲートウェイ"広場
—子供達の遊び場である芝生のスロープ
—屋内に配置されたカフェとショッピング・エリア
—"スノー・タンク"噴水

"X"タワーの頂部を構成する公共空間は空と結ばれる
—タワー23.5°の展望階にある"北極星"カフェ
—"日周圏"階段の付いた，内側のテラス
—地球と時間の動きに献じられたコンピュータ・スクリーン映像のある到着エリア，"窓のない部屋"
—木造のサウナを覆う，最頂部のヘリコプター・パッド（タワー90°）

ヒンジド＝スペース・アパートメント"X"タワー内の住宅は，フレキシブルで変更可能，機能的である。木製の軽く大きなピボット・ドアが様々に回転して，各フラットに，それぞれ異なる部屋やプライベートな寝室エリアを形成する。特別な集いには，"ヒンジド＝スペース"のドアを開け放てば，素晴らしい眺めの見える一室空間となる。夜は"ヒンジド＝スペース"のドアを閉ざせば，各自の寝室に分けられる。ガラス張りのバルコニー・エリアに付けられた"ヒンジド＝スペース"ドアは，夏や冬，開け放したり，閉ざしたりできる。

対のタワーの足元は開放され，ざらざらしたフィンランド産の赤い花崗岩を敷き詰めた広場の先，遠くに海の水平線が見える眺めを枠取る。ショップやカフェの下で，建物は南と東側に広がる近隣地区とつながる。タワー23.5°には，中央にその傾斜に沿って下から上まで通る"インクリネイター"があり，そのキャビン沿いにベンチが見物客を展望台やカフェテラスに導く。このタワーには，小さなフラットと，2つのタワーの連結部4層にワンフロア全体を占めるフラットがある。タワー90°には2基のエレベータが付き，上階にはサウナ・テラスとヘリポートがある。

タワーのガラス・カーテンウォールには，陽射しを防ぐため薄い色合いの，高断熱複層ガラスが使われる。太陽に面する側のエレベータは白を混ぜた緑色，他は黄色である。すべての部屋に開閉窓があり，自然換気できる。新しいタウン・センターの夜景は，両極端な季節が循環するこの場所に，暖かく，輝く存在感のある姿を見せてくれるだろう。

Entrance エントランス

"X" Towers forming gateway on plaza: earth's axis (Tower 23.5°) always points North Star in Vuosaari

"X" タワーは広場のゲートウェイを形成する：ヴオサーリにおいては，地軸（タワー23.5°）は常に北極星を指す

Interior of apartment アパート内部

NELSON ATKINS MUSEUM OF ART

Kansas City, Missouri, U.S.A.
Design: 1999–2004   Construction: 2002–05

The expansion of the Nelson Atkins Museum will occur through five new "lenses" forming new spaces, new viewpoints, and new angles of vision. From the movement of the body through the landscape and the free movement threaded between the light gathering "lenses" of the new addition, exhilarating new experiences of the Nelson-Atkins will be created. Glass lenses bring different qualities of light to the galleries, while the sculpture garden's pathways meander through them. Rather than an addition of a mass, we envision the new elements to be in complementary contrast:

In complementary Contrast

"Existing"	"New"
Opaque	Transparent
Heavy (stone weight)	Light (feather weight)
Hermetic	Meshing of interior and exterior
Inward views	Views into the landscape
Bounded	Unbounded
Directed circulation	Open circulation
Single Mass	Multiple transparent "lenses"

Day and Night: A Meandering Garden of Lights
The lenses inject light into the galleries during the day. At night the light of the galleries glows in the sculpture garden via the lenses.

New Entry: An Inviting Lantern
A new bright and transparent glass lobby invites the public into the experiences of the Nelson-Atkins Museum. A rubber ramp escalator facilitates circulation to the continuous levels of galleries step down into the garden. From the lobby a new cross axis creates connection through the existing building.

At night the glowing glass of the lobby provides an inviting transparency announcing events and activities. The new parking is lit by special lenses at the bottom of the reflecting pond.

Structure: Breathing
"T" at the heart of the addition's glass "lenses" is a structural concept merged with a light and air distributor concept. "Breathing T's" bring light down into the galleries along their curved undersides while carrying the glass in suspension and providing the place for the HVAC ducts. Sustainable building concepts include green roofs and double glass cavities for gathering sun heated air in winter or exhausting it in summer. Computer controlled screens on south glass and special translucent insulating materials insure the efficiency and seasonal flexibilities of the "lenses" structural stability is increased by slight turns in plan geometry. A continuous service level basement below all the galleries offers flexible access to all the "Breathing-Ts."

Circulation: Open and Free
All the main galleries of the addition are organized on a continuous flowing level with occasional views into the landscape of the sculpture gardens. Circulation and exhibition merge as one can look from one level to another; from inside to outside. The back and forth "meander" path in the sculpture garden above has its sinuous compliment in open flow on the continuous level of new galleries.

Art + Landscape + Architecture: A Walk in the Park
The potential of the Nelson-Atkins Museum expansion to engage the landscape of the Sculpture Garden makes the entire museum precinct the site of the visitor's experience. The flanking open landscape-connected addition brings the user deep into the qualities of the site on every visit.

The strong holdings of the Nelson-Atkins Museum in Oriental Art such as "Verdant Mountains" 1090 by Chiang Shen or "The North Sea" by Chou Ch'en demonstrate the timeless merging of art, architecture and landscape. The new addition will celebrate this fusion with the new Noguchi sculpture court, setting a binding connection to the existing Sculpture Gardens and the new addition.

This competition winning addition is composed of five interconnected structures as opposed to a single massive expansion. Traversing from the existing building across its sculpture park, the five built "lenses" form new spaces and angles of vision. From the movement through the landscape and threaded between the light openings, exhilarating new experiences of the existing Museum will be formed. Circulation and exhibition merge as one can look from one level to another, from inside to outside. The "meandering" path in the sculpture garden above has its sinuous compliment in open flow through the continuous level of new galleries. Glass lenses bring different qualities of light to the galleries while the sculpture garden's pathways wind through them.

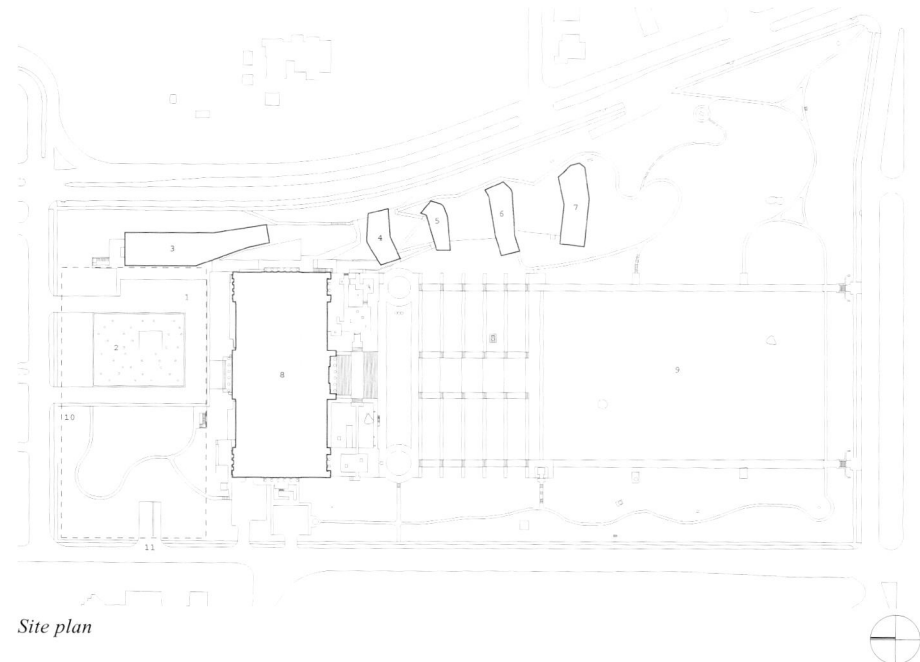

1 ENTRY PLAZA
2 REFLECTING POOL
3 LENS 1 UPPER LOBBY
4 LENS 2
5 LENS 3
6 LENS 4
7 LENS 5
8 EXISTING MUSEUM
9 EXISTING SCULPTURE LAWN
10 GARAGE BELOW
11 GARAGE ENTRANCE

Site plan

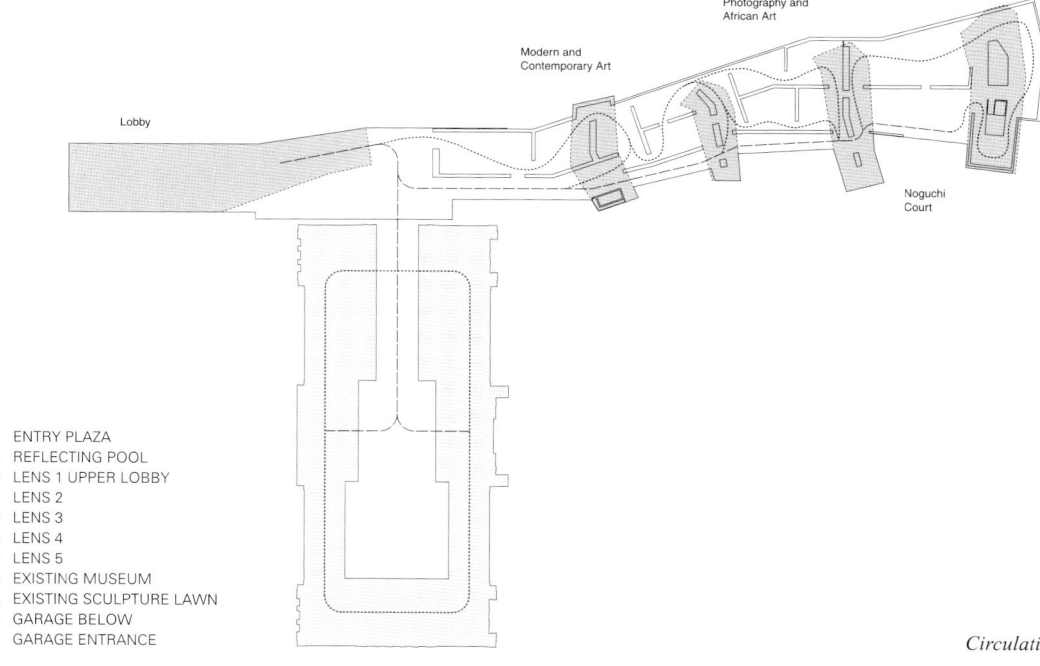

Circulation

G A PROJECT

コンペの優勝案となったネルソン・アトキンズ美術館の拡張計画は、新しい空間、新しい視点、新しい視角を形成する、互いに連結された5つのストラクチャー、"レンズ"によって展開されている。ランドスケープのなかを通り過ぎて行く身体の動き、光を集める"レンズ"のあいだを縫うように進む自由な動きから、生き生きとした、新しい美術館体験が生まれるだろう。ガラスの"レンズ"がギャラリーに多彩な光を運び込み、彫刻庭園の通路は"レンズ"を蛇行しながら抜けて行く。マスを加えるのではなく、新しいエレメントが、旧棟と補完的な対比を構成するような増築にしたいと考えた。

補完的な対比
〈既存のもの〉　　　　　〈新しいもの〉
不透明　　　　　　　　　透明
重い（石の重さ）　　　　軽い（羽の重さ）
密封された　　　　　　　メッシュ状の内部と外部
内向きの眺め　　　　　　風景に向かう眺め
拘束され、方向性を持つ導線
　　　　　　　　　　　　拘束されない、開かれた導線
単一のマス　　　　　　　多様で透明な"レンズ"

〈昼と夜：光の蛇行する庭園〉
"レンズ"は昼間、ギャラリーに光を差し入れる。夜は、ギャラリーの光は"レンズ"を透過して彫刻庭園のなかで輝く。

〈新しい入り口：招き寄せるランタン〉
透明ガラスに包まれた、明るい新ロビーが、来館者をネルソン・アトキンズ美術館の体験のなかへ招き入れる。ゴム製のランプ・エスカレータは、庭園へ降りて行くギャラリーを構成する、連続する様々なレベルへ向かう導線をスムーズなものにする。ロビーから延びる新しい横断軸が旧棟全体とのつながりをつくりあげる。

夜になると、ロビーの透明なガラスは内部の照明に輝き、イベントや活動の様子を外に知らせて、人を招き寄せる。リフレクティング・ポンドの底に付けられた特殊レンズが、新しい地下駐車場を明るく照らす。

〈構造：呼吸する"T"〉
増築部のガラス"レンズ"の中心に立つ"呼吸するT"は、光と大気の配達人という発想と構造上のコンセプトを合体させたものである。"呼吸するT"は光をその下側の湾曲に沿ってギャラリーに落とす一方、ガラス壁を支持し、空調ダクトの設置場所を提供する。サステイナブルな建物という基本的な考えには、グリーン・ルーフや冬には太陽熱に暖められた空気を集め、夏には排気する役割を果たす二重ガラスによる空隙の設置などが含まれる。南面するガラスに取り付けられたコンピュータ制御のスクリーンと、特殊な半透明断熱材が省エネルギー効率を確実にし、"レンズ"の構造的安定性を守る、季節に対応した柔軟性は、プラン・ジオメトリーのわずかな転回によって増加する。ギャラリーの下、地下に延びるサービス階は、"呼吸するT"へのフレキシブルなアクセスを提供する。

〈動線：開かれていて自由な〉
増築部のメイン・ギャラリーは、流れるように連続するレベルで構成され、ところどころ彫刻庭園の風景が飛び込んでくる。動線と展示スペースは、一方の階から他方の階を、内側から外側を見ることができるように結合されている。上の彫刻庭園の、前後左右に"蛇行する"通路を、新しいギャラリー・レベルの、なめらかに続く流れが間接的に補完する。

〈アート＋風景＋建築：公園のなかの散歩〉
彫刻庭園の風景と増築棟を組み合わせることが可能であったため、美術館の全領域を来館者の体験サイトへとつくりあげることができた。ガラスの両側面が風景に開き、風景と結びついた増築部は、訪れるたびに、敷地の多彩な魅力のなかに深く引き込んでくれるだろう。

1090年作のチャン・シェンの「青山」やチュー・チェンの「北海」など、美術館が所蔵する東洋美術の力強い作品は、アート、建築、風景の無限の融合に気付かせてくれる。新しくつくられるノグチ・スカルプチャー・コートが、既存の彫刻庭園と増築部を結び、この融合を現実のものとする。

1 LIBRARY
2 UPPER LOBBY
3 GARDEN DINING ROOM
4 SPECIAL EXHIBITIONS
5 LOWER LOBBY
6 MODERN & CONTEMPORARY ART
7 PHOTOGRAPHY
8 AFRICAN ART
9 SPECIAL EXHIBITIONS

Library floor

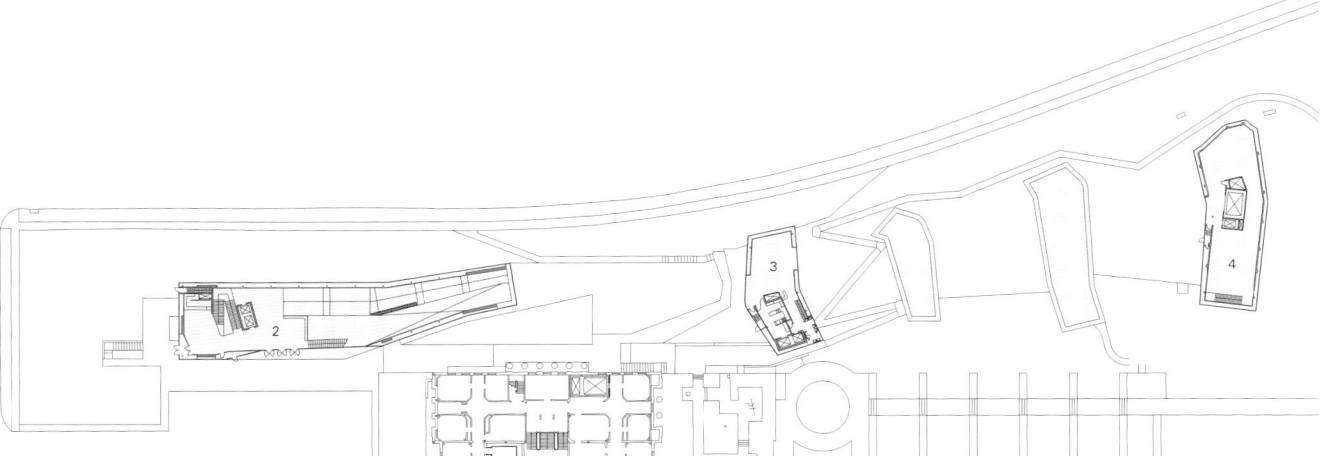

First floor

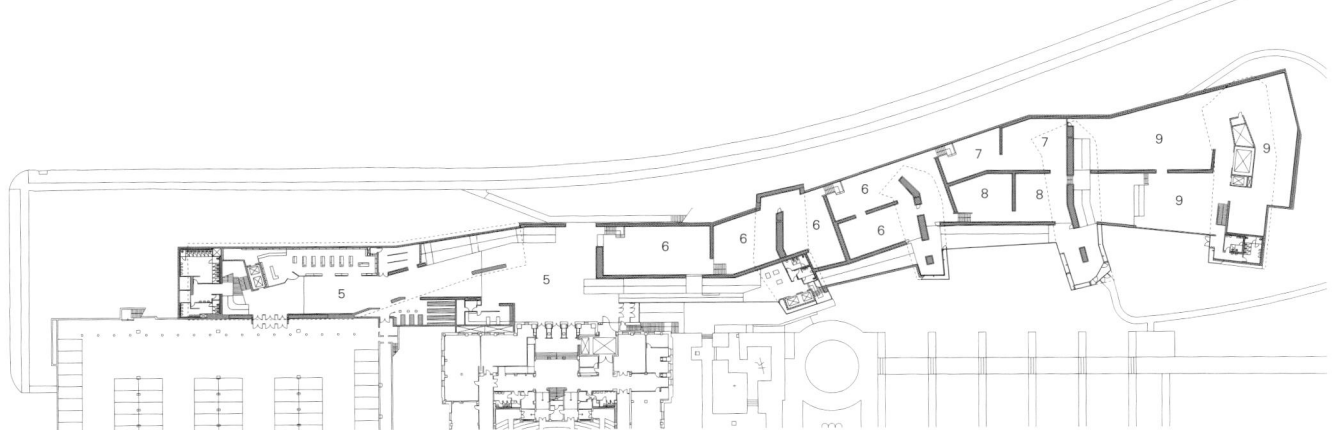

Ground floor

Architects: Steven Holl Architects—Steven Holl, principal-in-charge; Chris McVoy, partner-in-charge; Richard Tobias, Martin Cox, project architect; Gabriela Barman-Kraemer, Matthias Blass, Molly Blieden, Elsa Chryssochoides, Robert Edmonds, Makram El-Kadi, Simone Giostra, Annette Goderbauer, Mimi Hoang, Li Hu, Justin Korhammer, Linda Lee, Fabian Llonch, Stephen O'Dell, Susi Sanchez, Irene Vogt, Urs Vogt, Christian Wassmann, project team; Casey Cassias, partner; Greg Sheldon, project architect
Associate architect: Berkebile Nelson Immenschuh McDowell Architects
Client: Nelson Atkins Museum of Art
Consultants: Guy Nordenson and Associates, structural; Structural Engineering Associates, associate structural; Ove Arup & Partners, mechanical; W.L. Cassell Associates, associate mechanical; Renfro Design Group, lighting; Olin Partnership, landscape; Walter De Maria, site specific art installation
Program: addition to museum, garage, sculpture garden

Model: view from southeast　模型：南東より見る

View from reflecting pool: new building (Lens 1) on left, existing museum on right
水盤より見る。新棟（レンズ１）が左に，旧棟が右に建つ

Exploded axonometric

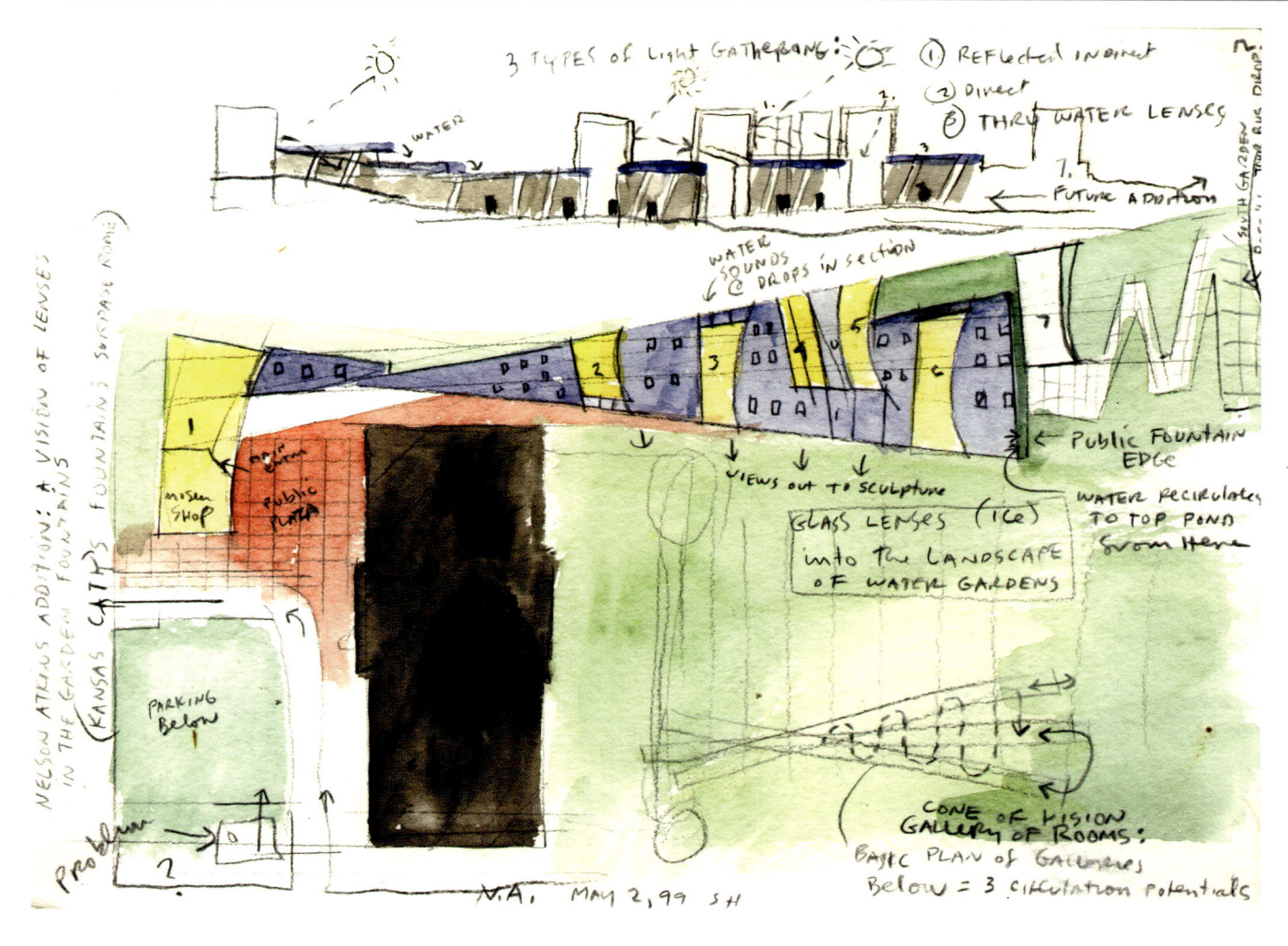

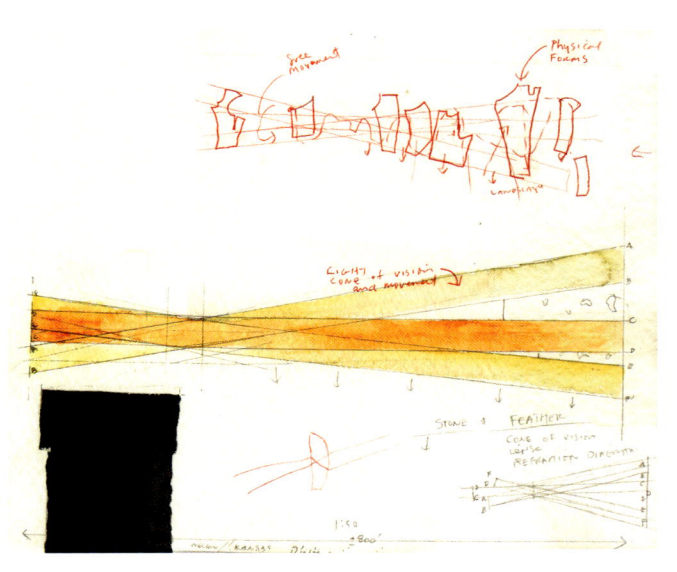

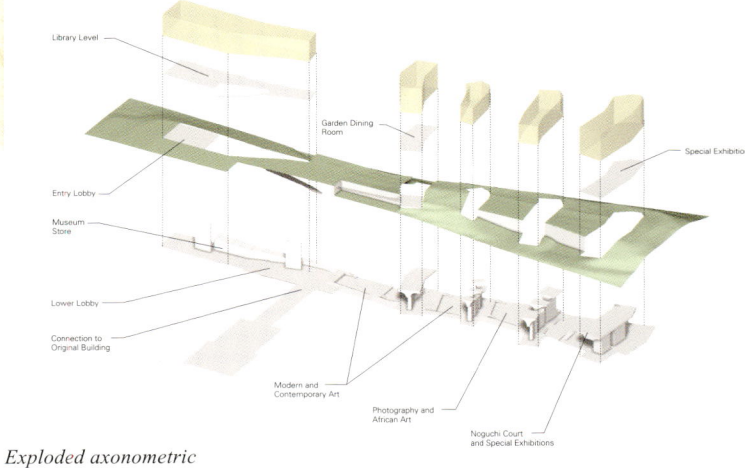

Model: new buildings like lantern ランタンのような新棟

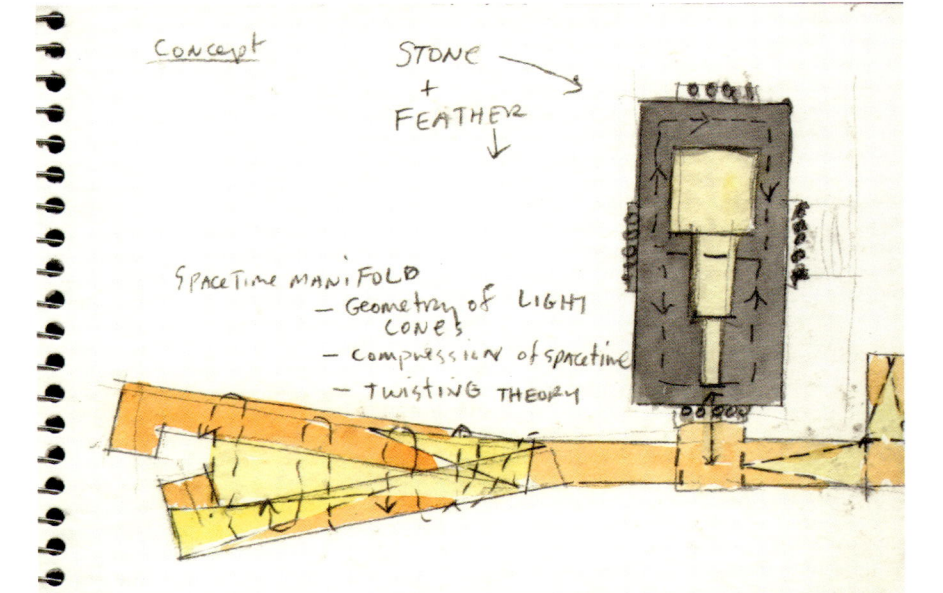

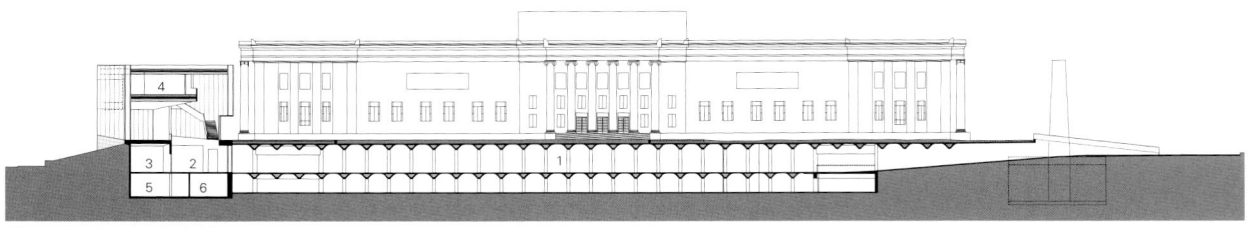

Cross section: main lobby/garage

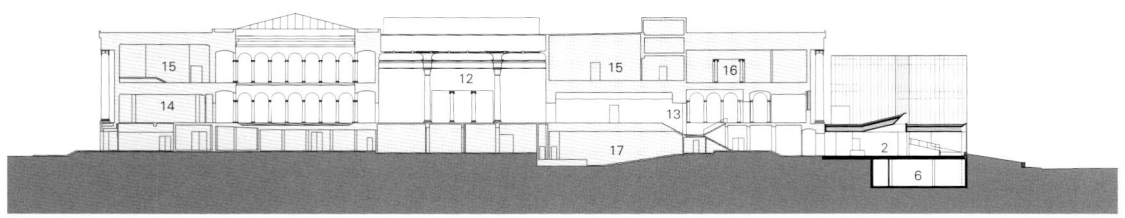

Cross section: lower lobby & existing building cross axis

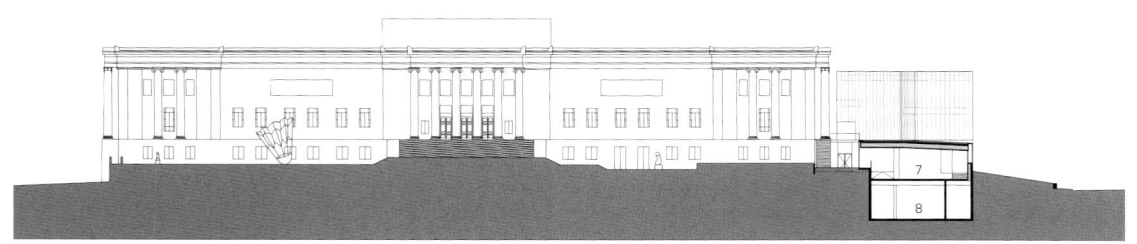

Cross section: modern & contemporary galleries

1	PARKING GARAGE	10	SPECIAL EXHIBITION
2	LOBBY	11	ART RECEIVING
3	MUSEUM STORE	12	EXISTING BUILDING
4	LIBRARY	13	NEW OPENING & STAIR
5	STACKS	14	EUROPEAN ART
6	MECHANICAL	15	ASIAN ART
7	MODERN & CONTEMPORARY ART	16	AMERICAN ART
8	COLLECTION STORAGE	17	AUDITORIUM
9	NOGUCHI COURT	18	PHOTOGRAPHY

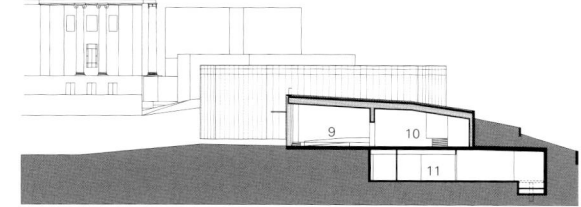

Cross section: Noguchi court/special exhibition

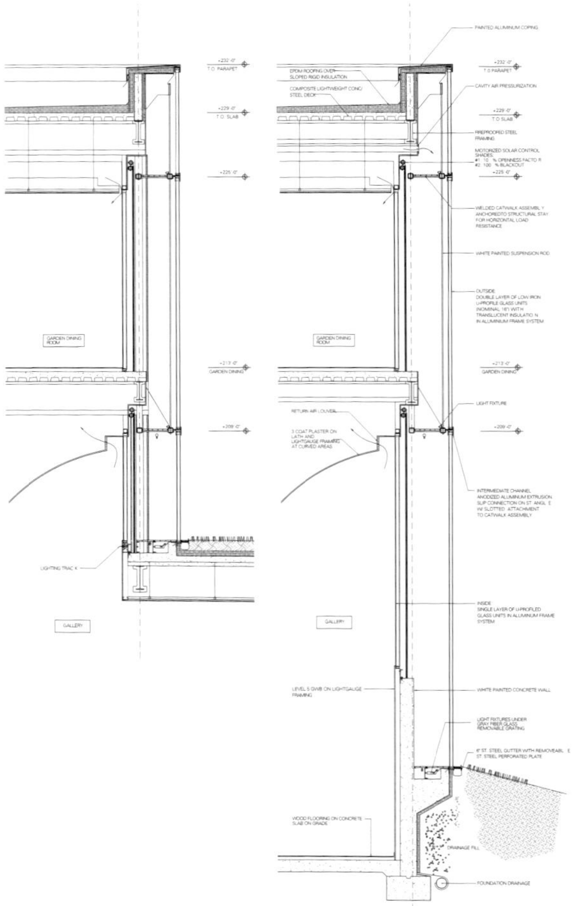

Wall section

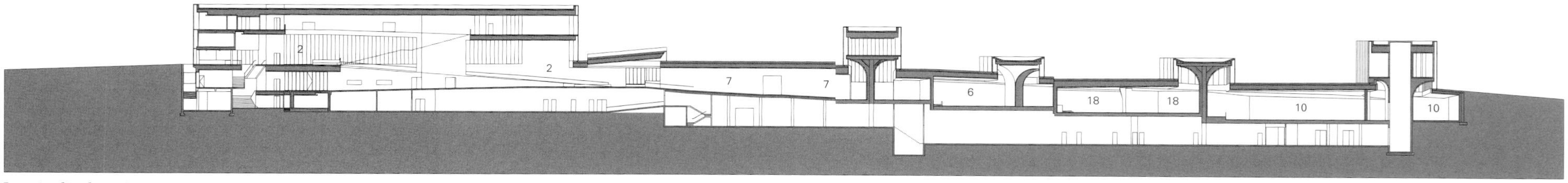

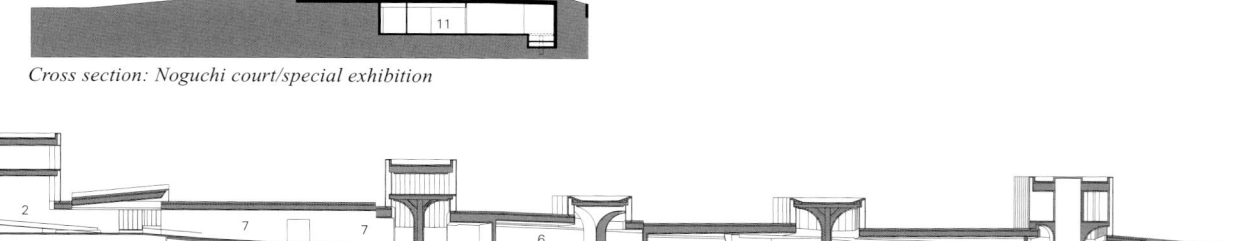

Longitudinal section

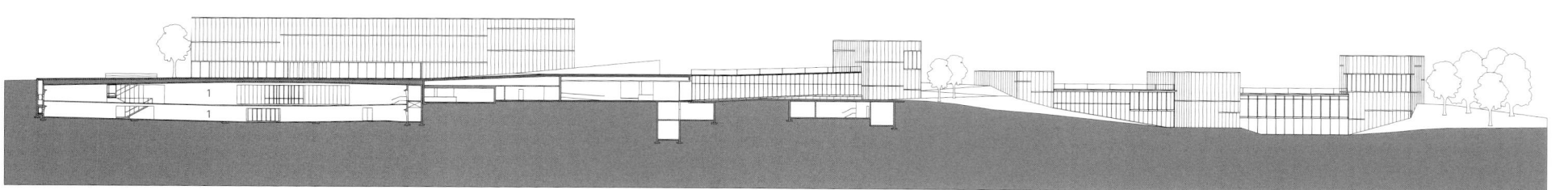

West elevation

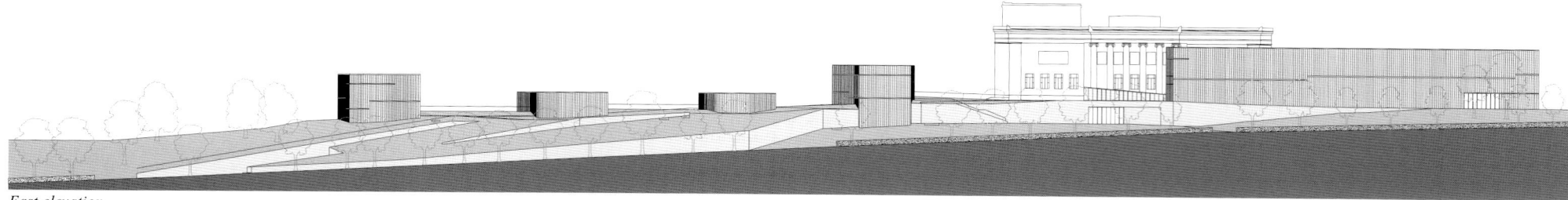

East elevation

39   GA PROJECT

"T" structure: sectional detail

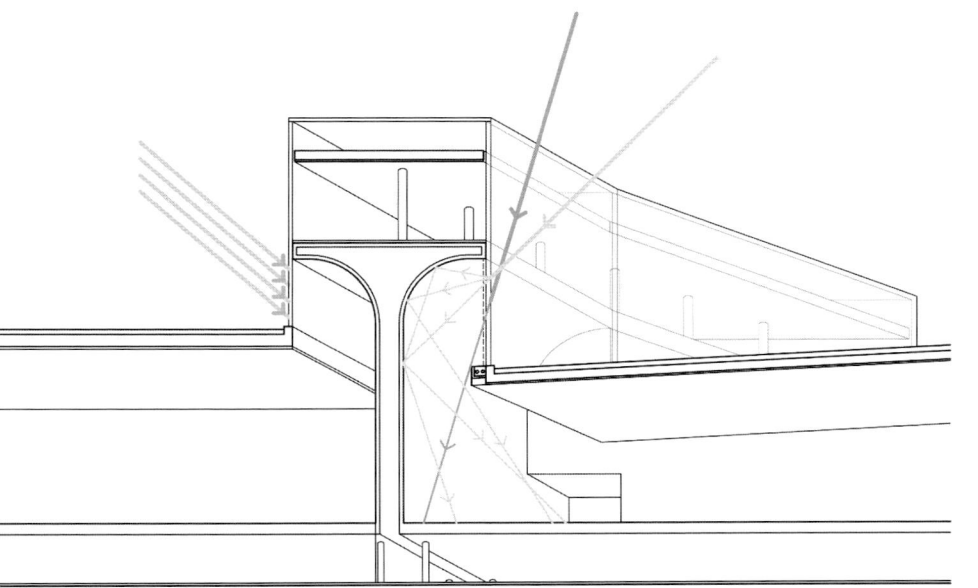

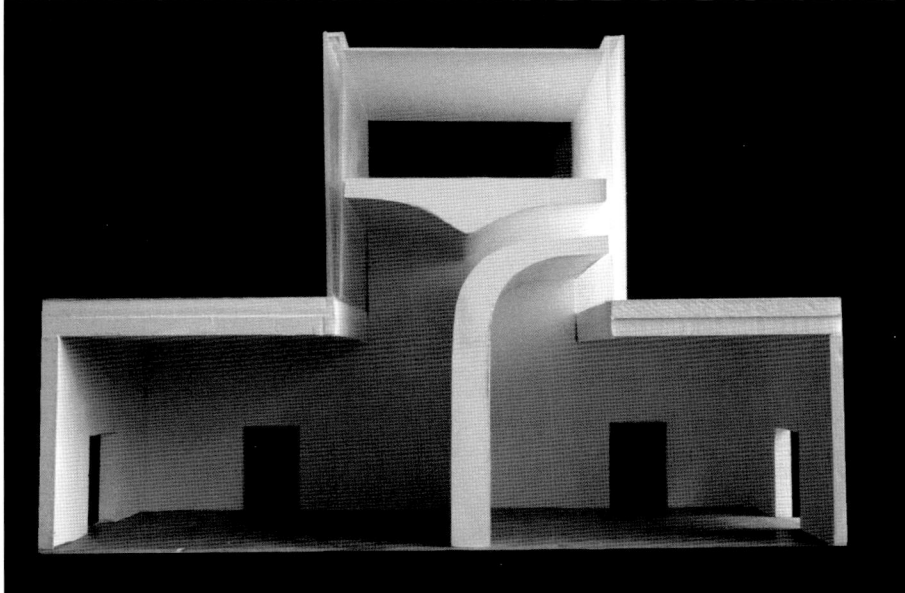

"T" structure: sectional model

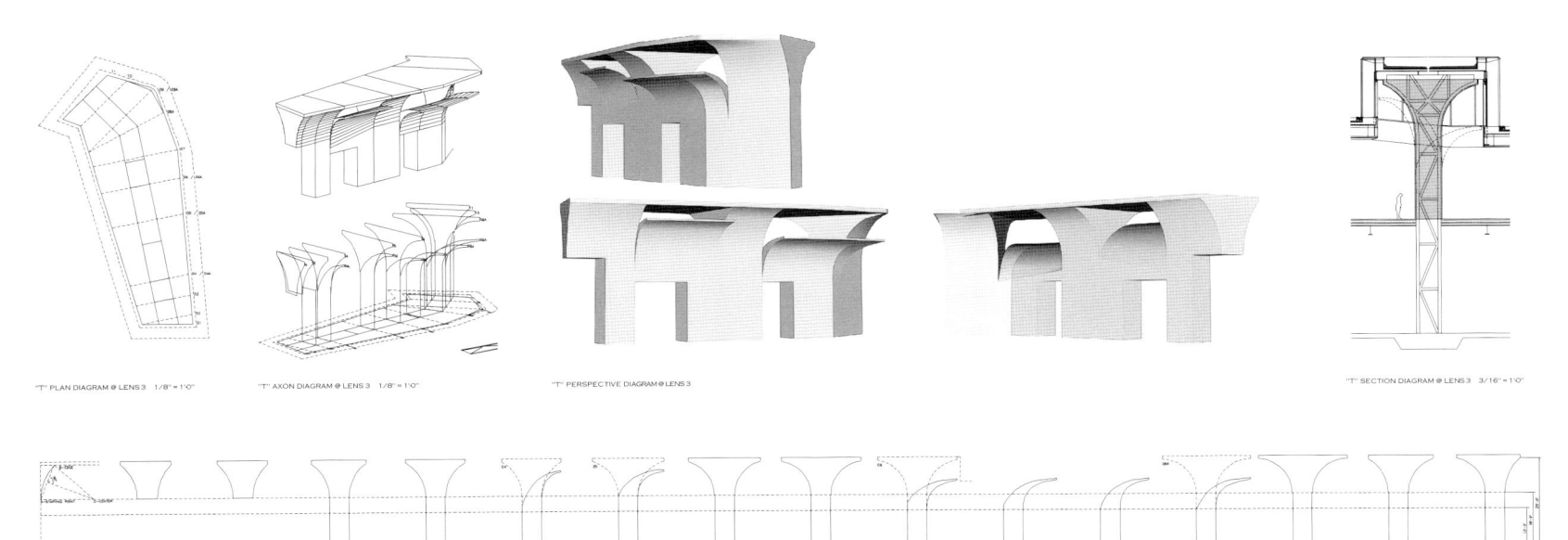

"T" PLAN DIAGRAM @ LENS 3   1/8" = 1'-0"   "T" AXON DIAGRAM @ LENS 3   1/8" = 1'-0"   "T" PERSPECTIVE DIAGRAM @ LENS 3   "T" SECTION DIAGRAM @ LENS 3   3/16" = 1'-0"

"T" structural analysis

Existing building: garage below reflecting pool　旧棟：水盤の下には駐車場がある

Construction site: "T" structure　工事中："T"ストラクチュア

Garage　駐車場

Gallery　ギャラリー

Noguchi court　ノグチ・コート

Reflecting pool　水盤

41

GA PROJECT

▽△*Noguchi court* ノグチ・コート

MUSEUM OF HUMAN EVOLUTION

Burgos, Spain
Design: 2000

Concept A
The body of the Museum of Human Evolution hovers above an "Urban Mirror"—a platform of water recycled from the Arlazon River. The river branches to the north, bringing water from the Atapuerca caves, thereby connecting the site to the caves, just as origin myths from the world's cultures are connected to water.

Concept B
A "Chromatic Space" is created between the urban mirror and the undersides of the museum and auditoriums. This dramatic urban space, with open walkways over water, serves as an enormous entry space from which one can see the entrances to all the lobbies. The Chromatic Space corresponds to the long span of time before humans first became conscious of their own evolution—this "layer of unconsciousness" is a place for reflection.

Concept C
For a visitor experiencing the museum, the content of exhibits is gradually revealed using different formulations of space. First, by recreating the actual environment of the Atapuerca caves. Second, a "Score of Darkness" is created alongside the cave reconstruction by light piercing the dark background spaces. Finally, advanced digital exhibition techniques explore new information and future projections.

Concept D
5 points of fusion occur where the organic form, inspired by the Atapuerca caves, merges and overlaps with the orthogonal forms derived from urban Burgos.
These merging points allow 5 places of programmatic flexibility and overlap. Circulation and exhibits can be rerouted according to the needs of specific events.

Concept E
The unity of man and nature is expressed in the void-solid reversal of the central museum geometry which extends out from the cave reconstruction. This argument against a non-dualistic consciousness is also expressed in the Arlazon River water connection at the urban mirror platform.

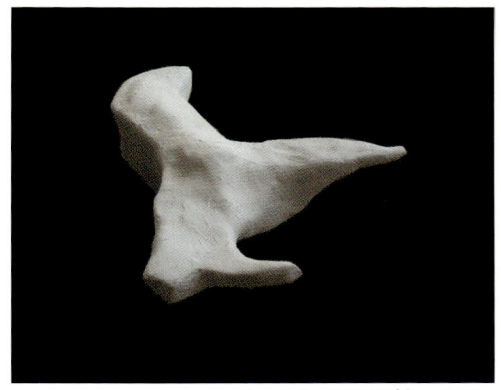

Concept model コンセプト・モデル

〈コンセプトA〉
人類史博物館の本体は，アルラソン川の水を再利用する水のプラットホーム"都市の鏡"の上を舞いあがるように覆う。川は北に分岐して，アタプエルカ洞窟から水を運ぶ。それによって，川に結びついた世界文明の発祥神話とまさに同じように，敷地は洞窟に結ばれる。

〈コンセプトB〉
"染色体空間"が"都市の鏡"と博物館本体及びオーディトリアムの下側面のあいだに生まれる空隙につくられる。水の上を，開かれた歩行路が走る，このドラマティックな都市空間は，巨大なエントリー・スペースの役割を持ち，そこからすべてのロビーへの入り口が見える。クロマティック・スペースは，人類が初めて自分たちの進化について意識するに至るまでの，長い時のスパンに相応する——この"無意識のレイヤー"は熟考するための場所である。

〈コンセプトC〉
来館者が博物館を身体で経験できるように，展示内容は，空間の様々な組立から徐々に現れてくる。最初に，アタプエルカ洞窟の実際の環境が再構成される。次に，暗い背景を持つ空間を刺し貫く光線が，再構成された洞窟の傍らに"暗黒のなかの亀裂"をつくりだす。最後に，最新のデジタルな展示技術で，新しい情報や予測される未来を探る。

〈コンセプトD〉
アタプエルカ洞窟に着想を得た有機的形態が，ブルゴスの都市構成から引き出された直交する形態と合流し重なり合う地点に5つの合流点が発生する。
　これらの合流点は，プログラムに柔軟に対応し重なり合う5つの場所をもたらす。

〈コンセプトE〉
人と自然の融和は，再構成された洞窟から外に広がる博物館の中心的ジオメトリー，ヴォイドとソリッドの逆転のなかに表現される。この，非二元論的意識と対立する主題は，プラットホーム"都市の鏡"の，アルラソン川の水とのつながりによっても表現される。

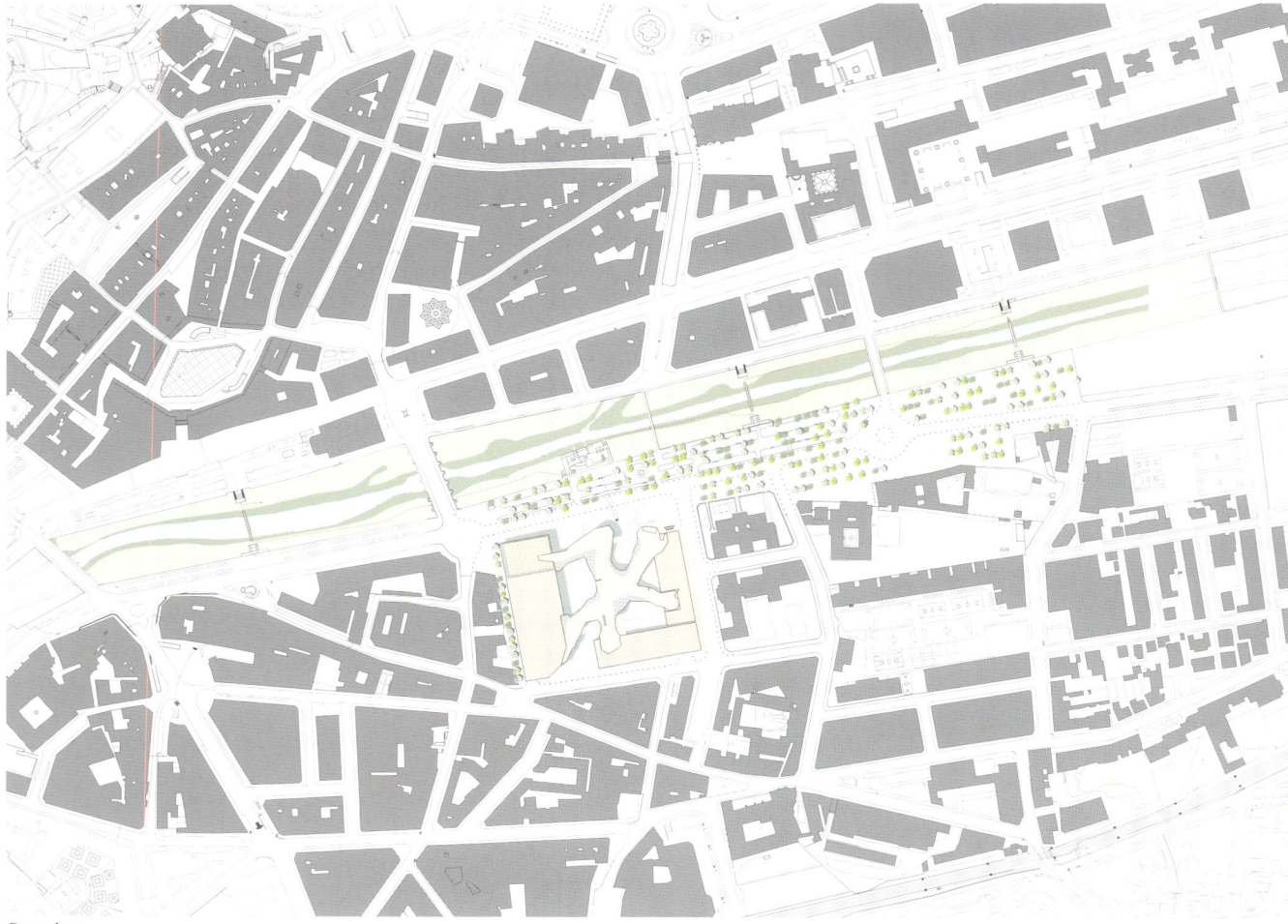

Site plan

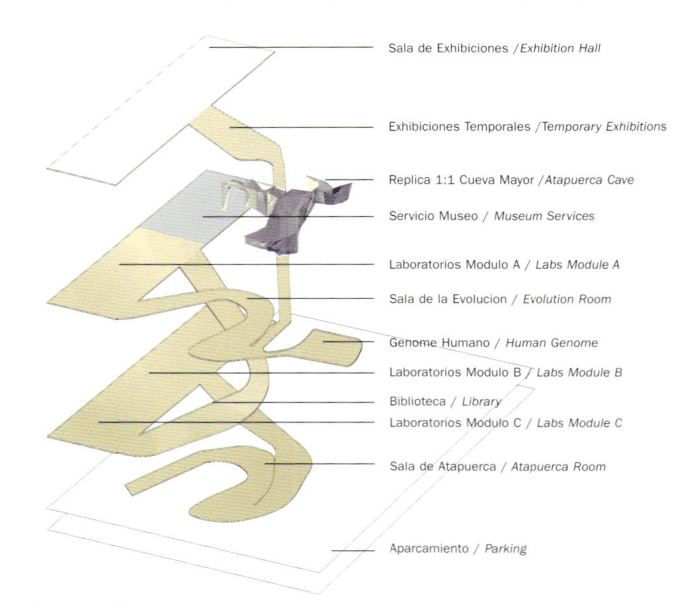

Program diagram

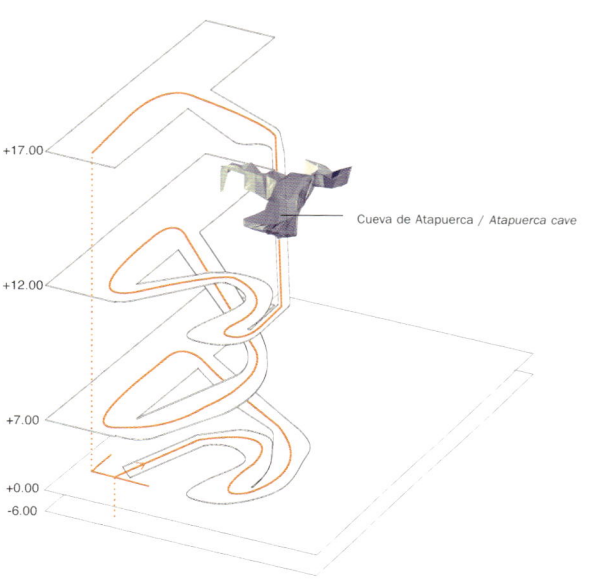

Sala de Exhibiciones / *Exhibition Hall*
Exhibiciones Temporales / *Temporary Exhibitions*
Replica 1:1 Cueva Mayor / *Atapuerca Cave*
Servicio Museo / *Museum Services*
Laboratorios Modulo A / *Labs Module A*
Sala de la Evolucion / *Evolution Room*
Genome Humano / *Human Genome*
Laboratorios Modulo B / *Labs Module B*
Biblioteca / *Library*
Laboratorios Modulo C / *Labs Module C*
Sala de Atapuerca / *Atapuerca Room*
Aparcamiento / *Parking*

Circulation

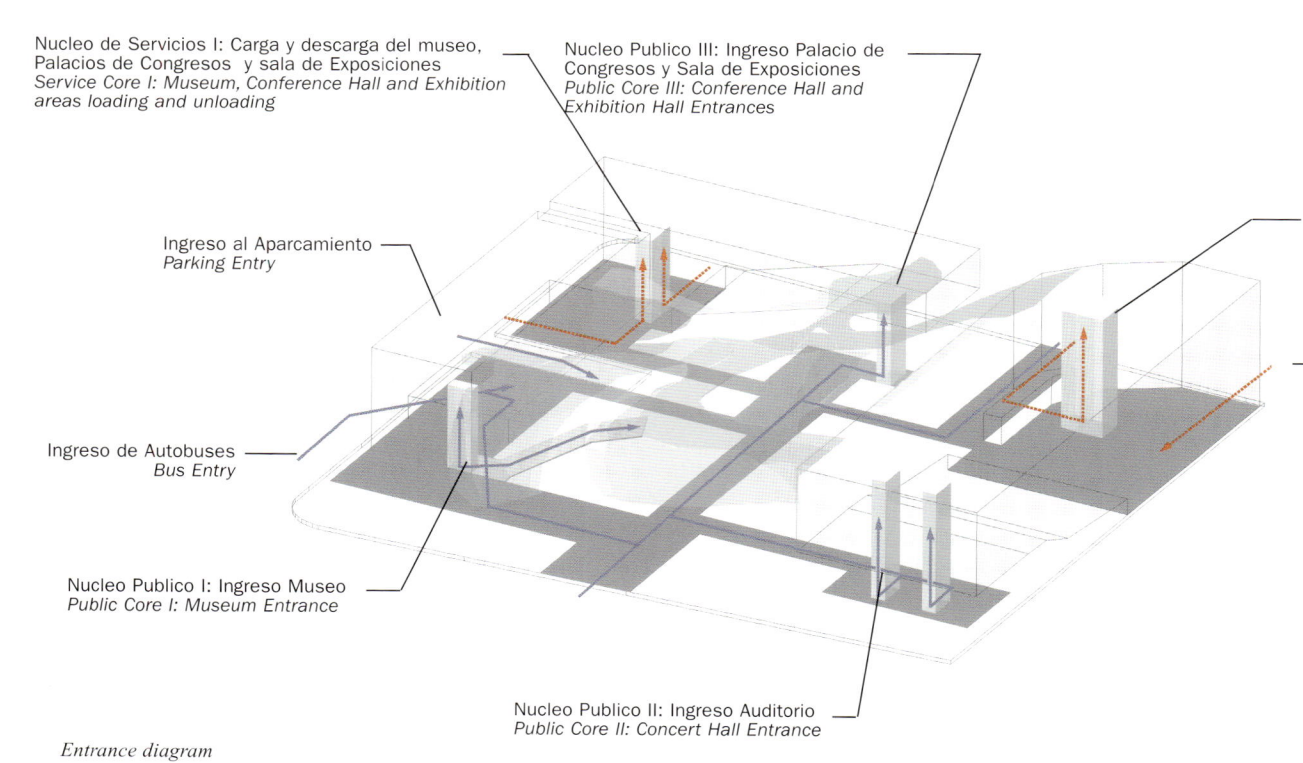

Cueva de Atapuerca / *Atapuerca cave*

Entrance diagram

Nucleo de Servicios I: Carga y descarga del museo, Palacios de Congresos y sala de Exposiciones
Service Core I: Museum, Conference Hall and Exhibition areas loading and unloading

Nucleo Publico III: Ingreso Palacio de Congresos y Sala de Exposiciones
Public Core III: Conference Hall and Exhibition Hall Entrances

Nucleo de Servicios II: Ingresos de Artistas y Personal del Auditorio
Service Core II: Performers and Auditorium Staff Entrance

Ingreso al Aparcamiento
Parking Entry

Carga y desgarga de Escenario
Stage Loading

Ingreso de Autobuses
Bus Entry

Nucleo Publico I: Ingreso Museo
Public Core I: Museum Entrance

Nucleo Publico II: Ingreso Auditorio
Public Core II: Concert Hall Entrance

Architects: Steven Holl Architects—Steven Holl, principal-in-charge; Benjamin Tranel, Fabian Llonch, Paola Iaccuci, Martin Cox, Aaron Cattani, Makram El Kadi, Ziad Jamaleddine, project team
Client: City of Burgos
Consultants: Guy Nordenson and Associates, structural; Ove Arup & Partners, mechanical
Program: galleries, conference hall, auditorium
Total floor area: 28,500 m²

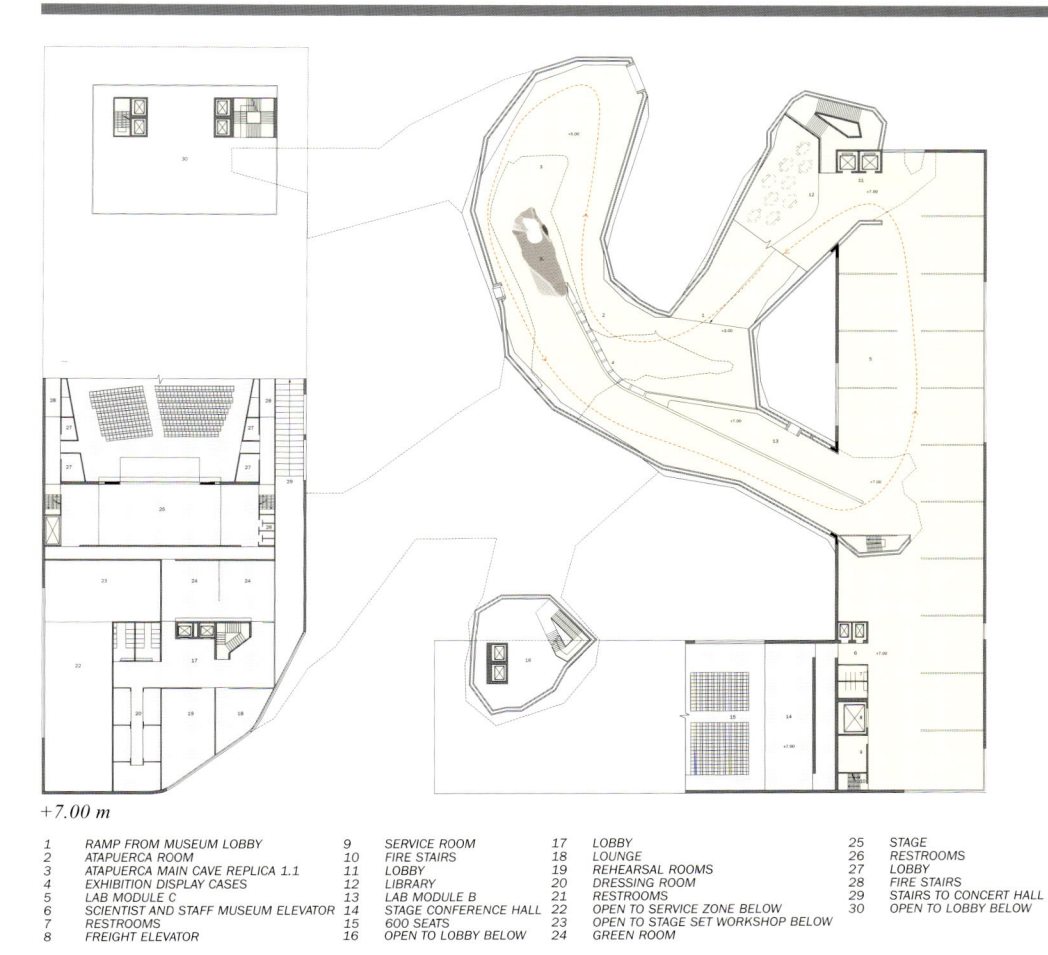

45 GA PROJECT

+7.00 m

1	RAMP FROM MUSEUM LOBBY	9	SERVICE ROOM	17	LOBBY	25	STAGE
2	ATAPUERCA ROOM	10	FIRE STAIRS	18	LOUNGE	26	RESTROOMS
3	ATAPUERCA MAIN CAVE REPLICA 1.1	11	LOBBY	19	REHEARSAL ROOMS	27	LOBBY
4	EXHIBITION DISPLAY CASES	12	LIBRARY	20	DRESSING ROOM	28	FIRE STAIRS
5	LAB MODULE C	13	LAB MODULE B	21	RESTROOMS	29	STAIRS TO CONCERT HALL
6	SCIENTIST AND STAFF MUSEUM ELEVATOR	14	STAGE CONFERENCE HALL	22	OPEN TO SERVICE ZONE BELOW	30	OPEN TO LOBBY BELOW
7	RESTROOMS	15	600 SEATS	23	OPEN TO STAGE SET WORKSHOP BELOW		
8	FREIGHT ELEVATOR	16	OPEN TO LOBBY BELOW	24	GREEN ROOM		

+17.00 m

1	LOBBY	15	MEETING ROOMS
2	EVOLUTION ROOM	16	OFFICE SPACE
3	TEMPORARY EXHIBITION	17	OPEN TO STAGE BELOW
4	EXHIBITION HALL	18	1700 SEATS AUDITORIUM
5	RESTROOMS	19	PROJECTION MEZZANINE ABOVE
6	FREIGHT ELEVATOR	20	OPEN TO VESTIBULE ABOVE
7	SERVICE ROOM	21	CAFE
8	FIRE STAIRS	22	RESTAURANT
9	600 SEATS CONFERENCE HALL	23	KITCHEN
10	RESTROOMS	24	RESTROOMS
11	SERVICE ROOM	25	RAMP THROUGH ATAPUERCA CAVE
12	LOBBY AND EXHIBITION SPACE	26	EXHIBITION SPACE
13	PRESS CONFERENCE	27	ATAPUERCA CAVE

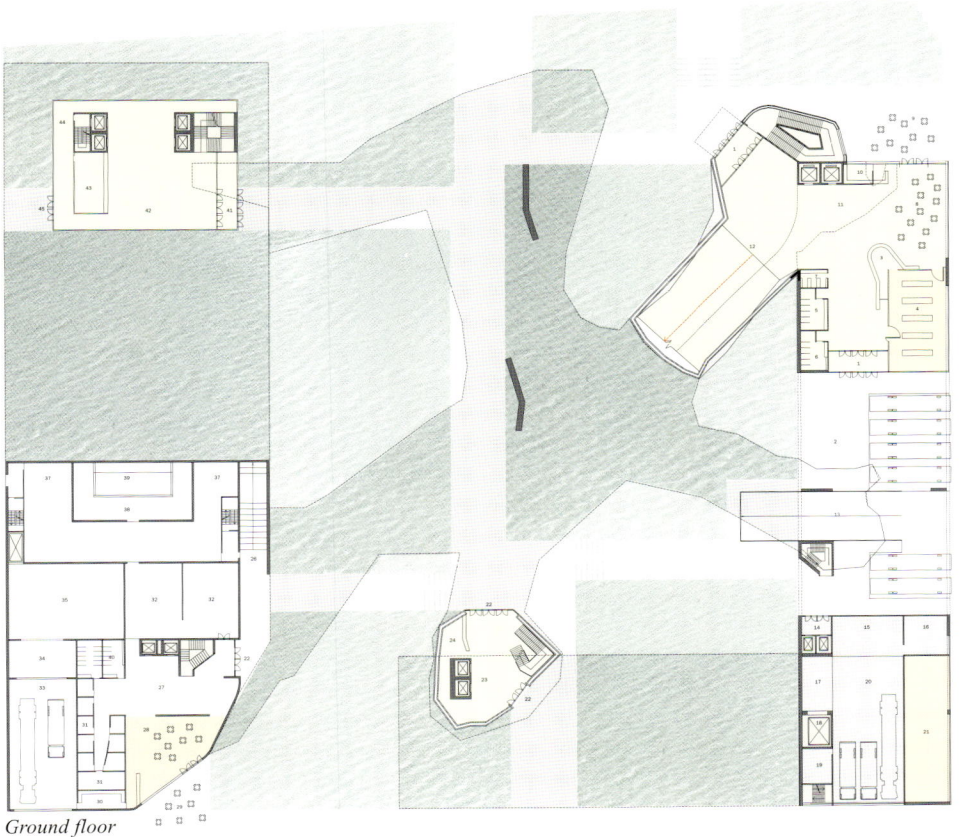

Ground floor

1	MAIN ENTRY	13	PARKING ENTRY	25	PERFORMERS & AUDITORIUM STAFF ENTRY	37	STORAGE
2	PRE-LOBBY	14	SCIENTISTS & MUSEUM STAFF ENTRY	26	STAIRS TO CONCERT HALL	38	UNDERSTAGE
3	TICKETING & INFORMATION	15	CRATING / UNCRATING	27	LOBBY	39	ORCHESTRA PIT
4	MUSEUM SHOP	16	COLLECTION STORAGE	28	STAFF CAFÉ	40	RESTROOMS
5	WOMEN'S RESTROOMS	17	LOADING / UNLOADING	29	TERRACE	41	CONCERT HALL MAIN ENTRANCE
6	MEN'S RESTROOMS	18	FREIGHT ELEVATOR	30	KITCHEN	42	LOBBY
7	COAT CHECK	19	REGISTRATION OFFICE	31	TUNING	43	TICKETING & COAT CHECK
8	CAFE	20	SERVICE ZONE	32	REHEARSAL ROOM	44	SERVICE STAIRS
9	TERRACE	21	RENTAL SPACE	33	SERVICE ZONE	45	SERVICE ENTRY
10	CAFE SERVICE	22	CONFERENCE HALL ENTRY	34	LOADING / UNLOADING		
11	MUSEUM MAIN LOBBY	23	LOBBY	35	STAGE SET WORKSHOP		
12	CONTROL POINT	24	TICKETING & COAT CHECK	36	HYDRAULIC ELEVATOR		

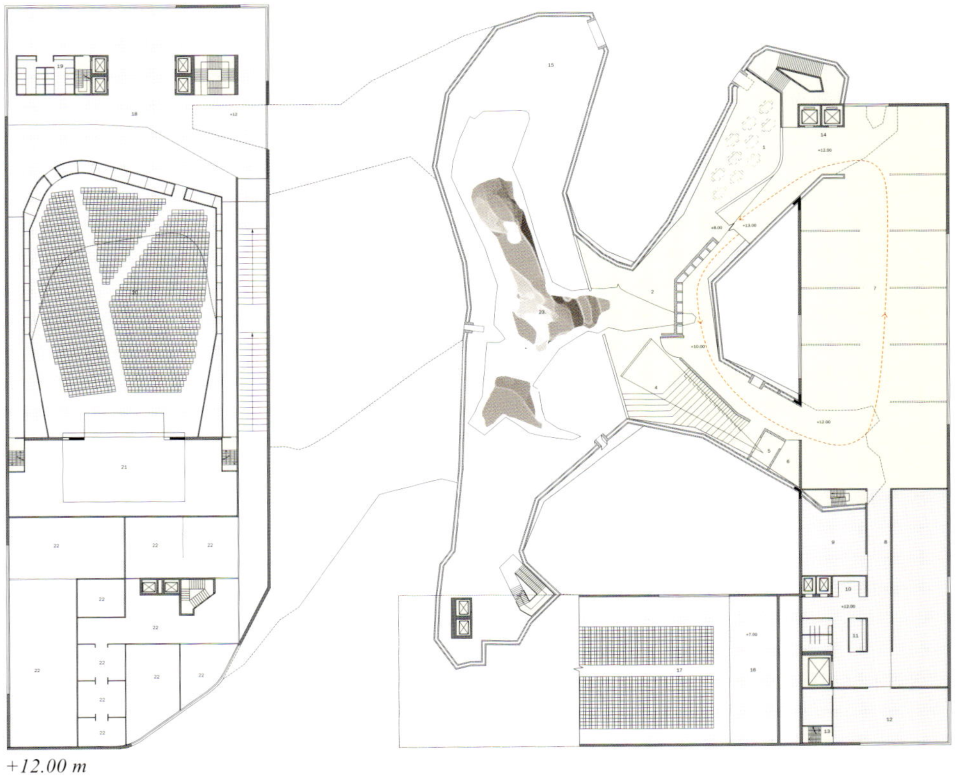

+12.00 m

1	LIBRARY	13	FIRE STAIRS
2	FOYER	14	LOBBY
3	EXHIBITION DISPLAY	15	OPEN TO ATAPUERCA ROOM BELOW
4	PROJECTION / MEETING ROOM	16	STAGE CONFERENCE HALL
5	PROJECTION BOOT	17	600 SEATS
6	TRANSLATION BOOT	18	LOBBY AUDITORIUM
7	LABS MODULE A	19	RESTROOMS
8	MUSEUM STAFF AND RESEARCH	20	1700 SEATS AUDITORIUM
9	SCIENTIFIC AND TECHNICAL SERVICE ROOM	21	OPEN TO STAGE AUDITORIUM BELOW
10	LOUNGE	22	OPEN TO BELOW
11	KITCHENETTE	23	ATAPUERCA CAVE
12	SERVICE AREAS		

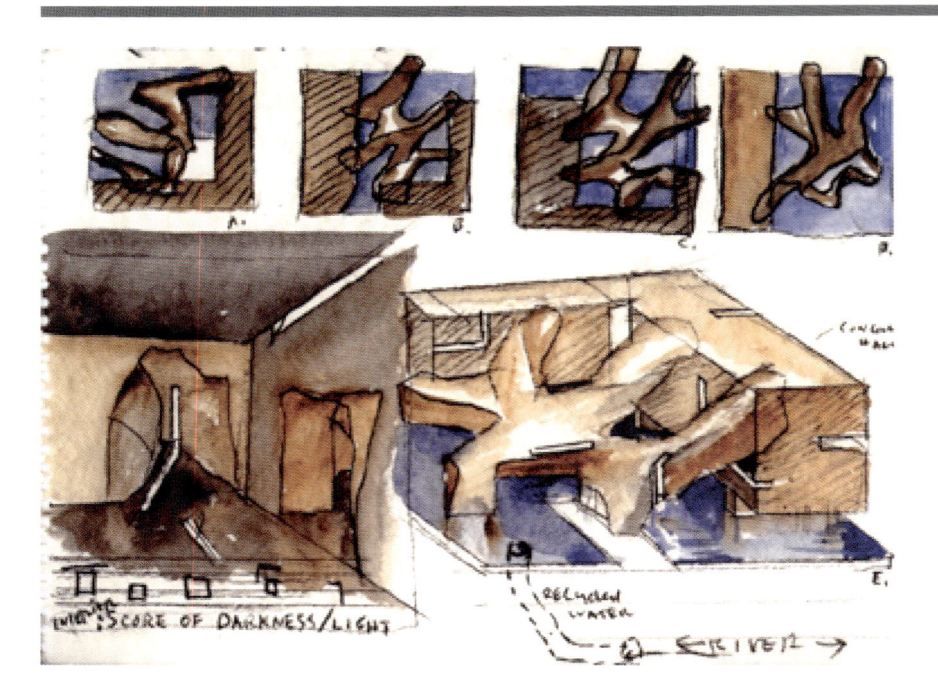

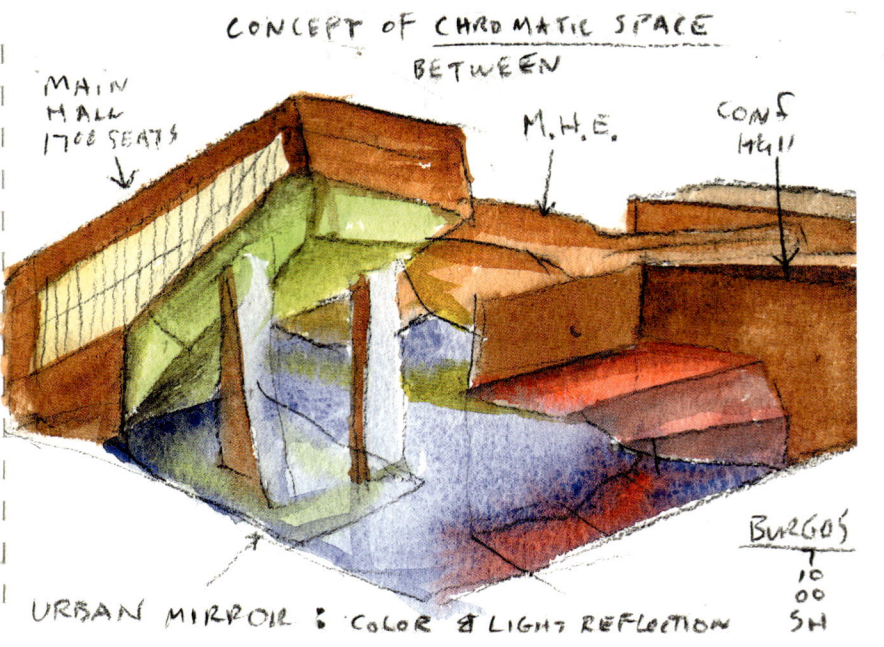

Sketches: *study of "Atapuerca cave"*
スケッチ：“アタプエルカ洞窟”のスタディ

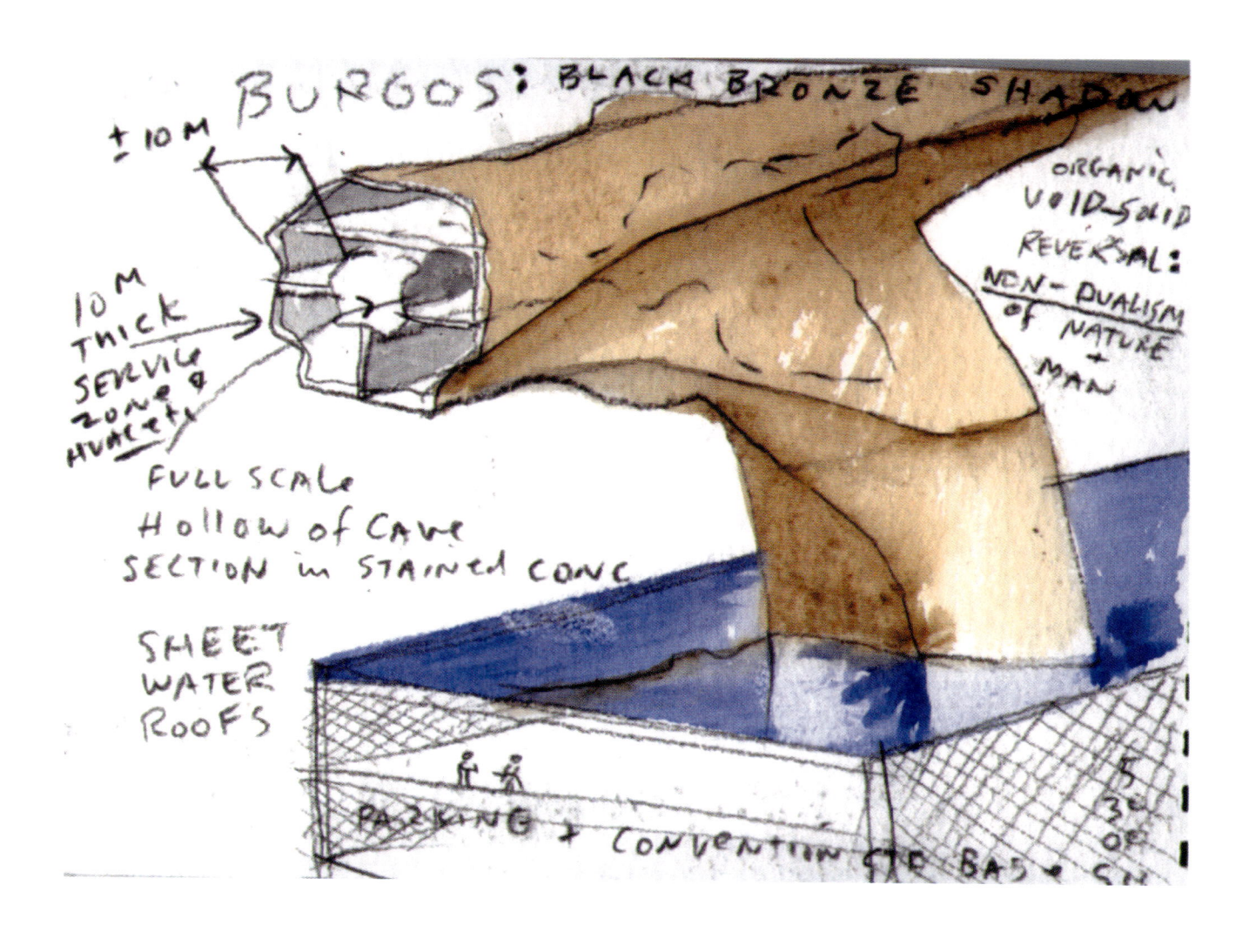

BURGOS 8/13/00 S. Holl

Model 模型

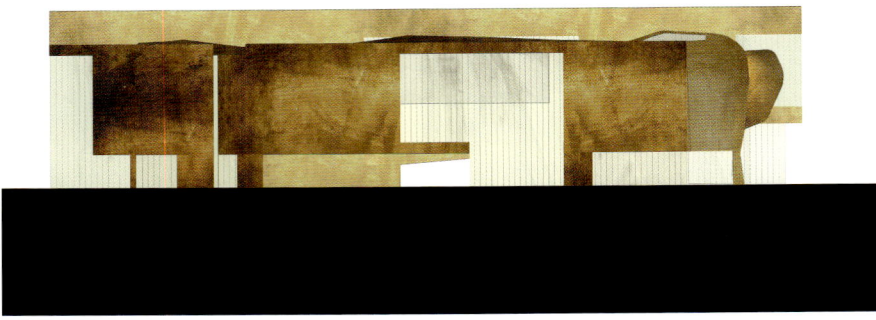

East elevation

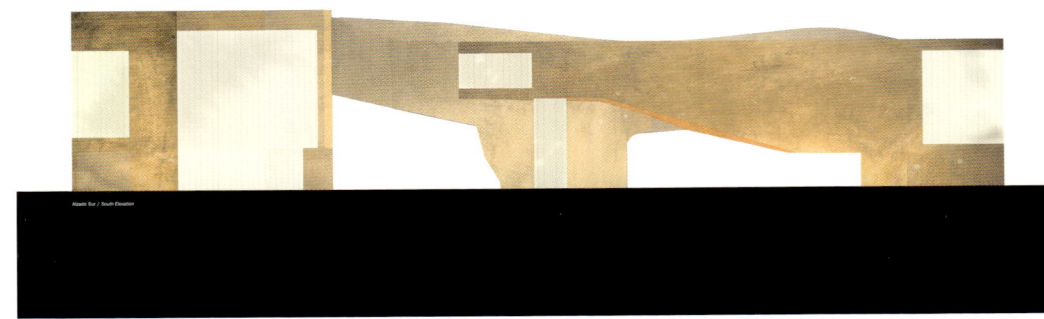

South elevation

West elevation

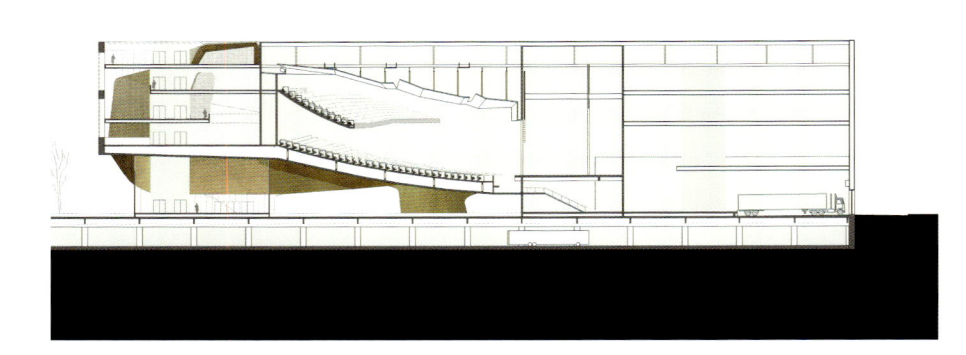

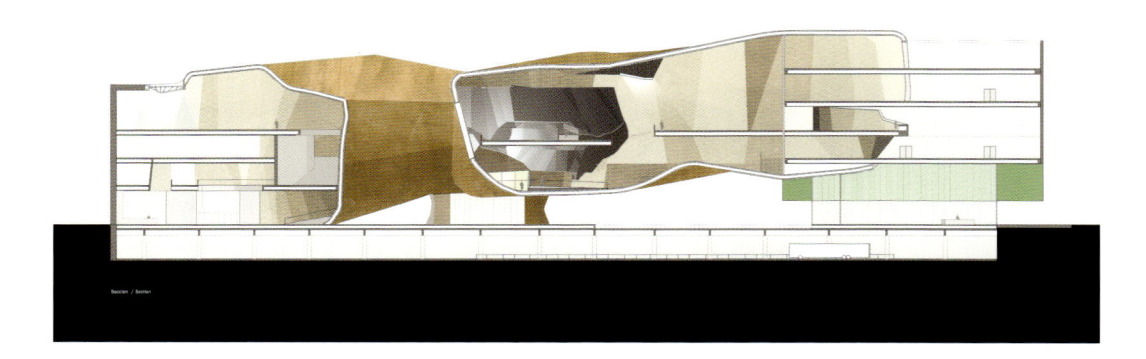

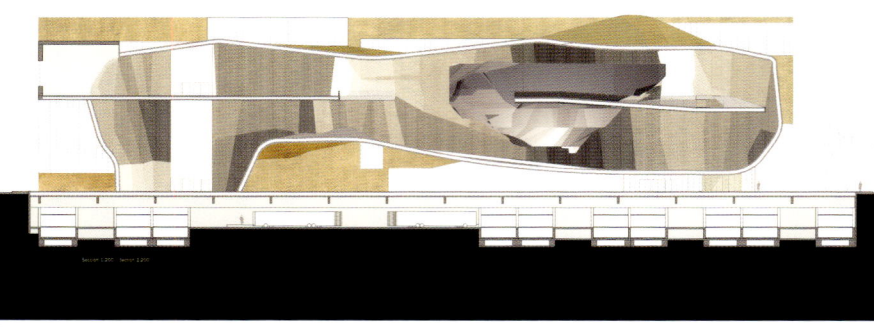

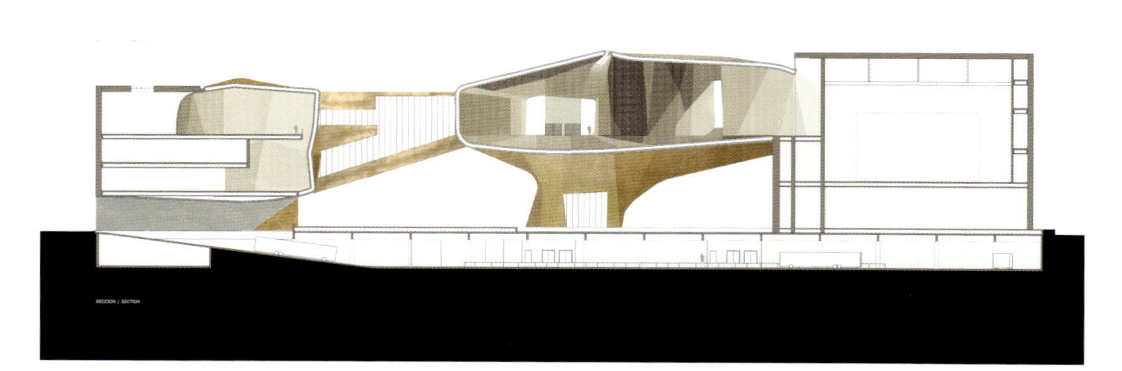

Sections

"Chromatic Space" between "Urban Mirror" (platform of water) and museum is entry space and serves dramatic urban space. Interior images of museum are below

水のプラットホーム"アーバン・ミラー"と建物本体の間の"染色体空間"はエントリー・スペースであり、ドラマチックな都市空間を提供する。下は博物館内部

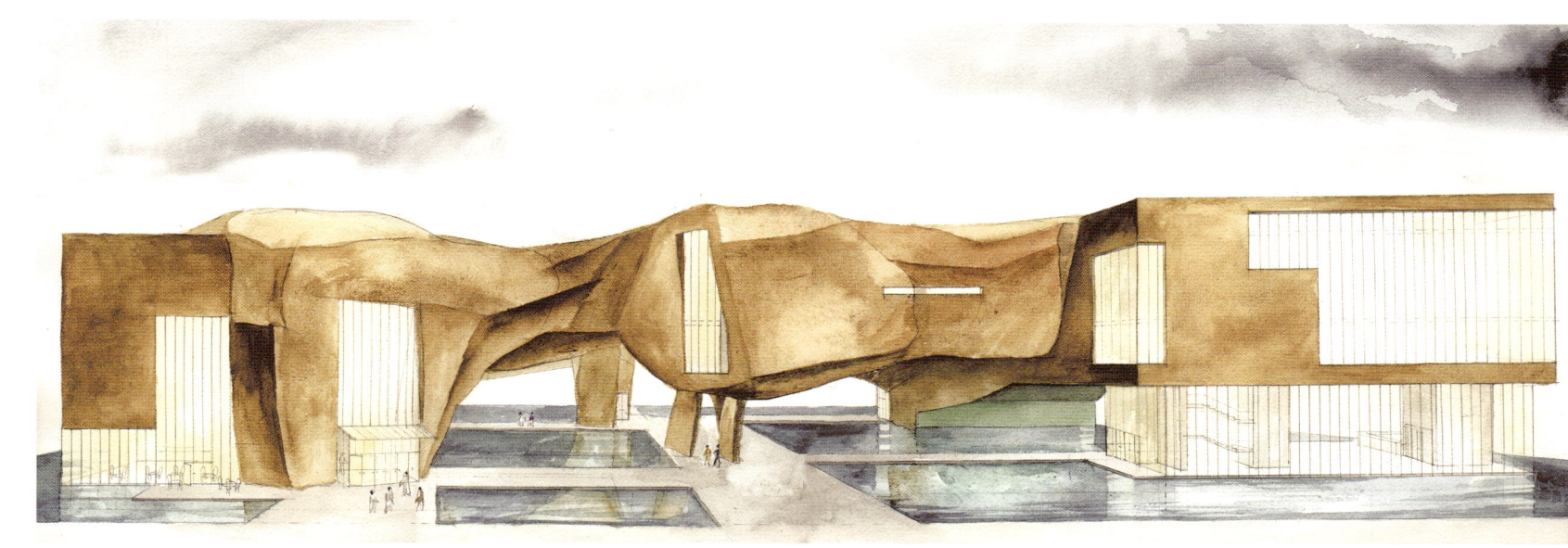

North elevation 北面

Under cave 洞窟下部

Atapuerca cave アタプルカ洞窟

"Urban mirror" アーバン・ミラー

MUSÉE DES CONFLUENCES

Lyon, France
Design: 2001

Aerial view 上空より見る

Distant view 遠景

Night view 夜景

The building form is a response to the unique aspects of the site. Its thinness and tapering off, the wide space of flow of the converging Rhone and Saone Rivers, the horizontality and organic turbulence are all aspects responded to in the building section of the new museum. The building's geometry moves toward horizontal vectors like that of the rivers.

The concept aims for a convergence of four geophysical aspects:
 1. Matter: the in and out of physical exhibition materials
 2. Energy: the main entry hall of public flow
 3. Configuration: the auditorium and main orientation
 4. Correlation: the education tower-classrooms for study and deeper evaluation.

These four vectors join in a central horizontal turbulence from which a suspended taper emerges horizontally cantilevered above with the flowing rivers reflected on its underside

It is an open concept of flowing within the architecture with spaces in liquid discourse. Interior passages should intervene and cross-cut. Exhibitions are held within parentheses walls bounded by intersecting potential. The building sections aim at relationships working at the root level, where things and formulations merge.

The steel framed structure utilizes standard sections due to new computer programs producing each joint effortlessly in complex geometries. The building skin is a special golden patina copper alloy with a natural patina's positive response to typical urban air pollution. Glass walls are double with an energy recycling of the inner air space.

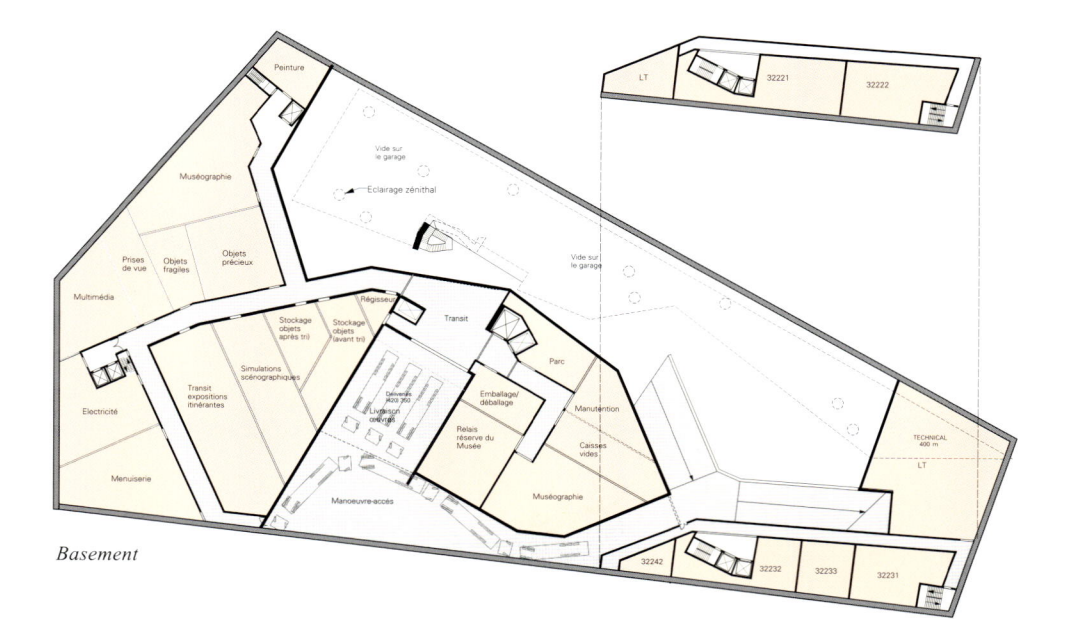

Mezzanine (entrance from city)

Ground floor (entrance from park)

Basement

Site plan

GA PROJECT

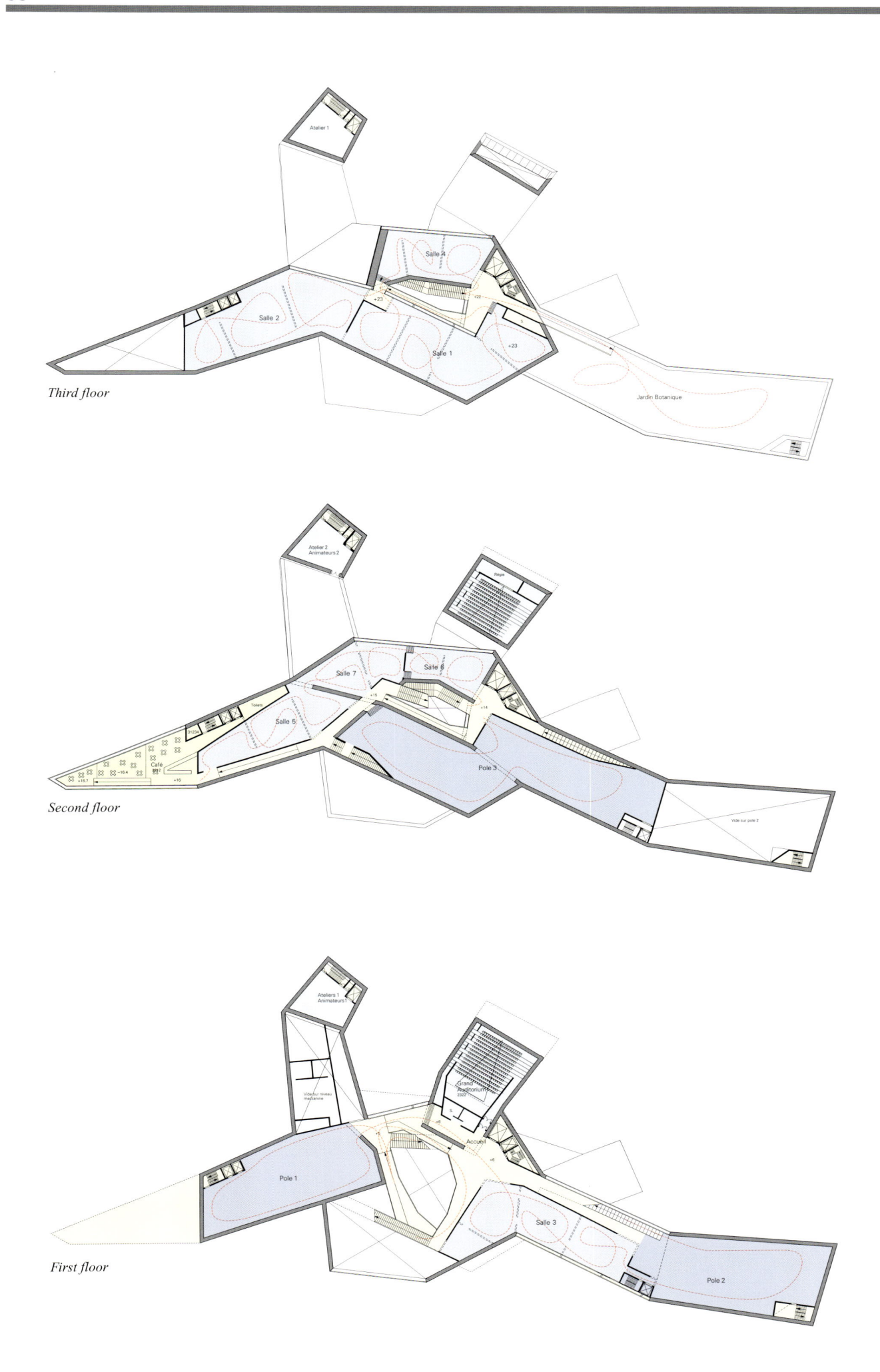

Third floor

Second floor

First floor

建物の形は，特別な敷地状況に対する応答である。先端がすぼまった小さな土地，ローヌ川とソーヌ川が合流する広い川幅，水平性，生成展開する乱流，こうした様相のすべてが，新しいミュージアムの建築構成のなかに取り込まれる。建物のジオメトリーは，川と同じように，水平方向のベクトルで動く。

4つの地球物理学的様相の集合を目指すコンセプト：

1）物質：物理的表現材料の見え隠れ
2）エネルギー：メイン・エントランス・ホールの人の流れ
3）相対的配置：オーディトリアムと主要方位
4）相互関係：学習と深い評価のための教育タワー＝クラスルーム

以上4つのベクトルは，中央に生まれている水平な乱流のなかで合体する。そこから，上方に，先端が細くなった形態がキャンティレヴァーで水平に延び出し，その下側面には川の流れが反射する。

これは，流体の話法で構成された建築空間における，流れを主題とするオープン・コンセプトである。内部通路は，空間に割り込み，空間を分断しながら進むだろう。互いに交差する可能性によって連結される，括弧のように挟み込まれた壁の内側が展示空間となる。建物の各部は，ルート・レベルで有効に作用する関係に照準をあてる。そこでは物体と系統的表現が融合する。

新しいコンピュータ・プログラムは，複雑なジオメトリーを持つジョイントを簡単につくれるので，鉄骨枠組構造には標準規格の部材を用いる。外壁は，艶のある金色の特殊銅合金を用い，都会に特有な大気汚染への実際的な応答として自然な緑青を帯びさせる。二重ガラスの壁は，中央にエア・スペースをとり，エネルギーを再利用する。

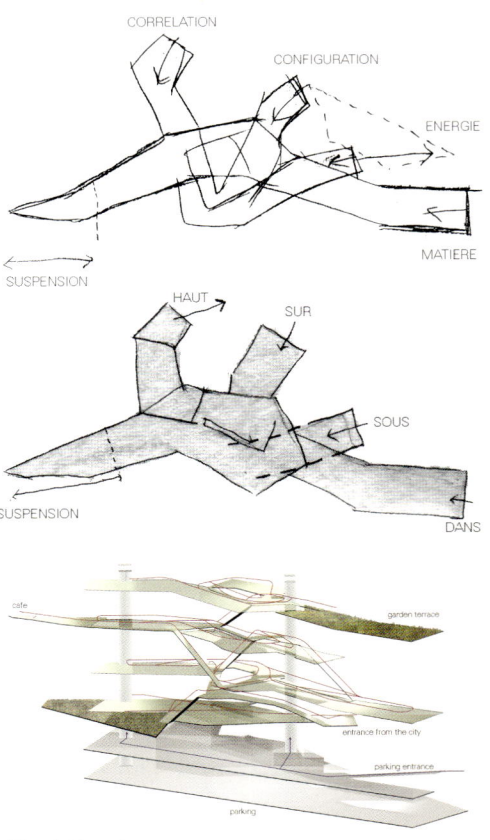

Circulation diagram

Cross section 1

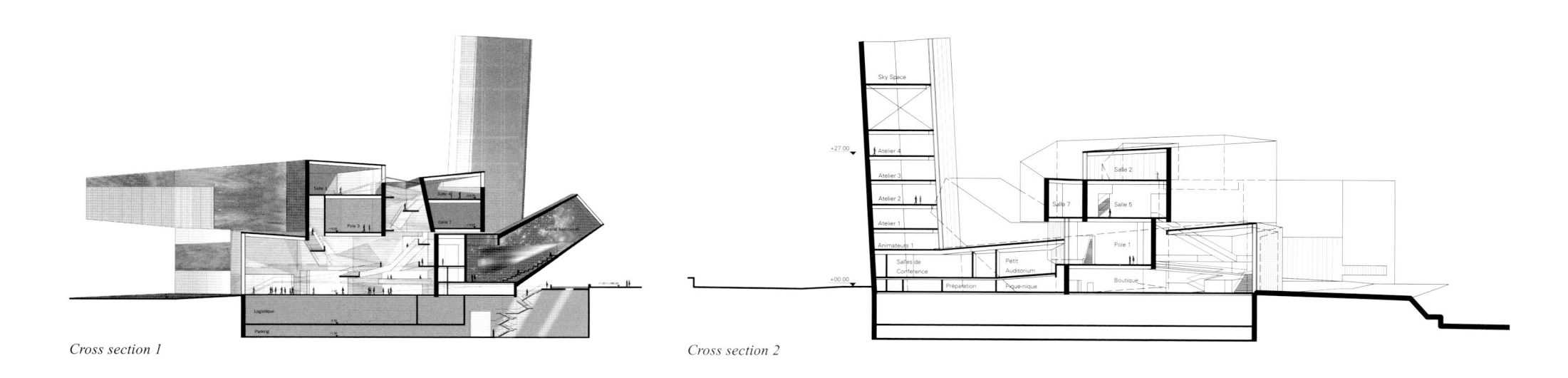

Cross section 2

GA PROJECT

Architects: Steven Holl Architects—Steven Holl, principal-in-charge; Timothy Bade, project architect; Annette Goderbauer, Mathew Johnson, Makram El-Kadi, Ziad Jamaleddine, Christian Wassmann, project team
Associate architect: Pierre Vurpas Associates
Consultants: Jacobs Serete (Paris), Phillipe Averty, structural; Guy Nordenson and Associates, associate structural

West elevation

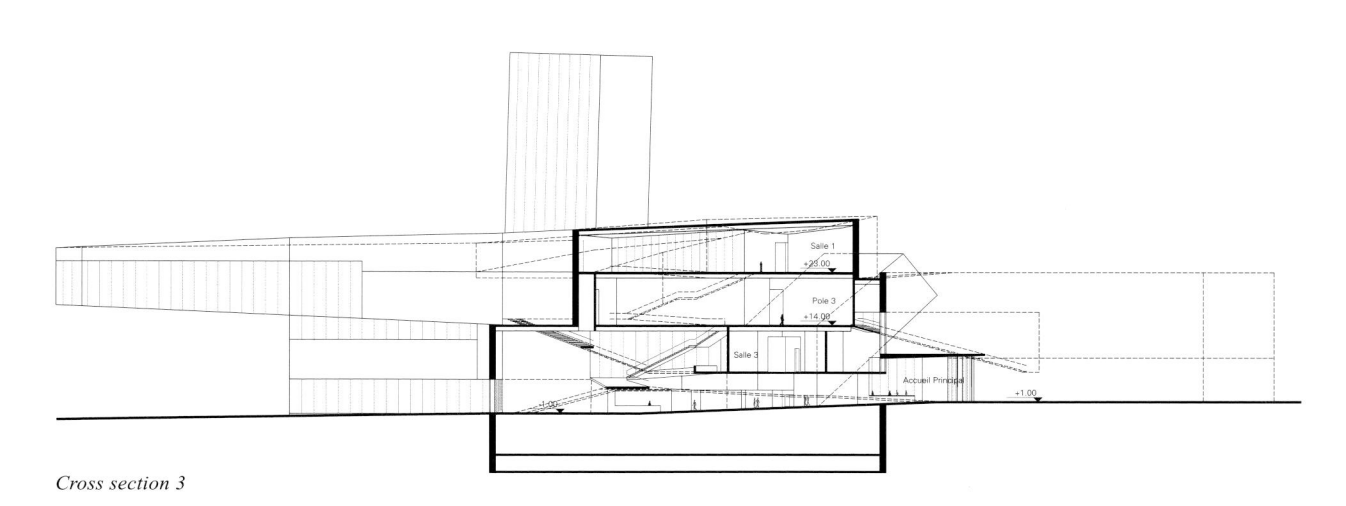

Cross section 3

South elevation

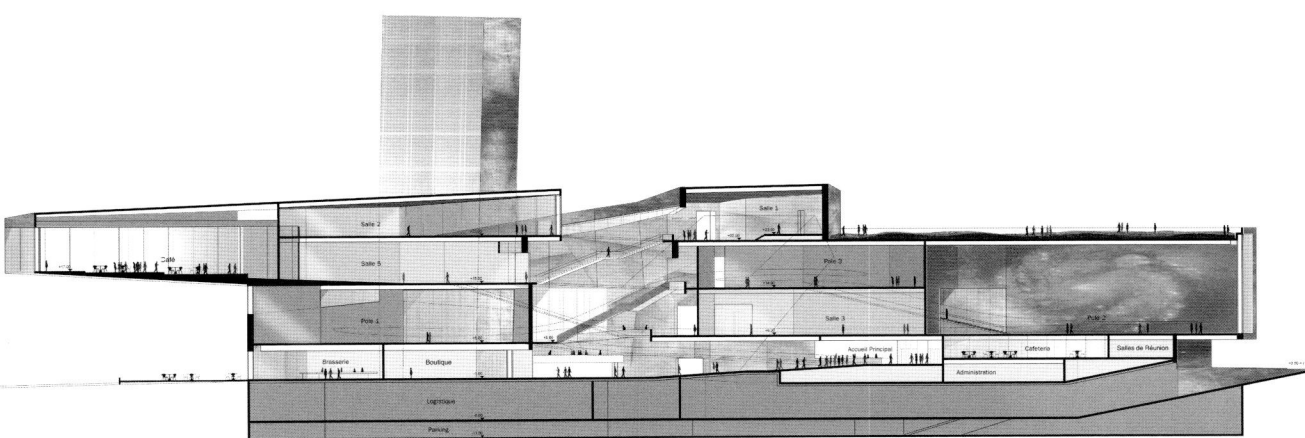

Longitudinal section

Entrance hall エントランス・ホール

Gallery ギャラリー

Entrance hall エントランス・ホール

Cafe カフェ

Downward view toward Rhone and Saone Rivers ローヌ川とソーヌ川を見下ろす

Entrance from city 街側エントランス

CORNELL UNIVERSITY DEPARTMENT OF ARCHITECTURE

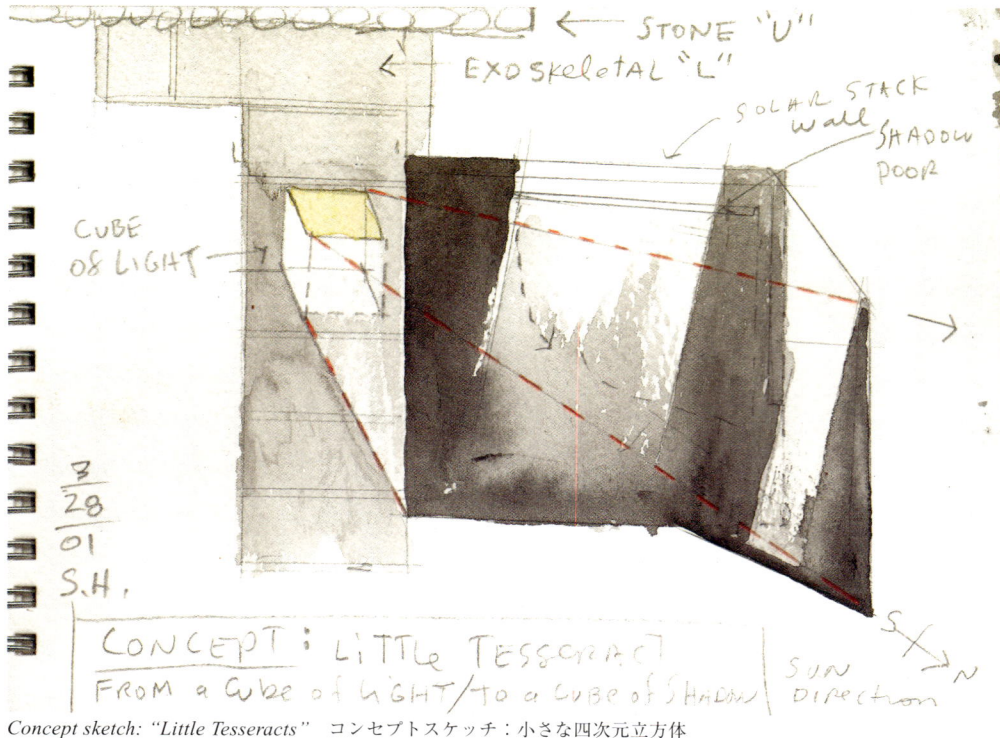

Ithaca, New York, U.S.A.
Design: 2001–

Concept sketch: "Little Tesseracts"　コンセプトスケッチ：小さな四次元立方体

Concept sketch: Two Tesseracts in New York　コンセプトスケッチ：ニューヨークの2つの四次元立方体

View from gorge 峡谷からの眺め

View over existing building, Sibley Hall 既存棟，シブレー・ホール越しに見る

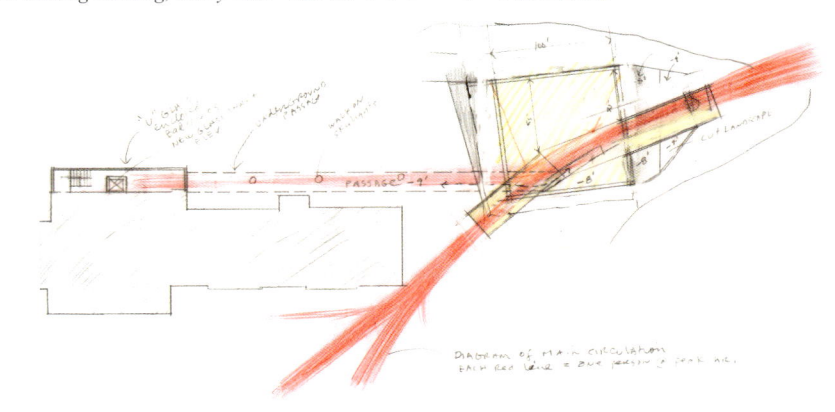

Model: south elevation 模型：南面

The site for the new Department of Architecture building, Milstein Hall, is located at the northeast corner of the Arts Quad, north of the Fall Creek Gorge Bridge, a main thoroughfare for pedestrian traffic onto campus. The new Milstein Hall offers a campus passage at its ground plane which is open to all and makes a new connection to the existing architecture school building, Sibley Hall. Students traveling through the Arts Quad can encounter exhibits of ongoing work in the school, see student projects in the shop, or attend an architecture lecture which is announced along the passage. The shop and lecture hall open directly to the new campus passage, facilitating the "social condenser" aspect of this passage.

The upper levels of the new Architecture School provide a special view connection to the gorge, the campus, and the distant views of Lake Cayuga. This view connects to the Finger Lakes Region's amazing topography.

Concept: Tesseract or Hypercube (An Open Bracket)

Scientifically a Tesseract is the four dimensional analogue to a cube (a square is to a cube as a cube is to a Tesseract). Internally this cube3 develops non-Euclidean properties which are experientially evident in the overlapping interior perspectives. The Review Rooms, the heart of an architecture studio education, are in the central overlapping cubes.

The loft-like studio spaces form an Open Bracket made operative by the infrastructural Tesseract Zone which is pulled inside out forming the west facade. The Tesseract Zone is embedded in the Open Bracket as a shifting intermittent section with alignments to the landscape of the site: The bottom of Fall Creek Gorge, the distant view of Lake Cayuga, the angle of the sun (47.5° at Equinox).

Construction in precast concrete planks and beams is complimented by the simplicity of structural channel glass planks on three facades (with translucent insulation) and juxtaposed with aluminum in different states for the Tesseract wall (foamed aluminum, bead-blasted, and direct digital-cut sheets). The translucent insulation in the glass planks brings softly molded light into the studios, while the rooms of Tesseract wall can be fully darkened to accommodate digital media.

The design incorporates many sustainable building elements, such as a ventilated cavity between the channel glass along the east and south facades. During the summer, a natural chimney effect exhausts the facades at the parapet. Closed in winter, these walls bring in solar heat. Natural cross ventilation is via 3′ x 3′ operable windows in shadow boxes which let in the winter sun and shade out summer sun. Photovoltaic cells on the roof are directly connected to ceiling fans in the studios for summer cooling.

Site model　敷地模型

Architects: Steven Holl Architects—Steven Holl, principal-in-charge; Stephen O'Dell, project architect; Tim Bade, Jason Frantzen, Annette Goderbauer, Li Hu, Paola Iacucci, Matt Johnson, Chris McVoy, Chris Otterbein, Christian Wassmann, Aislinn Weidele, project team
Consultants: Guy Nordenson and Associates, structural
Total floor area: 70,000 sq.ft.

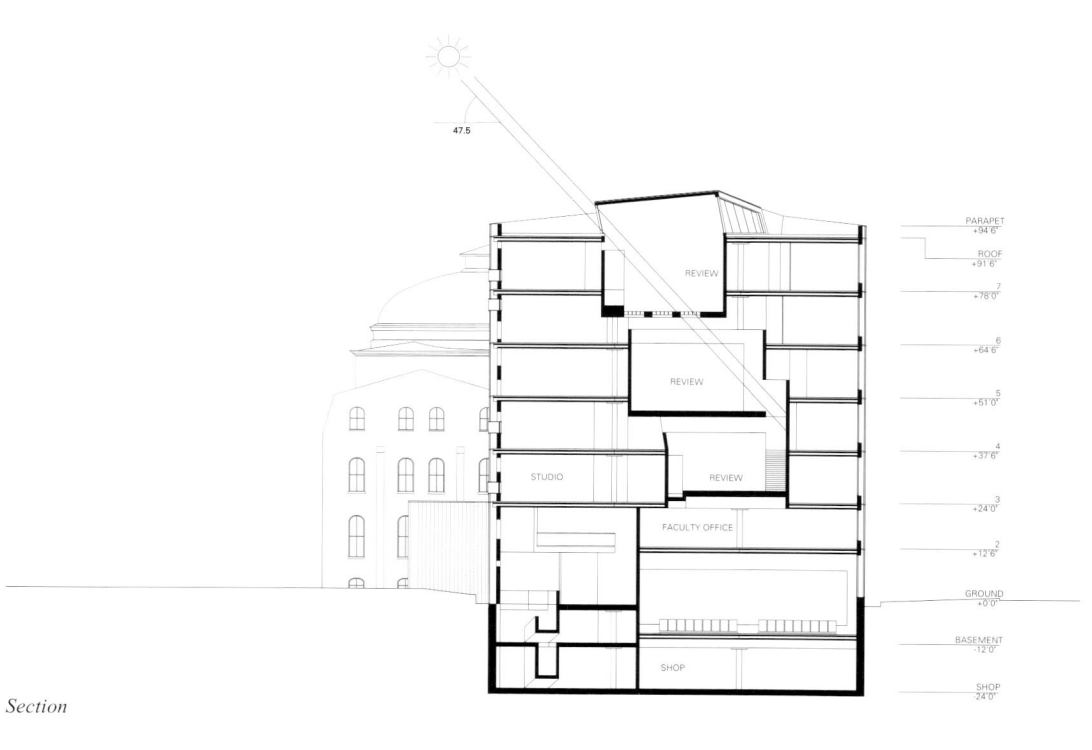

Section

Model: west elevation　模型：西面

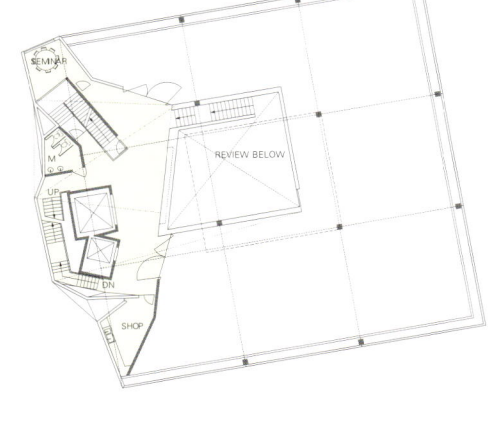

+64'-6"

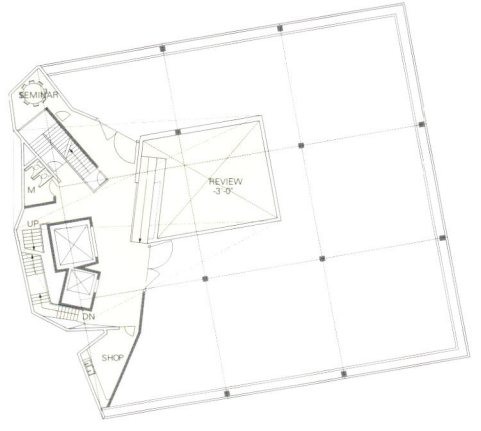

+51'-0"

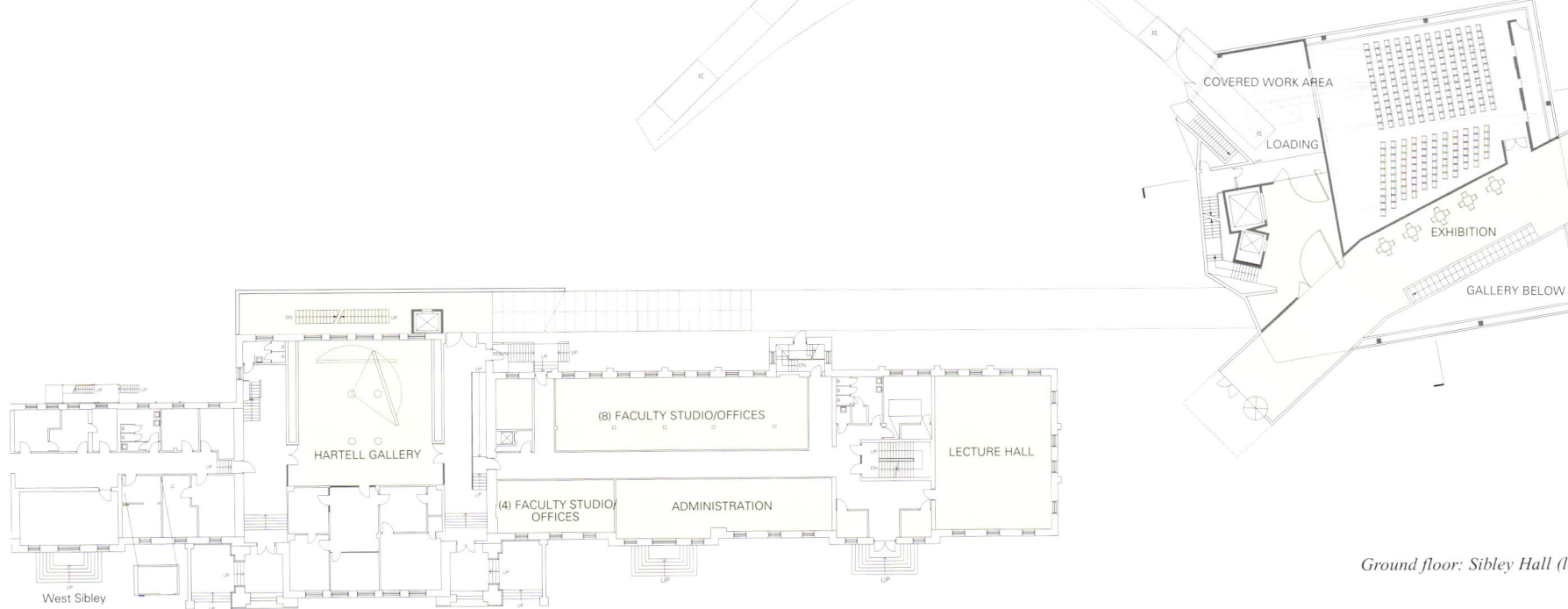

Ground floor: Sibley Hall (left) and Milstein Hall (right)

0 5 10 20 40

GA DOCUMENT

Model: west view 模型：西より見る

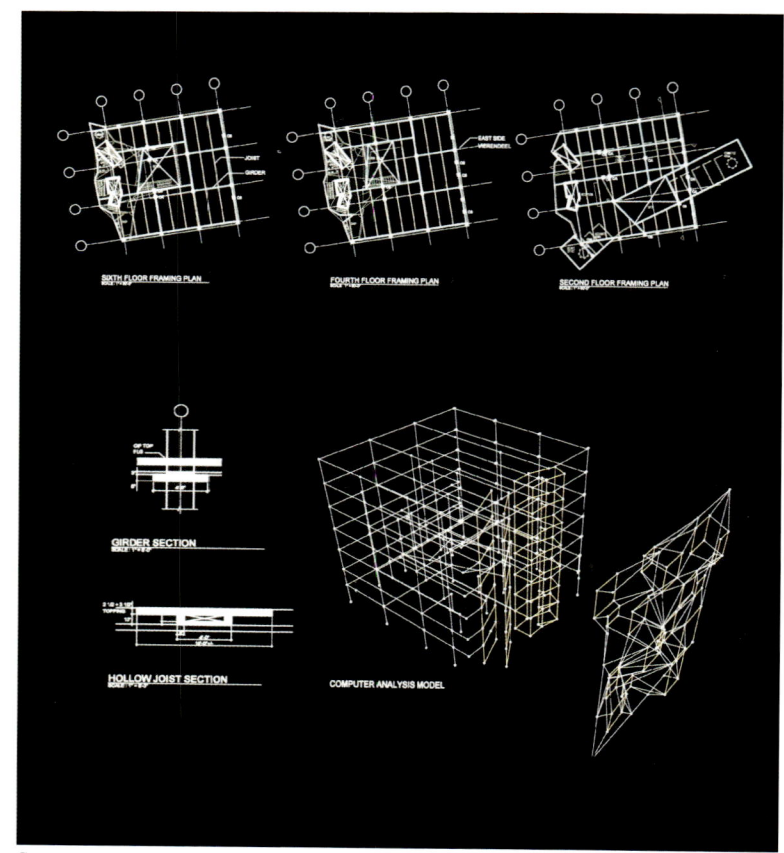

Studio スタジオ

Structure

Milstein Hall has function as campus passage to existing building, Sibley Hall
ミルスタイン・ホールは、既存棟、シブリー・ホールへの通過動線となる

Auditorium オーディトリアム

Staircase 階段室

Campus passage 学生通路

TOOLENBURG-ZUID LIVING IN THE 21ST CENTURY

Schipol, The Netherlands
Design: 2001–

Aerial view 上空より見る

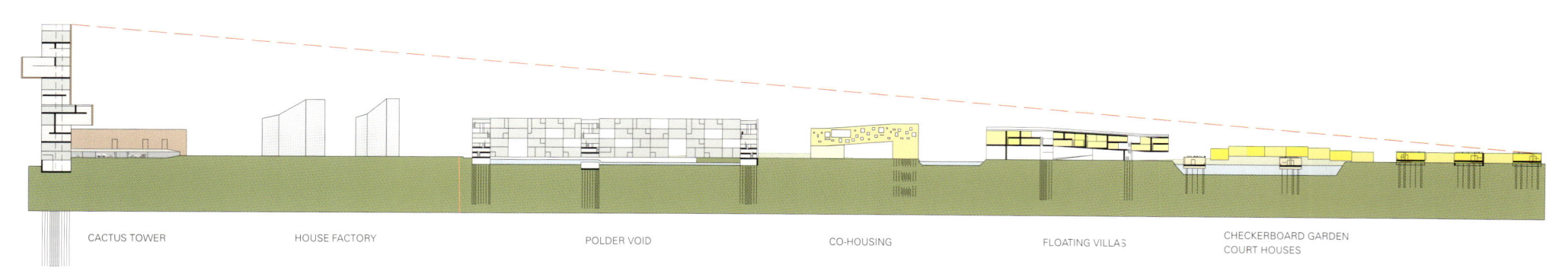

Site section

CACTUS TOWER — HOUSE FACTORY — POLDER VOID — CO-HOUSING — FLOATING VILLAS — CHECKERBOARD GARDEN COURT HOUSES

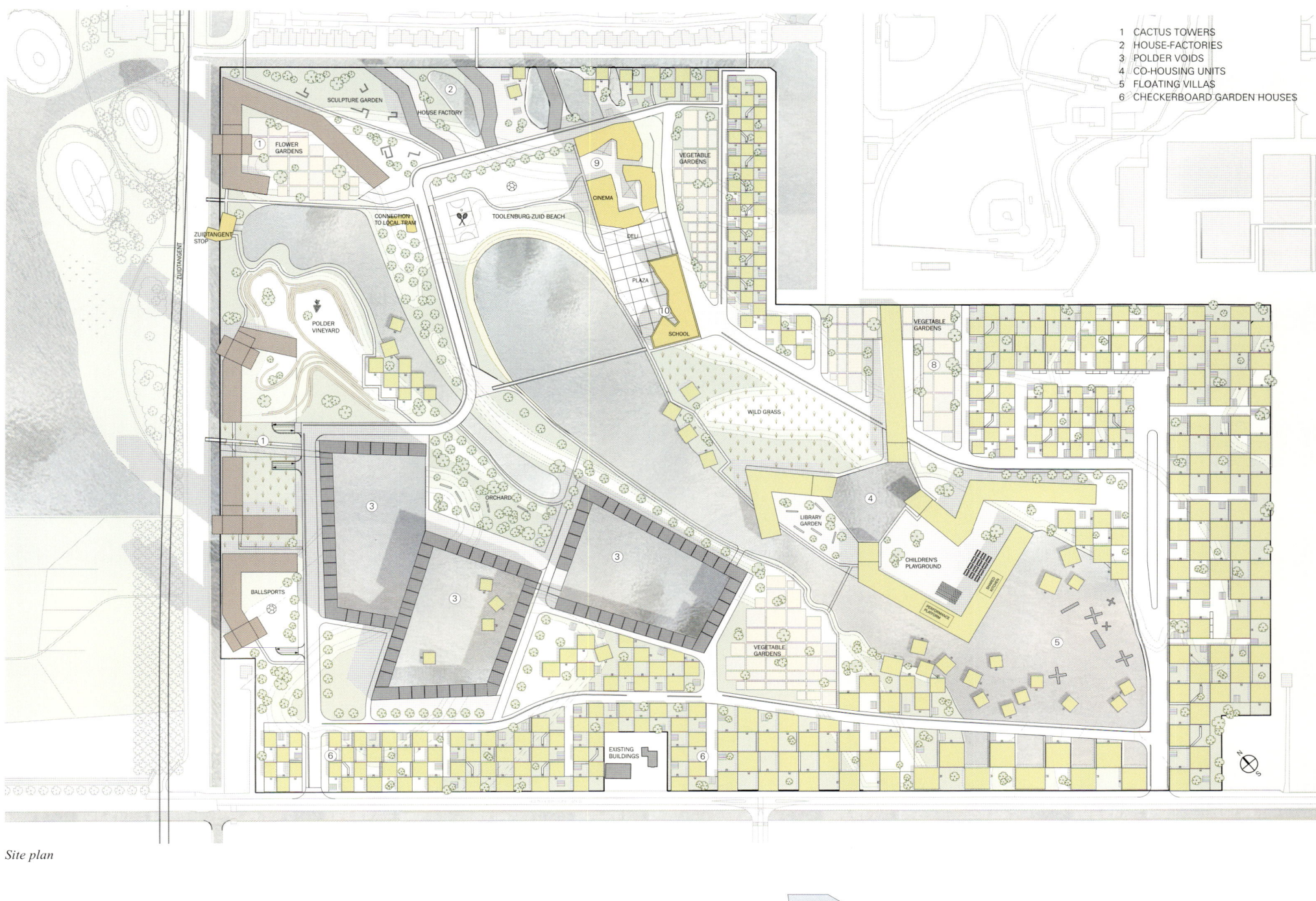

GA PROJECT

1 CACTUS TOWERS
2 HOUSE-FACTORIES
3 POLDER VOIDS
4 CO-HOUSING UNITS
5 FLOATING VILLAS
6 CHECKERBOARD GARDEN HOUSES

Site plan

Alternative living

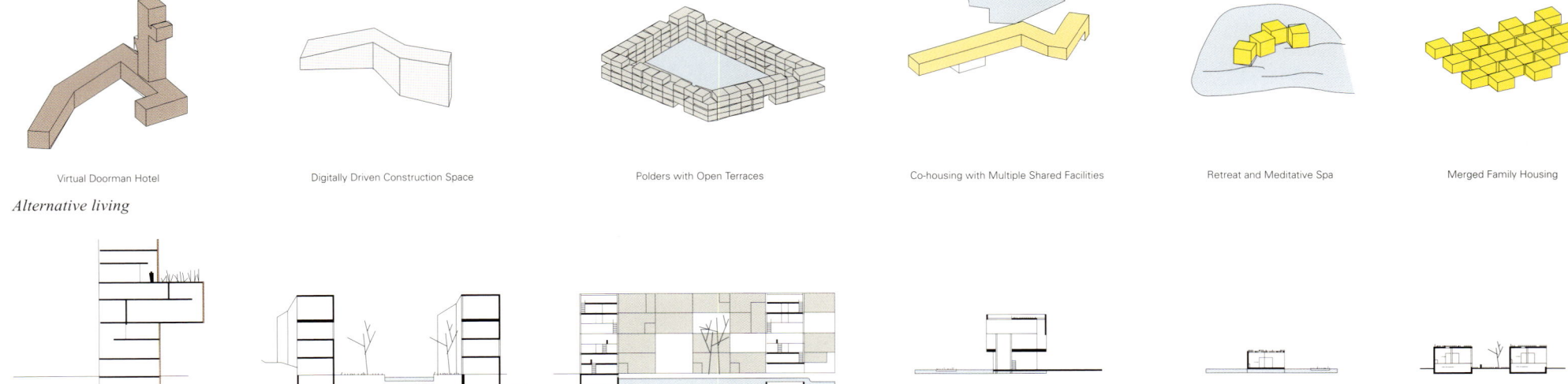

| Virtual Doorman Hotel | Digitally Driven Construction Space | Polders with Open Terraces | Co-housing with Multiple Shared Facilities | Retreat and Meditative Spa | Merged Family Housing |

Relationship to green spaces

| Terrace Garden | Braqueted Garden Spaces | Polder Water Courts | Roof Gardens, Water Gardens Below | Floating Gardens Nearby | Private Courtyards and Roof Gardens |

Space-Time-Information

At the beginning of the 21st Century the new Toolenburg-Zuid is envisioned as a hybrid zone oriented toward world citizens. The site is linked to Schipol International Airport by a high speed transit connection which connects to a local interactive electric tram—a horizontal elevator—on the site. This connection to the international transportation network has the effect of collapsing time and space.

As a global site, owners will be able to remain virtually connected to their homes across space and time. For example, a doctor from Hong Kong can connect on line to his loft in Toolenburg-Zuid to check on his garden. Travelers on layover from Schipol airport can visit the site in a one hour tour as part of the Haarlemmermeer building exposition. Fiber-optic wiring will allow each home to be both an object of destination and a subject of communication.

Combinatory & Crossbred Living

The new Toolenburg-Zuid is envisioned as a site for programmatic hybridization, allowing for unlimited variety of life styles and living arrangements. The project provides tower-lofts for the global commuter, courtyard houses for the family commuter with two children and a dog, and the house factory for the young sculptor in need of a workspace. The range of specialized housing types, such as co-housing for groups of single-parent families, celebrate the vital and dynamic residential community which results from the contemporary diversity of family arrangements. Flexibility of house design will allow for different programs and ways of living, thus increasing the useful lifespan of the buildings.

Planning Concepts

Competition scheme

The competition-winning scheme for Toolenburg-Zuid was based on three principal planning concepts:

- 20 % Water

The polder is returned to 20% water in the form of a large calligraphic cut. The earth displaced for the water calligraphy is used to create a topological earth calligraphy. These two giant marks become the new site, a globalized future carved from the polder's liquid pre-history.

- Ascending Section

Like the distant ascending jets, an ascending section moves across the site at a 5° angle, reaching a total height of 80 m in the Cactus Towers which overlook the adjacent site's lake recreation area. This sectional ascent, with the bearing angle from north to south, maximizes sunlight in all sections. Distant views of Schipol jets taking off can be seen from all new housing.

- Six Housing Types for 21st Century Living

This series of six (6) different building types present a diversity of program on a large scale. The range of variables in each basic type is digitally stretched to the point of transforming (almost morphing) into other types: Cactus Towers, Polder Voids, Co-Housing Arms, Floating Villas, Checkerboard Villas and House-Factories.

During this follow-up phase, Steven Holl Architects was directed to produce a modified plan to take account of three aspects: variety of housing, quality of open space, and access and circulation.

Landscape as Ecological Engine

The ecological aspirations of the competition scheme are further developed through the intensification of the water-landscape. Instead of a typical suburban development where the open space is merely a means of spearating houses, that then acquires garden and recreation functions, the landscape sanctuary of Toolenburg-Zuid is designed as an ecosystem that acts in symbiosis with the architecture.

Through the management of the water resources on site, drinking-water supply is conserved and surface run-off is minimized. Rainwater is harvested and used for irrigation; a biological system of plants and pools assisted by solar-powered pumps allows for reuse of grey water from the housing; a fantastically rich landscape of wet and dry with gardens for flowers, vegetables or medicinal plants is provided for the residents' use. As a result the site itself becomes a model for new ways of living.

Further, each building type will be designed to maximize its particular ecological possibilities. For example, polder voids take advantage of geothermal heating and cooling while the cactus towers exploit their height to produce wind power.

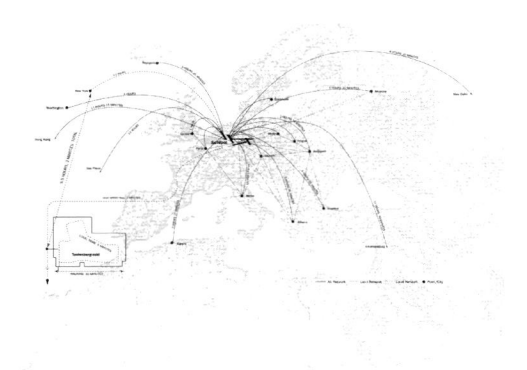

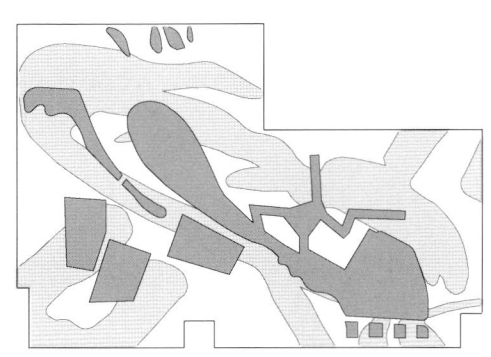

Concept and site

Architects: Steven Holl Architects—Steven Holl, principal-in-charge; Martin Cox, associate-in-charge; Gabriela Barman-Kramer, project architect; Molly Blieden, Matt Johnson, Makram El-Kadi, Jason Frantzen, project team; Chris Otterbein, The Orchard Group, model fabrication

Site

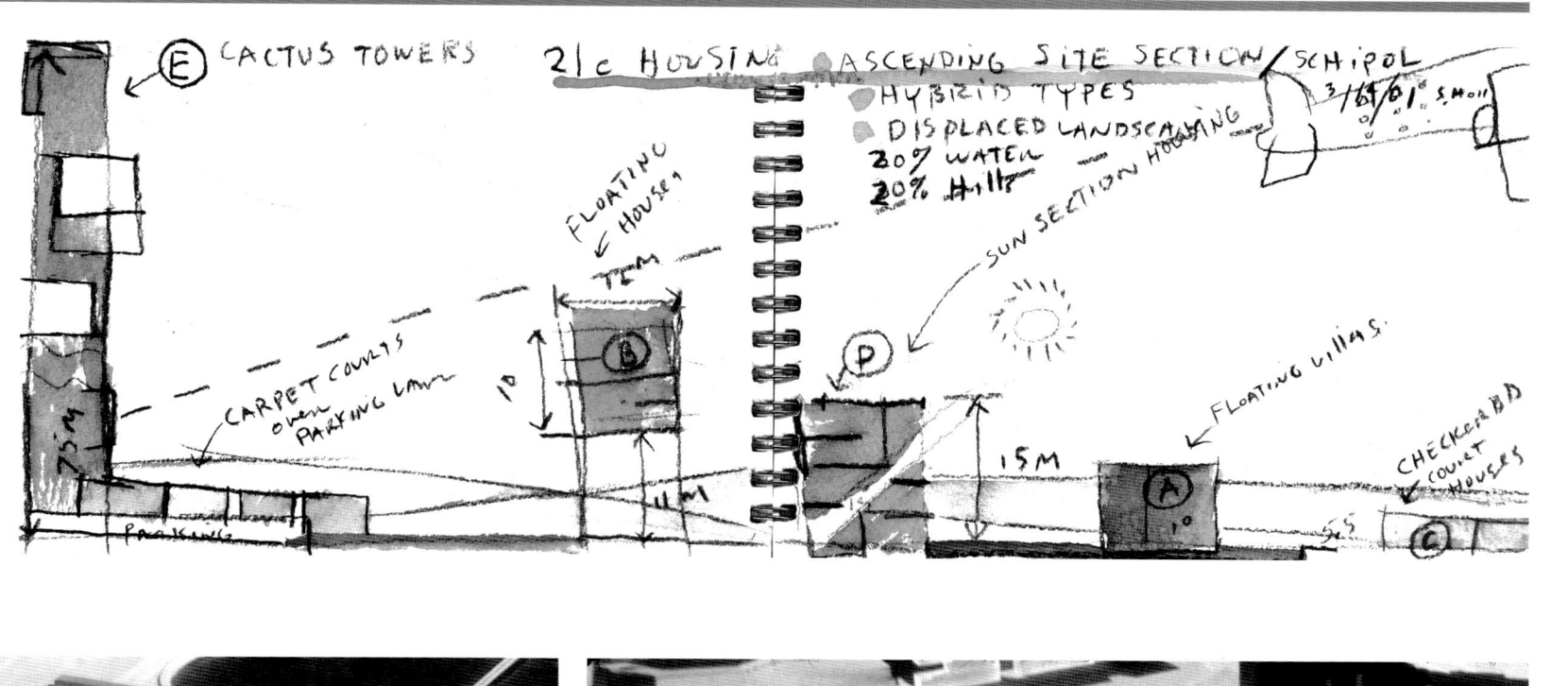

Models of alternative livings 各住戸タイプの模型

Cactus Towers and Polder Voids カクタス・タワー&ポルダー・ヴォイド

Sketch: Cactus Towers スケッチ：カクタス・タワー

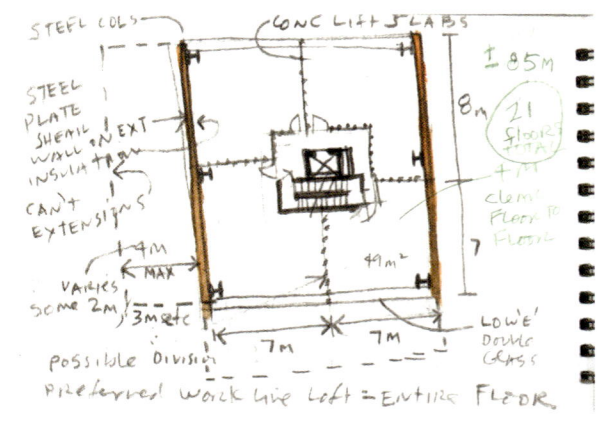

View from wild grass 野草地より見る

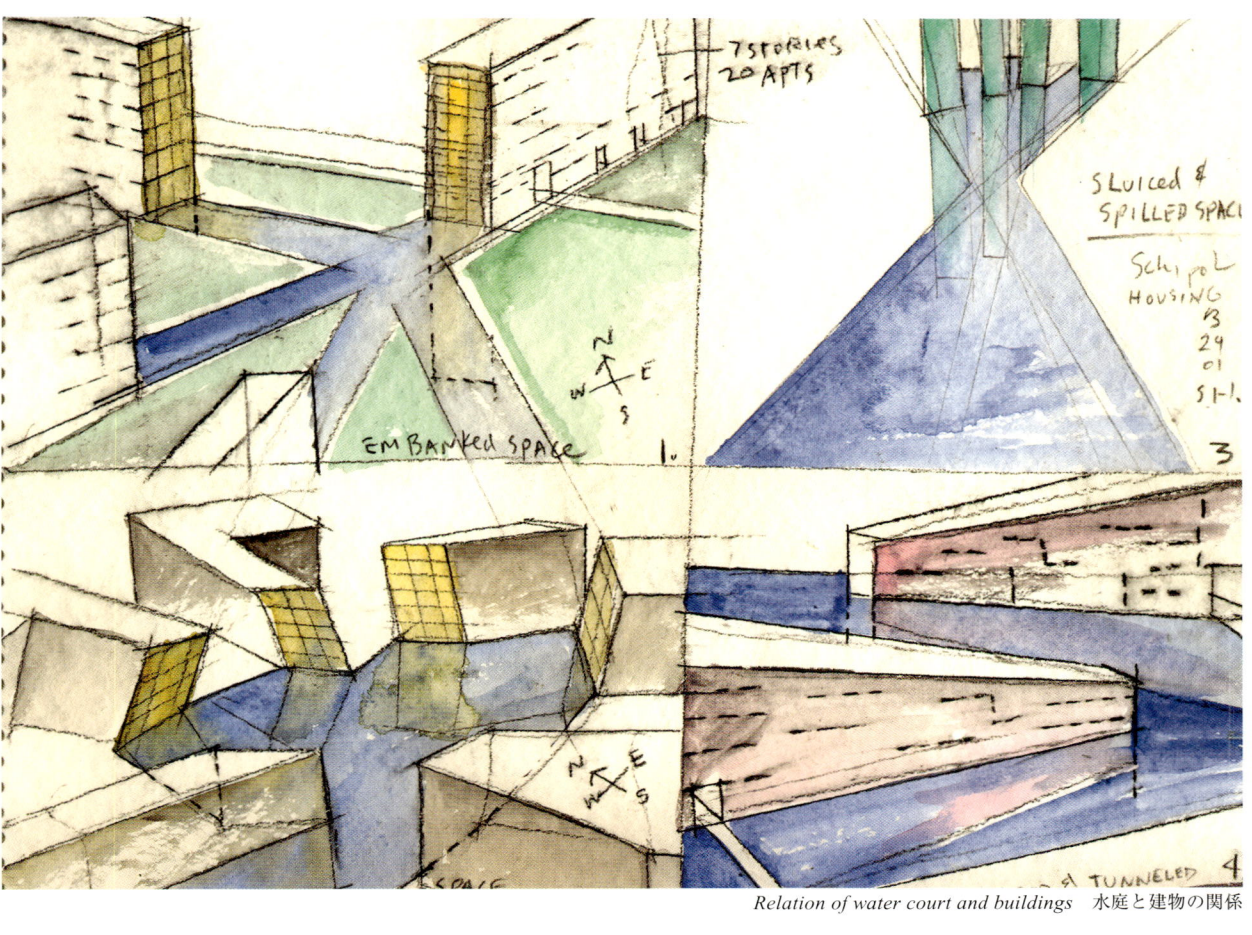

Relation of water court and buildings 水庭と建物の関係

View toward Cactus Tower from Co-Housing コー・ハウジングよりカクタス・タワーを見る

View toward Cactus Tower from lake　湖よりカクタス・タワーを見る

View toward site from outside　敷地外側より見る

View toward Cactus Tower from Checkerboard Garden Houses チェッカーボード・ガーデンハウスよりカクタス・タワーを見る

Water court of Polder Voids ポルダー・ヴォイドの水庭

PINAULT FOUNDATION

Paris, France
Design: 2001

The Overall Planning of Île Seguin:
The transformation of the Renault Factory site which built out Île Seguin will have a social/public ideal equal to the Art Foundation's ideals.

In reflection of the great social history of the site (factory worker's labor history, Paris 1968, etc.) the northeast majority of the island is envisioned as a free global university. Talented students from any nation (especially focused will be those countries presently working on various Renault car elements) will win scholarships to include their free journey to Île Seguin for studies. Various technology companies underwrite teaching and institutional costs including dormitory housing of the island.
(Note: The buildings could house other University Functions.)

The morphological form of the university is envisioned as a flipped outline of the south western 1/3 of the island. This "hinge and flip" form produces a large park and sculpture gardens along the southern and sunny edge of the transformed Île Seguin. Five "Thrown Voids" connect its form to the Foundation's geometry.

Concept:
The concept for the Pinault Foundation on Île Sequin, Paris is a salute to Stephane Mallarme's epic poem Un Coup De Des (A Throw of the Dice)

Simple rectangular galleries in a range of sizes in fine proportions and light are joined around five "thrown" armature spaces. These shaped voids form a vast internal spatial sequence. Here we imagine collaborating on new permanent artworks with artists such as Walter de Maria, James Turrell, Richard Serra, etc.

Around the Foundation at the edge of Île Seguin are located cafes and terraces connected by a continuous electric tram. The activities of the sitting and moving crowds loop the site and are near the water's edge, while the heart of the Foundation is a 'spiritual refuge'.... a place of personal reflection .... a place free of the noise and smell of automobiles. Free in a zen-like emptiness of poetic reverie.

While the overall reads as one building, the internal concept is of three types of major spaces each inserted into the other (thing within a thing within a thing).

The largest spaces (A) are shaped voids without specific functions which makeup the large sculpted internal sequence through the foundation. Here we imagine collaborating on new permanent artworks with artists such as Walter de Maria, James Turrell, Richard Serra, etc.

The new gallery spaces (B) are scaled in a more intimate way to best frame more intimate artworks. The galleries are of various sizes making a variety of simple rooms for art.

The service spaces (C) include reading and study areas, cafes, bookstores, film rooms, etc. connected to the public loop around the perimeter of the foundation. We envision these spaces can be open longer than the foundation itself, for now we call them the 24-hr spaces.

Moving from the deep "shaped voids" at the heart of the Foundation (A) to the brackets of the simple galleries (B) the outer edges (C) wrap the foundation in 24hr spaces which provide glowing facades reflected in la Seine day and night seven days a week.

〈スガン島の全体計画〉
スガン島にあるルノー工場跡地の転換計画には、ピノー芸術財団の理想と同じ社会的／公共的理想を持たせたいと考えた。

労働者の社会主義的な運動の場ともなった（パリ、1968年の5月革命など）、敷地の歴史を反映させて、島の北東部の大半を世界自由大学として構想する。あらゆる国からの才能豊かな学生に（現在、ルノー車の多種多様な部品を製造している国が優先されるだろう）学ぶためにスガン島への旅費を含めて奨学金を与える。様々な技術関連企業が、教育、管理事務コスト、島の寄宿舎の費用を負担する（注：建物にはその他の大学機能も収容できる）。

大学のモルホロジカルな形態は、島の南西部3分の1を裏返した場合の輪郭を想定して描かれている。この"ヒンジとフリップ"による形態構成は、スガン島の南側や日当たりのよい縁に沿って広い公園や彫刻庭園をつくりだす。5つの"投げられたヴォイド"が、その形態を財団のジオメトリーに接続する。

〈コンセプト〉
パリ、スガン島に計画されたピノー財団のためのコンセプトは、ステファヌ・マラルメの叙事詩、『骰子一擲』への挨拶である。

精緻な均整を持ち光に満たされた様々な大きさの、骰子のように単純な矩形のギャラリーは、5つの"擲げられた"甲冑のような空間の周りで接合される。これらの象られたヴォイドは巨大な内部空間のシークエンスを形成する。ここでは、ウォルター・デ・マリア、ジェームズ・タレル、リチャード・セラなどのアーティストとの恒久的な作品の共同制作を行うことを想像している。

スガン島の縁にある財団を囲むように、トラムで結ばれたカフェやテラスが並ぶ。座ったり、行き来する人々の動きは、輪を描き、水辺近くを占め、一方、財団の中心部は"スピリチュアルな退避場所"……一人沈思黙考する場所……騒音や車のガソリンの匂いから解放された場所となる。禅に似た空のなかでの詩的瞑想の自由。

全体は一つの建物に見えるが、内部のコンセプトは互いに一方のなかに挿入された、入れ子状の3つのタイプの主要空間で構成される。

一番大きいスペース（A）は特別な機能を持たない象られたヴォイドで、財団全体を貫く大きな彫刻的シークエンスをつくりだす。

新しいギャラリー・スペース（B）は、それより小さな作品を枠取るに相応しい、より親しみやすいスケールを備える。様々な大きさのギャラリーは、アートのための多彩でシンプルな空間をつくりあげるだろう。

サービス・スペース（C）は、財団の周縁部を囲むパブリックなループに接続し、読書や学習のためのエリア、カフェ、書店、フィルム・ルームなどがある。

これらのスペースは財団本部よりも長い時間オープンできるようにしたいと考えている。目下、私たちはこれらを、24時間スペースと呼んでいる。

財団の中心部、奥まった場所にある"象られたヴォイド"（A）からシンプルなギャラリー（B）空間である"ブラケット"に進んでくると、外周部（C）が財団を24時間スペースで包み、セーヌ川に、1週7日間、昼も夜も、輝くファサードを投影する。

GA PROJECT

Architects: Steven Holl Architects—Steven Holl, principal-in-charge; Annette Goderbauer, project architect; Asako Akazawa, Arnault Biou, Jason Frantzen, Li Hu, Mathew Johnson, Brian Melter, Olaf Schmidt, Aislinn Weidele, project team
Consultants: Jacobs Serete (Paris), Guy Nordenson and Associates (New York), structural; Ove Arup & Partners (New York), mechanical; Orchard Group (New York), model fabrication

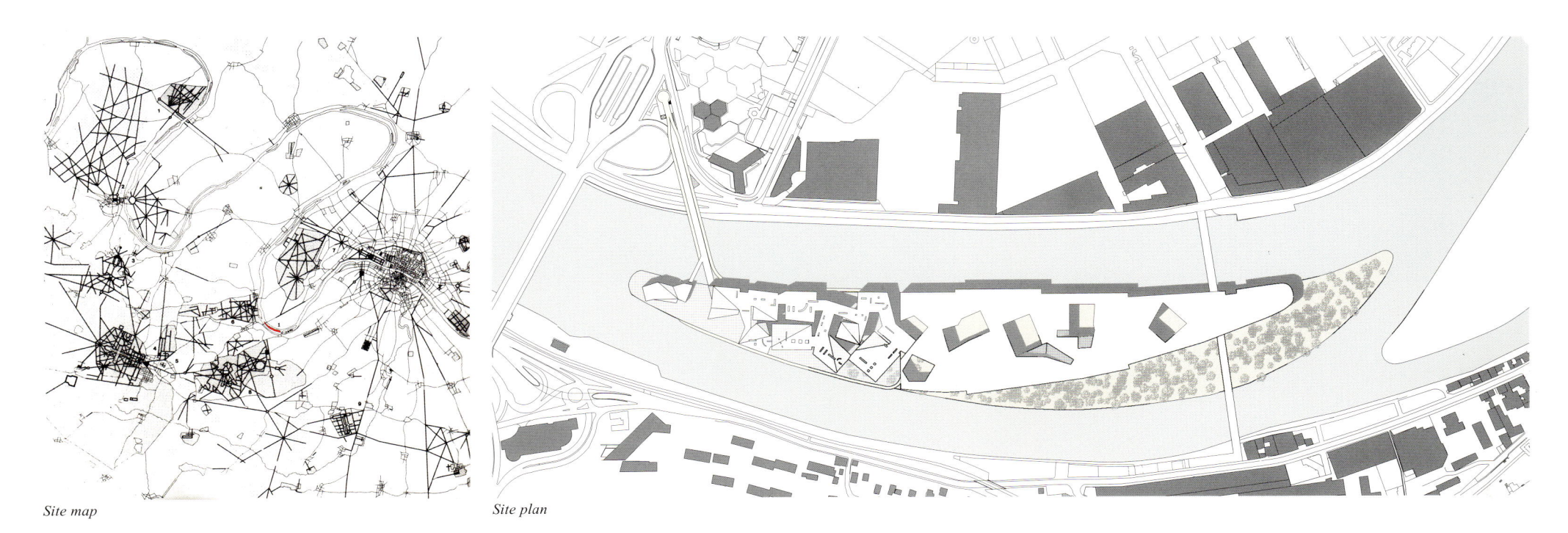

Site map

Site plan

Night view of elevation 立面夜景

Aerial view　上空より見る

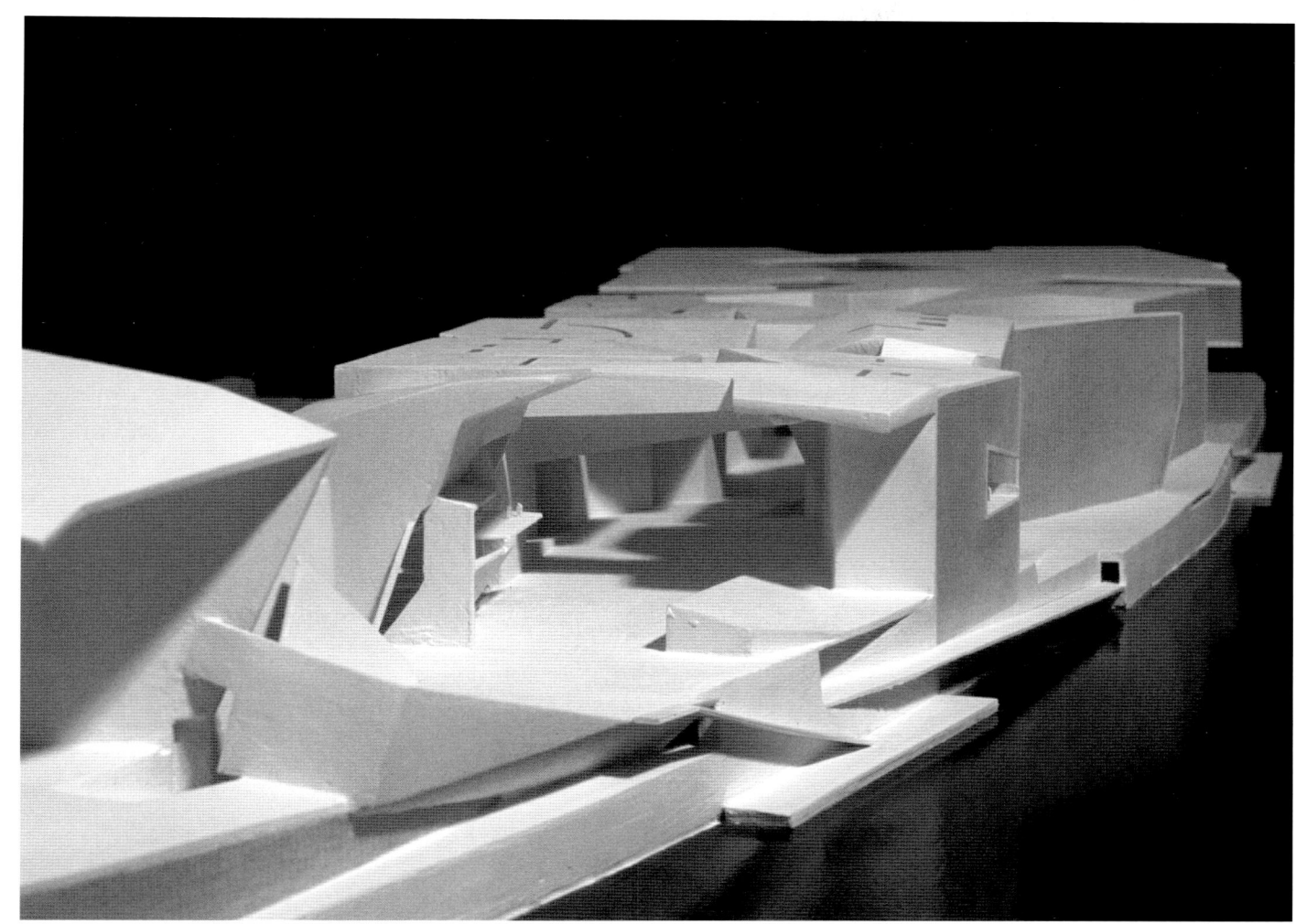

75 | GA PROJECT

Entrance plaza エントランス・プラザ

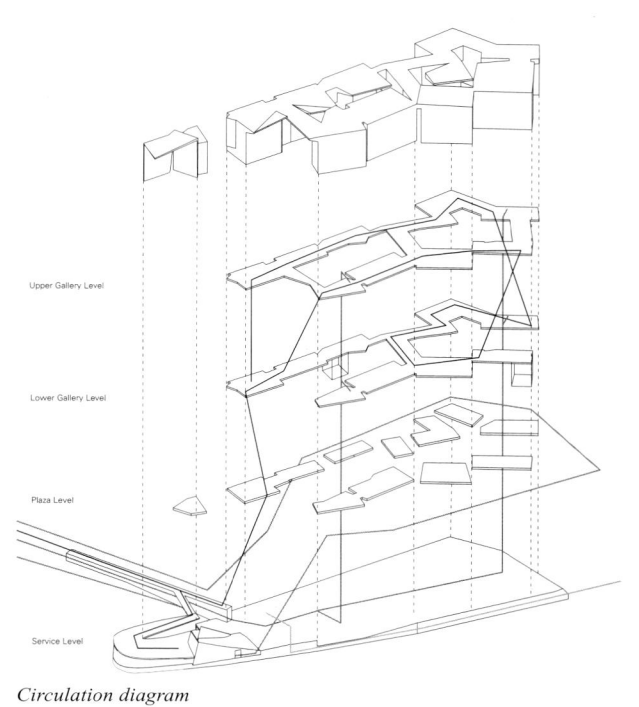

Circulation diagram

Night view of east end 東端部夜景

Lower gallery level +48

1 GALLERY AND BREATHING SPACE
2 RECEPTION
3 TICKETING
4 CHILDRENS' SALON 1
5 LIBRARY SALON 2
6 LIBRARY SALON 3
7 BOOKSTORE + ÎLE SEGUIN ORIENTATION

Ground level +41

1 RECEPTION	•MULTIMEDIA	EXHIBITIONS
2 TRAM STATION	8 EDUCATIONAL WORKSHOPS	•PUBLIC PROGRAMS
3 BOOKSTORE/BOUTIQUE	9 VIDEO CAFE	12 OFFICES
4 CONVENIENCES	10 SHARED SERVICES	•DIRECTION/CONSERVATION
5 LIBRARY	FOR MANAGEMENT	•VIP RECEPTION
6 TELEVISION STATION	11 OFFICES	
7 OFFICES	•ADMINISTRATION	
•COMMUNICATIONS	•COLLECTIONS AND	

Basement +34

Roof

Upper gallery level +56

1 GALLERY AND BREATHING SPACE
2 SALON CAFE
3 LIBRARY SALON 1

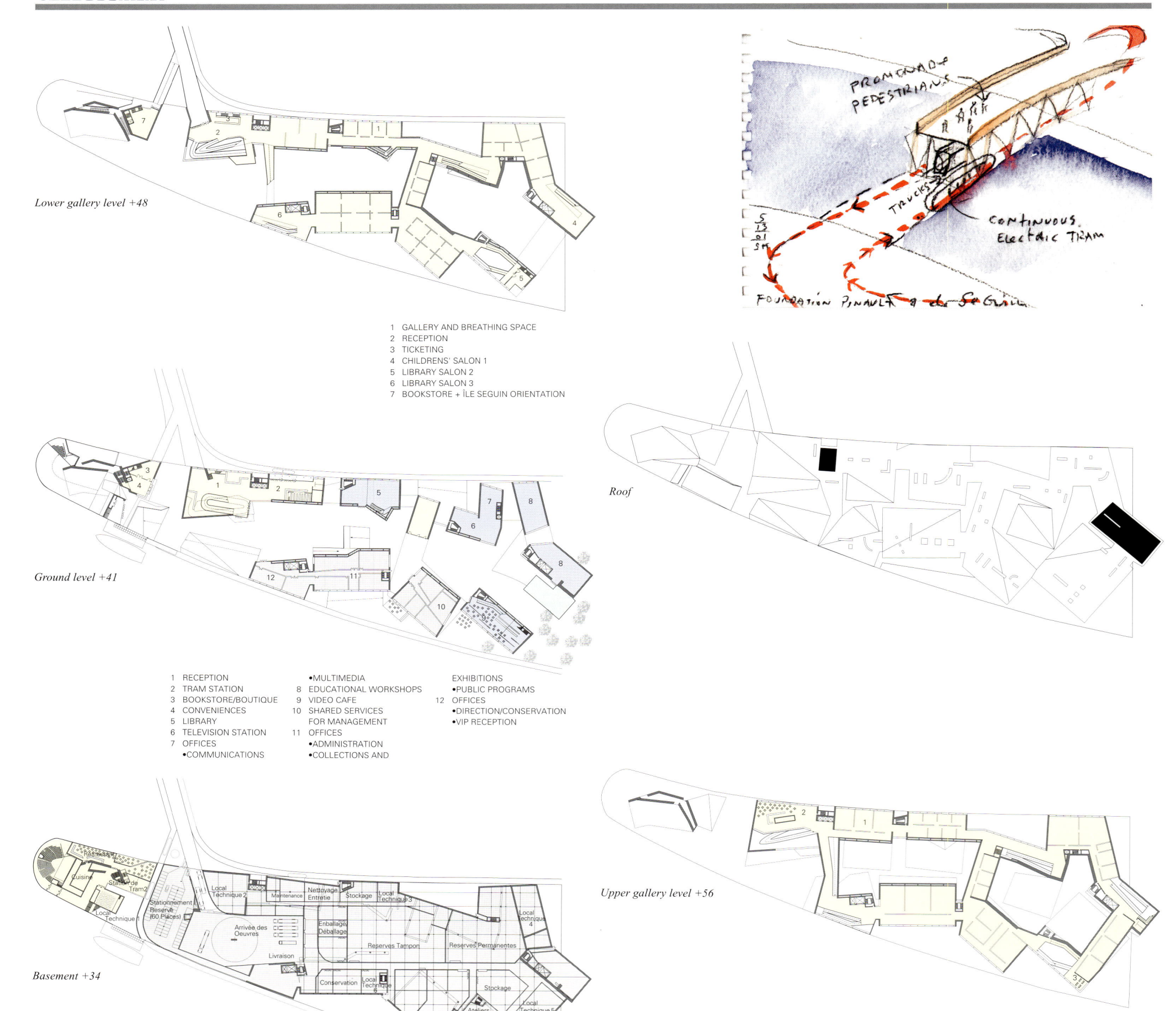

GA PROJECT

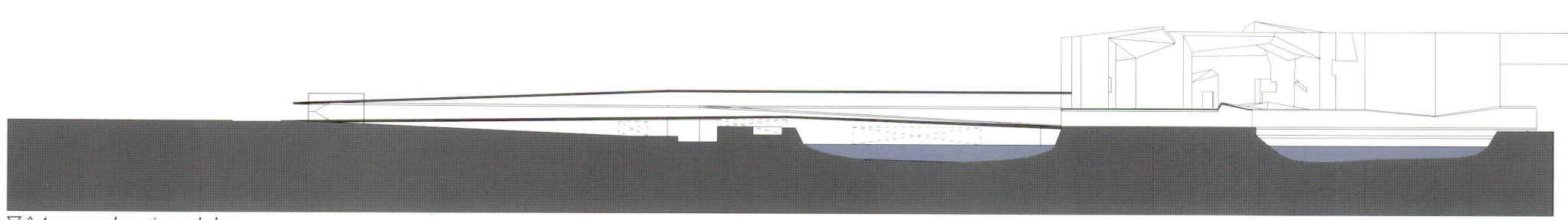

△▽ *Access road: section and plan*

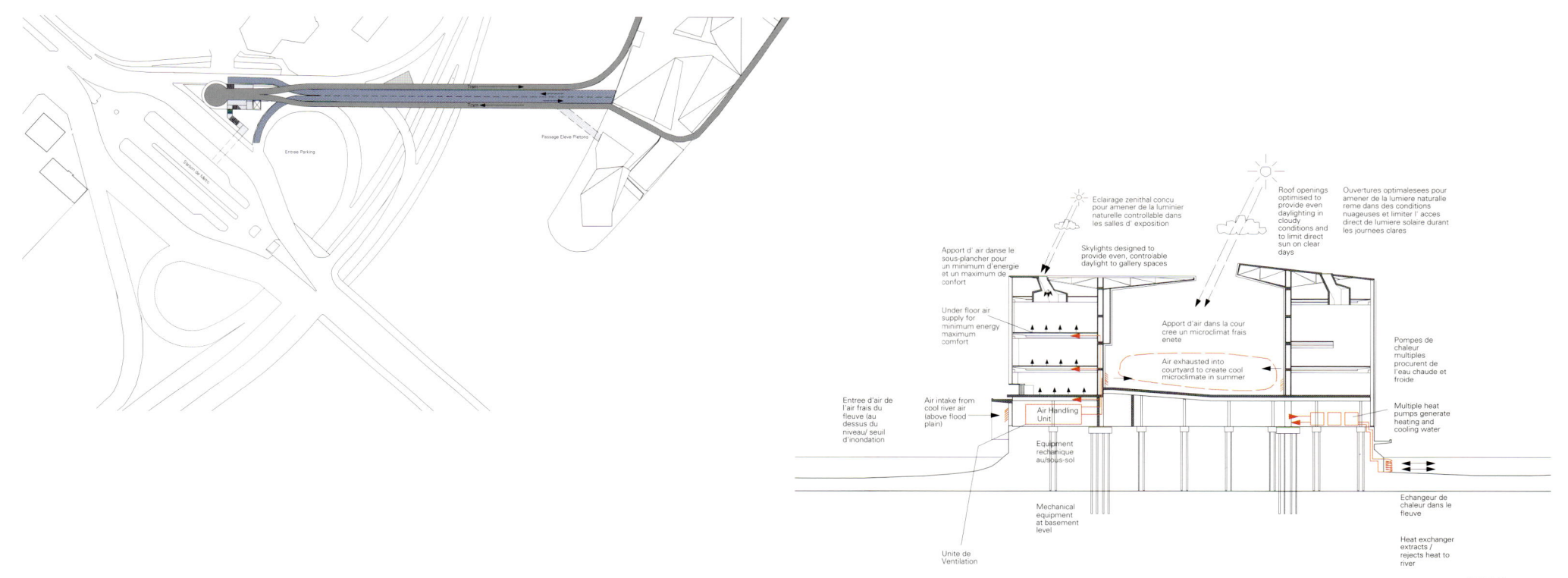

HVAC system

1 UPPER GALLERY LEVEL
2 LOWER GALLERY LEVEL
3 LIBRARY
4 OFFICE
5 BUILDING LOGISTICS
6 ARRIVAL OF ART WORK
7 PROCESSING OF ART WORKS

1 UPPER GALLERY FLOOR
2 LOWER GALLERY FLOOR
3 RESPIRATION SPACE
4 COMMON SERVICES
5 WORKSHOPS
6 PERMANENT STORAGE

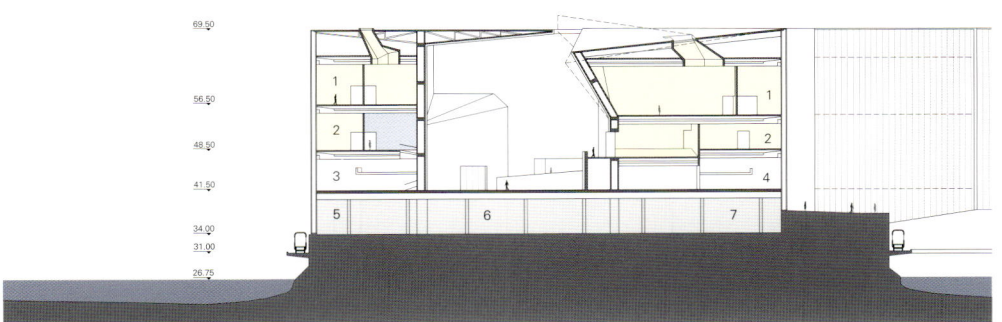

Section 1

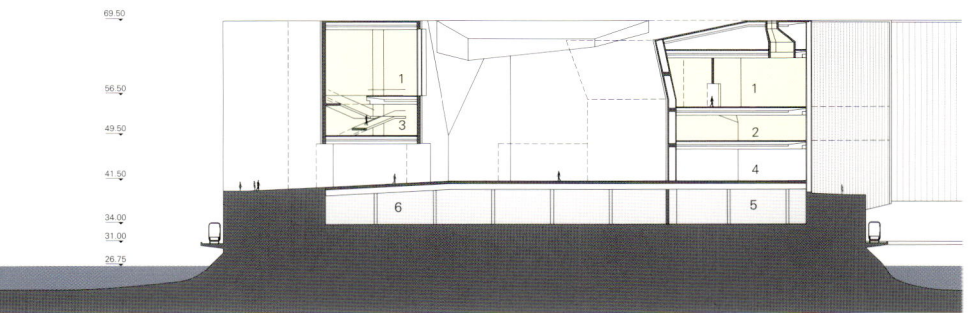

Section 2

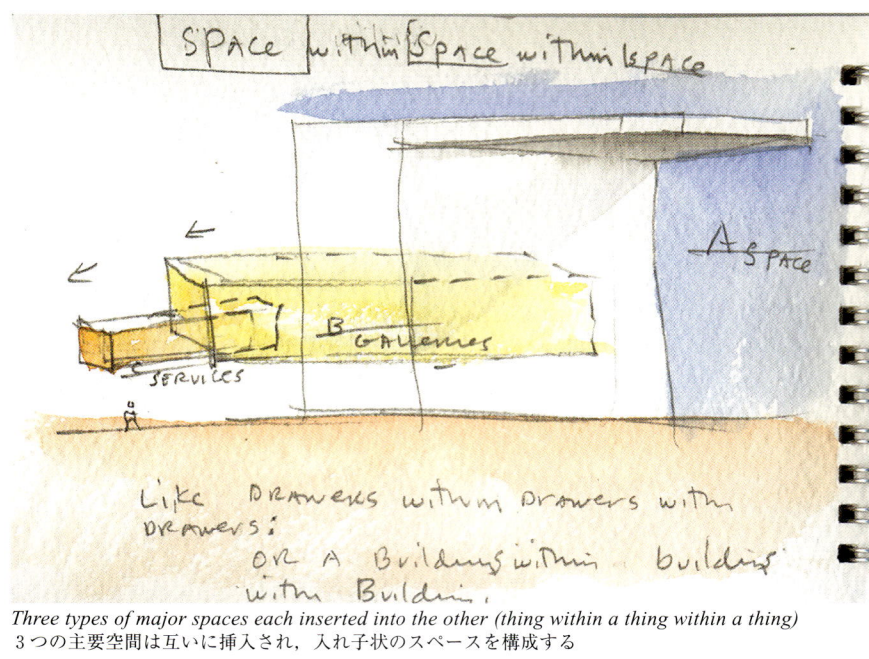

Three types of major spaces each inserted into the other (thing within a thing within a thing)
3つの主要空間は互いに挿入され，入れ子状のスペースを構成する

View of east edge 東端を見る

Approach from Seine River セーヌ川からのアプローチ

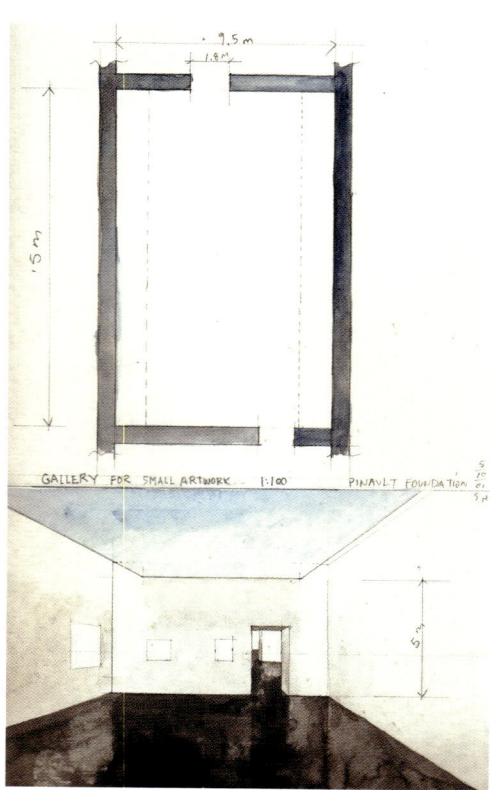

Small gallery 小ギャラリー

79 GA PROJECT

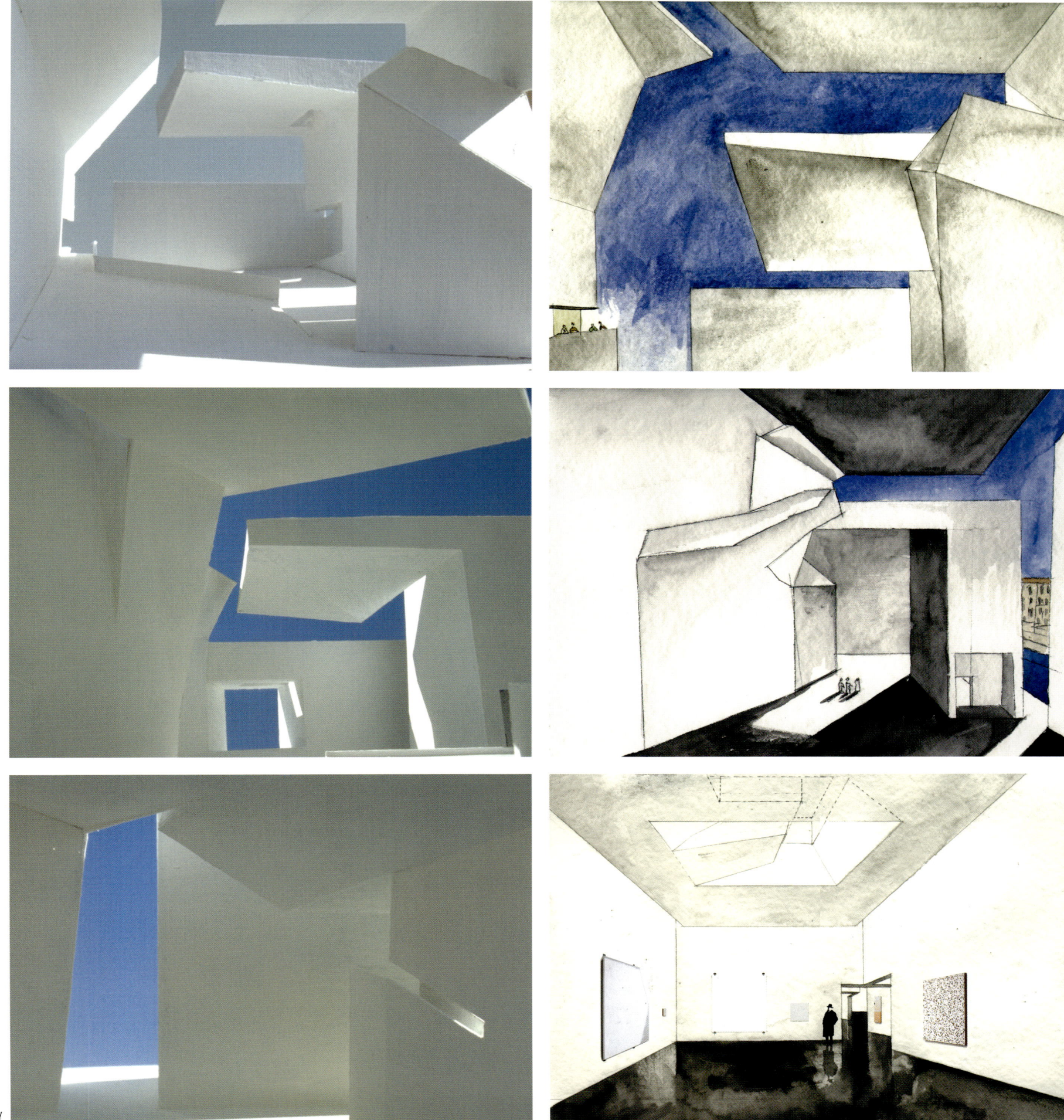

Spaces each inserted into the other
入れ子状の空間

LACMA
LOS ANGELES COUNTY MUSEUM OF ART

Los Angeles, California, U.S.A.
Design: 2001

Model: north view　模型：北より見る

GA PROJECT

The expansion of the Los Angeles County Museum of Art, California's largest public institution devoted to art, should be a social condenser for greater Los Angeles. Unlike the Getty Museum, LACMA can open directly to the public on the street, inviting all groups and ages into the world of liberating and enriching experiences of art.

We envision a new identity for LACMA which is concentrated in the dramatic inspiring qualities of its inner spaces. In order to draw the outside-in, we turn portions of the inside out in a vast public space—a "Y" shaped Canyon—free to the public and open 24 hours. Open to Wilshire Blvd. at street level on the south, to a New Park on the north and rising to the Japanese Pavilion and the La Brea Tar Pits on the east, the Canyon is seen as an initiating space lined with descriptive screens previewing current museum exhibitions. All along the edges, the social programs of the museum are exposed—a day care center, young adult services, community programs center, handicapped services, information and referral, education referral center, etc. With the restaurants opening to the New Park and a mini-cinemateque devoted to avant-garde film, this "Cultural Canyon" would serve as a forum for the city. At the crossing a generous new central lobby orients the entire LACMA Complex and connects directly to the new parking.

The light modulators form a new geometric landscape on the roof sprinkled with water pools and benches reclaiming the building site as public park. The geometrical landscape looks onto a new topological water garden laced with water fountain landscaping, which covers the parking area. The entire recirculating system of the garden is powered by the Photo Voltaic cells embedded in the glass walls of the new extensions (avoiding brown-out shutdown). Rooms for the outdoor Sculpture Garden are formed naturally by the rows of trees which, due to their recessed pockets, bring light and natural ventilation to parking below.

The new LACMA is formed of three landscapes:
- The geometrical landscape of the light monitors over the luminous platform.
- The topological water gardens and sculpture terraces over the parking.
- The geological landscape of the ancient tar pit history of the site.

While the "Y" shaped Canyon draws in three directions, its fissure coheres the culturally diverse Art Centers within the new and existing buildings. The flow of people of all communities which comprise 21st Century Los Angeles bring these continents together in a conceptual river through the new Cultural Canyon.

The position, mass, and re-centered circulation of the new elements binds all LACMA fragments together with great economy. The grand platform of fine proportioned galleries sliced by the orienting Cultural Canyon, a social condenser lined with transparent services, will add a new glowing public presence along Wilshire Blvd.

Model: northeast view 模型：北東より見る

Model: southeast view 模型：南東より見る

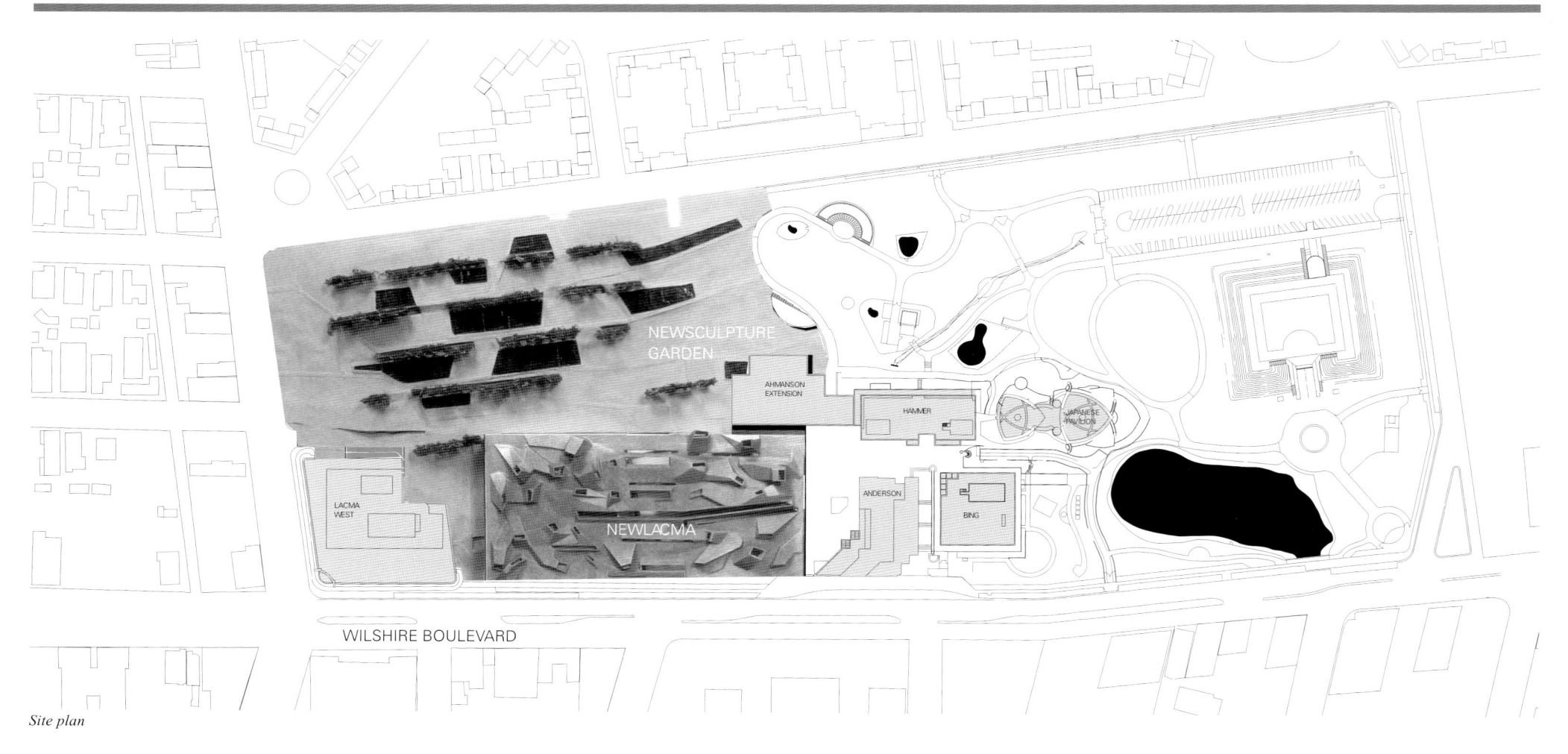

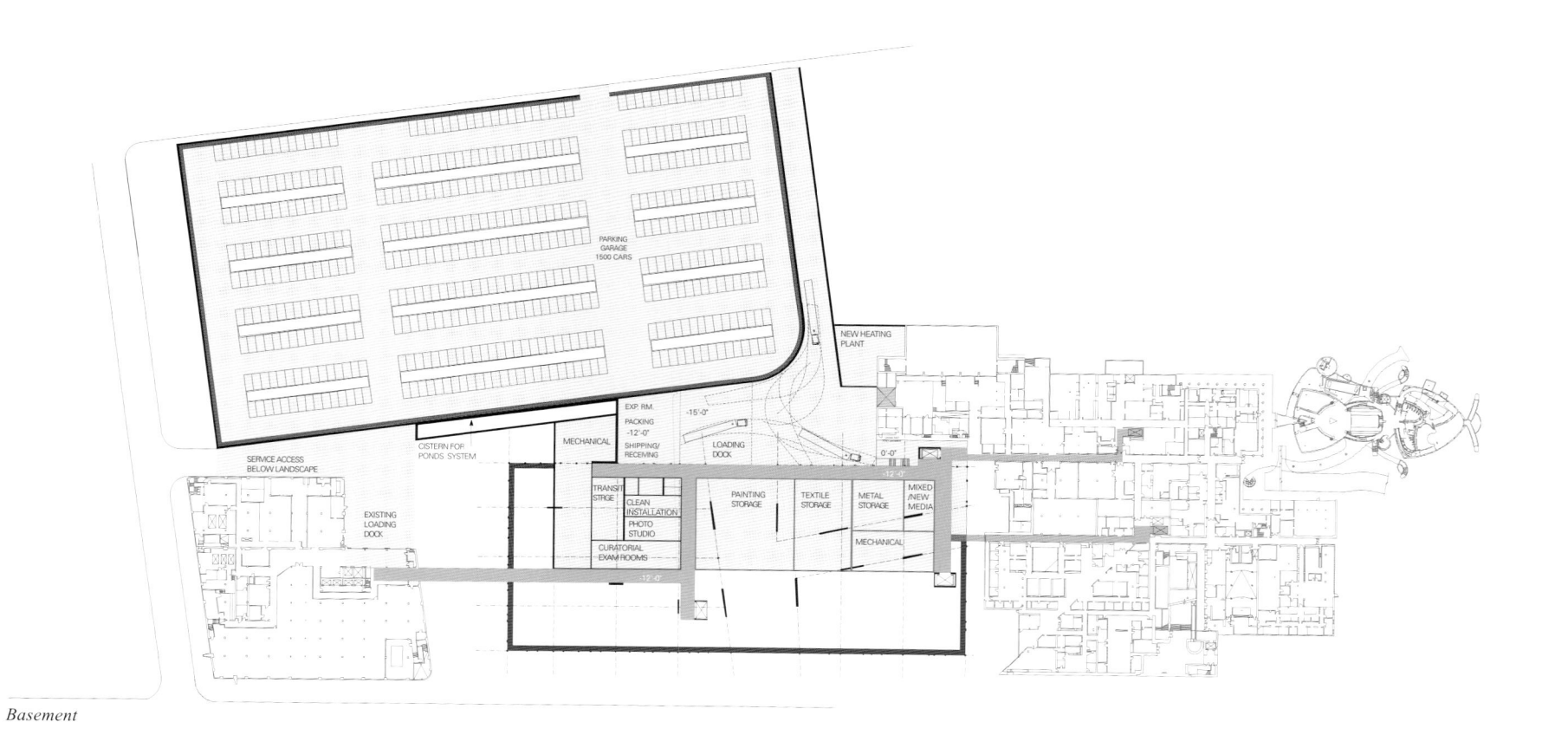

Site plan

Basement

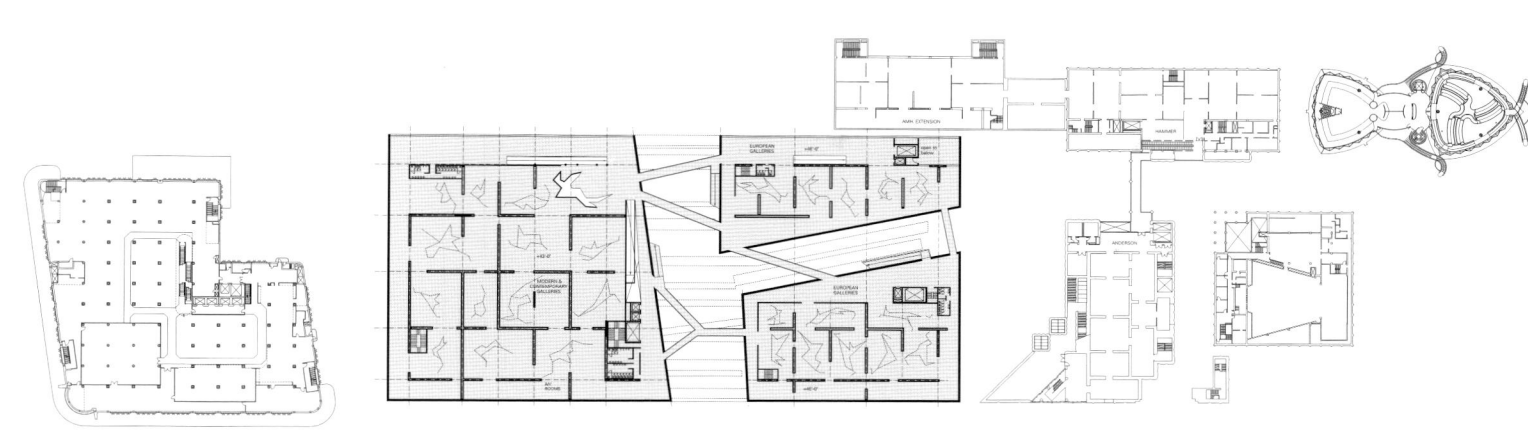

Upper floor

Mezzanine

Ground floor

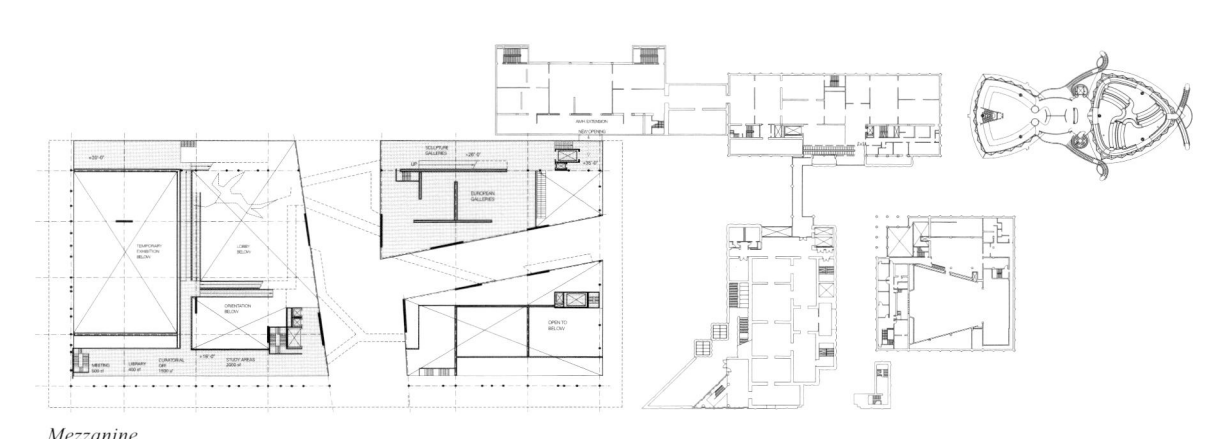

アート専門の公共施設としてカリフォルニア最大の規模を持つ，ロサンジェルス郡美術館の増築棟は，グレーター・ロサンジェルスのソシアル・コンデンサーとなるだろう。ゲッティ美術館とは異なり，LACMAは道路に面して街に直接開かれ，あらゆるグループや年齢層の人々を，アートの解放的で心を豊かにする体験へと招く。

　内部空間をドラマティックで，人を元気づけるものにすることに集中し，LACMAの新しい個性をつくろうと考えた。戸外を屋内に引き込むために，内部の一部を広大なパブリック・スペース（"Y"形の谷）として外に向け，自由に入れる，24時間オープンの場所とした。南側の道路レベルはウィルシャー大通りに，北側はニュー・パークに面し，東側の日本館とラ・ブレア・タール・ピッツに向かって上昇するキャニオンは，美術館で開催される展覧会について予告紹介するスクリーンと整列して，美術館のスタート地点となる。美術館の社会プログラムはすべて，周縁部に沿って並んでいる——デイケア・センター，若年層成人のためのサービス，コミュニティ・プログラム・センター，身体に障害のある人へのサービス，インフォメーションとリファレンス，エデュケーション・リファレンス・センター等々。ニュー・パークに面したレストラン，前衛映画専門のミニ・シネマと共に，この"文化の谷"は街のフォーラムとして活躍するだろう。交差部のところで広々とした新しい中央ロビーが美術館の全部門に方位を向け，新しいパーキングと直接連結する。

　水盤やベンチを散りばめ，公園として建築敷地を活用した屋上に，光を調整するモニターが，幾何学的なランドスケープをかたちづくる。ここから，パーキング・エリアの上につくられた，噴水が点在する，地形を生かした新しい水の庭を見晴らせる。庭の水の循環システムはすべて，増築棟のガラス壁に埋め込まれた光電池によって作動する（節電による運転停止を避けるため）。屋外の彫刻庭園は，木立の列で自然にかたちづくられ，その後退した窪みから，下のパーキングに外光や外気が運び込まれる。新しいLACMAは3つのランドスケープによって形成される：

——明るく輝くプラットホームの上に広がる，光モニターの幾何学的なランドスケープ

——パーキングの上に広がる，地形を生かした水の庭と彫刻テラス

——遠い昔のタール坑の歴史を物語る敷地の地質学的なランドスケープ

　"Y"形のキャニオンが3方向から人を誘い込む一方で，その亀裂は，多様な文化領域を持つアート・センターを新旧の建物内に結びつける。21世紀のロサンジェルスを構成するすべてのコミュニティから訪れる人々の流れが，これらのコミュニティを，新しい文化の谷を走り抜けるコンセプチュアルな川のなかで一つに結びつける。

　新たに増築されたエレメントの位置，マッス，再調整された導線は，LACMAの断片化された構成を，大幅な経費を節減しながら一つに束ねる。分かりやすいサービス部門に沿って並ぶソシアル・コンデンサー，方向性を持つ"文化の谷"によって切り分けられた，見事な均整を持つギャラリーを納めた広大なプラットホームは，ウィルシャー大通りに沿って，生き生きした新しい公共施設として加わるだろう。

GA DOCUMENT

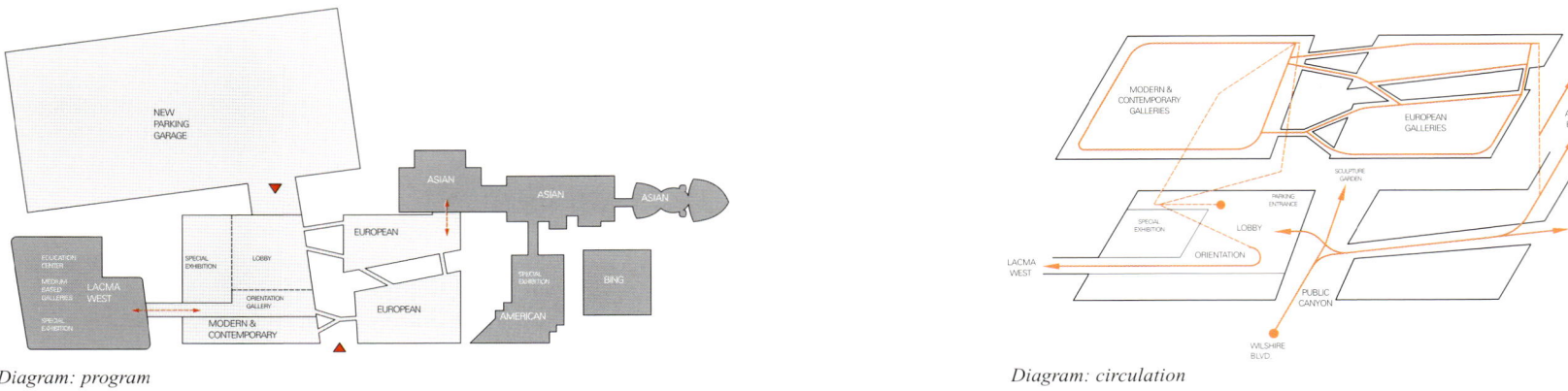

Diagram: program

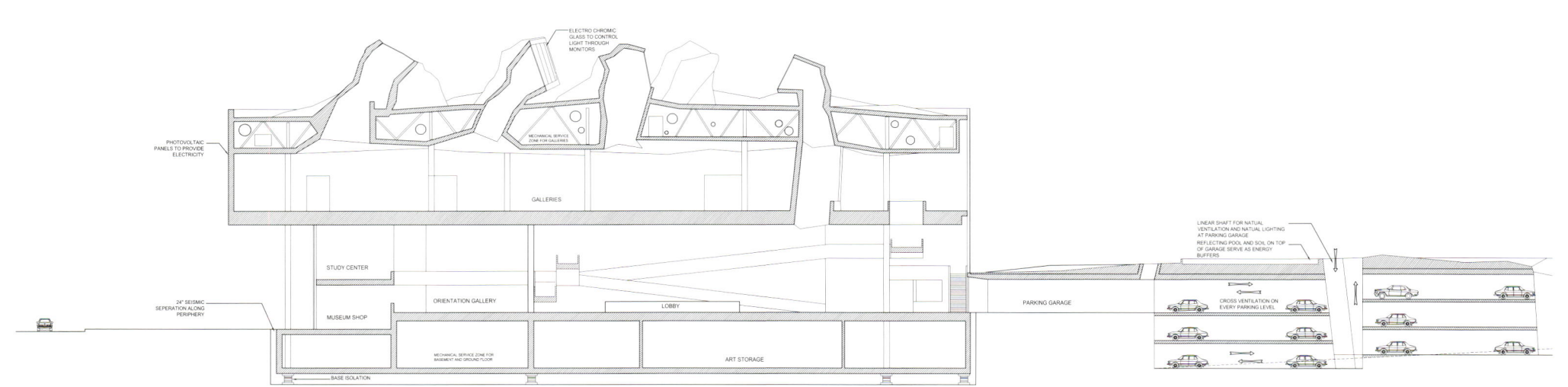

Diagram: circulation

North-south section: detail

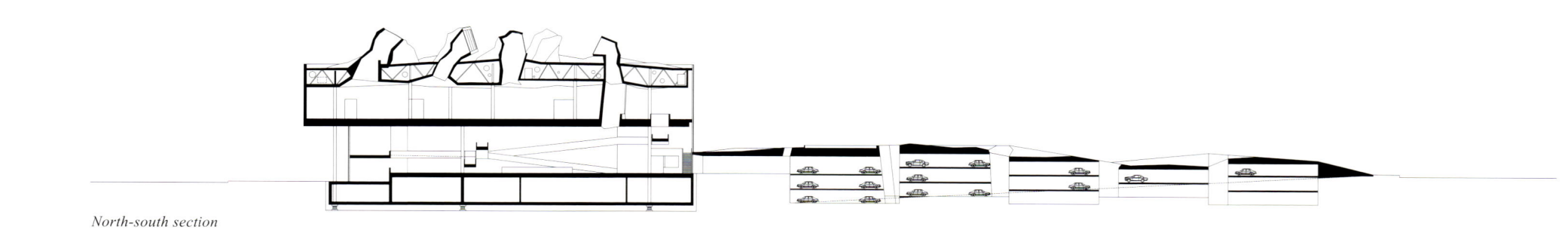

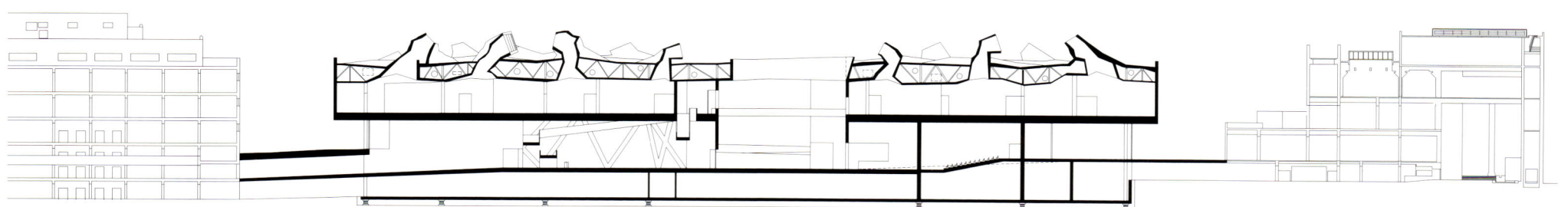

North-south section

East-west section

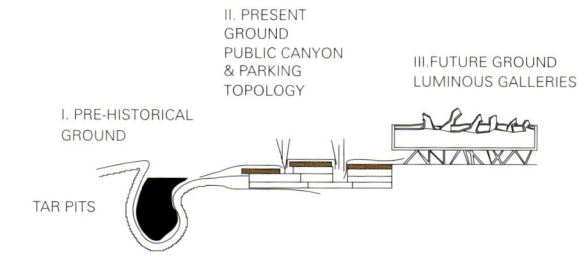

GA PROJECT

85

I. PRE-HISTORICAL GROUND — TAR PITS
II. PRESENT GROUND PUBLIC CANYON & PARKING TOPOLOGY
III. FUTURE GROUND LUMINOUS GALLERIES

1. THREE GROUNDS

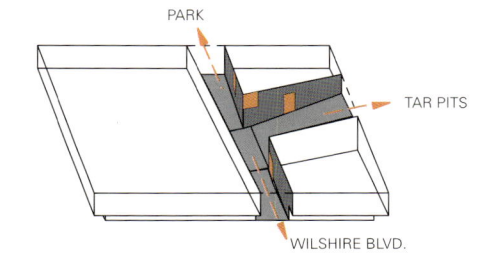

2. INITIATING SPACE & PUBLIC CANYON OPENING DIRECTLY TO THE PUBLIC STREET. FREE & INVITING ALL ETHNIC GROUPS & AGES INTO THE LIBERATING WORLD OF ART
   - PARK
   - TAR PITS
   - WILSHIRE BLVD.

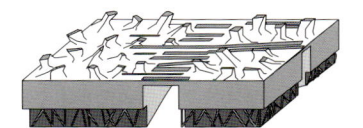

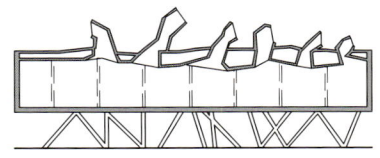

3. CONTINUOUS LUMINOUS PLATFORM OF GALLERIES. A NEW FLEXIBLE LEVEL BASED ON AN IDEAL GALLERY PROPORTION OF 34'x55'x21' HIGH EACH WITH A NATURAL LIGHT MODULATOR

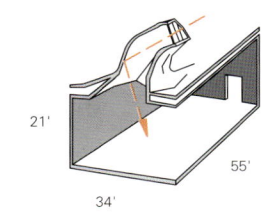

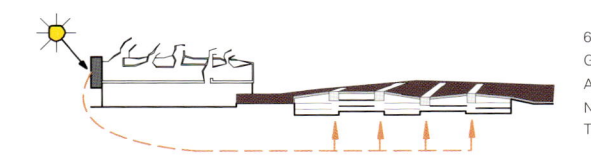

4. LIGHT MODULATORS DUE TO TWIST IN SECTION BRING DIFFUSED NATURAL LIGHT (BLACK OUT CAPACITY)

5. GEOMETRICAL LANDSCAPE OF LIGHT MODULATORS FORM NEW PUBLIC ROOF TERRACES (GEOMETRICAL MOUNTAINS)

6. TOPOLOGICAL LANDSCAPE OF GRAND NEW WATER GARDENS OVER THE NEW PARKING SECTION. ALL FOUNTAINS & PONDS POWERED BY SOLAR P.V. FACADE OF NEW BUILDING (BROWN OUT PROOF, SUN GENERATED LIKE THE ORIGINAL GEOLOGICAL LANDSCAPE OF THE TAR PITS.)

Program: concept

Architects: Steven Holl Architects—Steven Holl, principal-in-charge; Chris McVoy, partner-in-charge; Li Hu, project architect; Asako Akazawa, Makram El Kadi, Jason Frantzen, Brian Melcher, Olaf Schmidt, Christian Wassmann, project team
Client: Los Angeles County Museum of Art
Consultants: Guy Nordenson and Associates; Orchard Group, model fabrication
Program: musem expansion

NEW RESIDENCE AT SWISS EMBASSY

Wasington D.C., U.S.A.
Design: 2001–03   Construction: 2004–05

The scheme placed first in the competition of ten Swiss-American team's designs for the replacement of the Washington D.C. residence of the Swiss ambassador.

It is not only to be a private house but also a cultural gathering place on which standards and self-image of a country are measured.

Sited on a hill with a direct view through the trees to the Washington monument in the distance, a diagonal line of overlapping spaces drawn through a cruciform courtyard plan was the conceptual starting point. Official arrival spaces and ceremony spaces are connected along this diagonal line on the first level, while private living quarter functions are on the level above.

Materials are charcoal integral color concrete trimmed in local slate and sand-blasted structural glass planks.

Constructed according to Swiss "Minergie Standard", the south facades use passive solar energy. The roof is a "sedum" green roof with PVC panels.

The existing natural landscape will be clarified with new walkways and trees, while the plateau of the residence defines an arrival square, a reception courtyard and an herb garden.

ワシントンDCのスイス大使公邸を建て替えるために，スイス，アメリカ両国から選ばれた建築家10人によるコンペの1等入選案。

私邸であると同時に，スイスの国家水準とセルフイメージを測る文化的な集いの場所となる。

木立を抜けて真っ直ぐ前方にワシントン・モニュメントを望む丘に位置し，十字形の中庭型プランから引き出された折り重なる空間がつくる対角線が基本構想の出発点となった。公的な客が到着する場と儀式用のスペースはこの対角線に沿って1階に並び，私的な生活空間は2階にある。

材料には，地元産のスレート，サンドストンで縁取りしたチャコール色のカラー・コンクリート，サンドブラストした構造用ガラス厚板を用いる。

スイスの省エネルギー基準に従って，南面にはパッシブソーラーを使用。塩化ビニル・パネルと，"シーダム（ベンケイソウ）"の緑色の屋根。

もとの自然景観は，新しい歩行路と木立で整え，建物の建つ台地は，客が到着する広場，レセプション・コートヤード，ハーブ園を明快に分けるだろう。

Site map

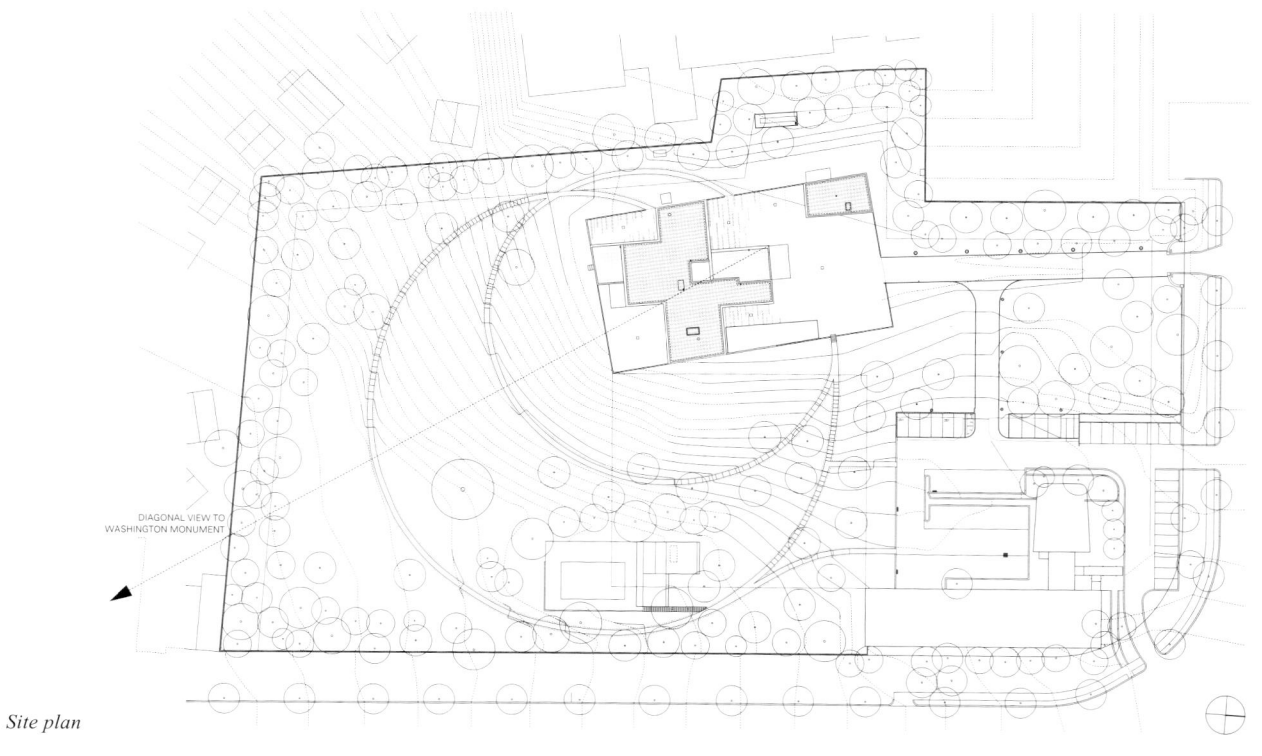

Site plan

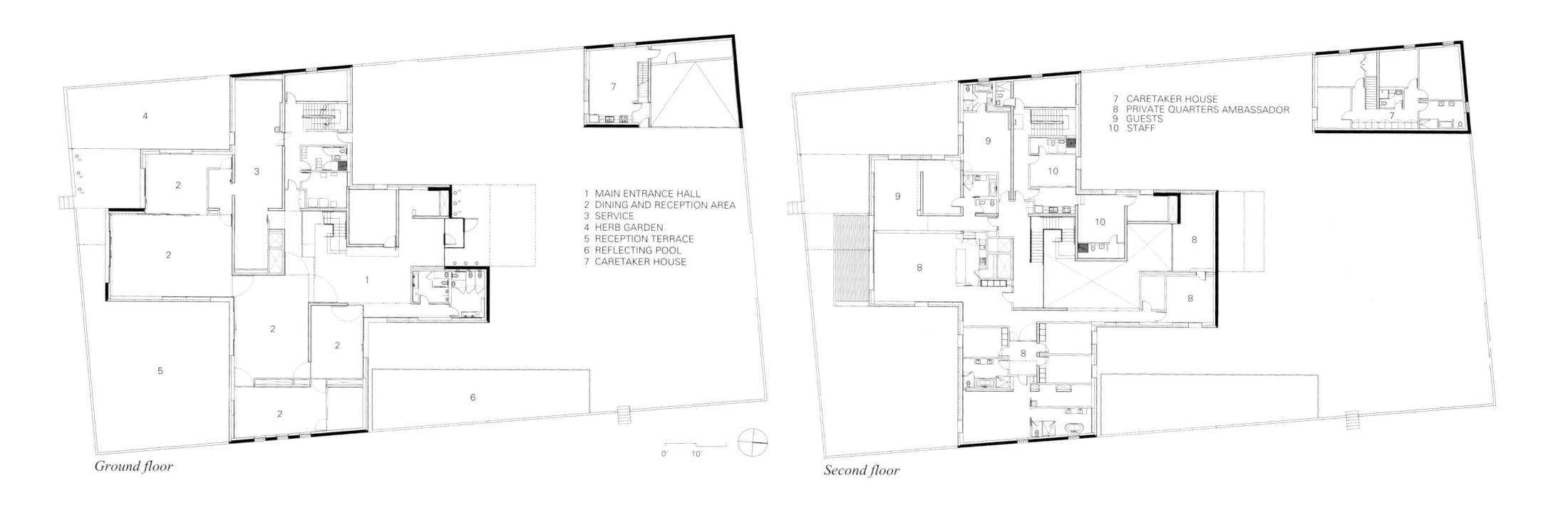

GA PROJECT

1 MAIN ENTRANCE HALL
2 DINING AND RECEPTION AREA
3 SERVICE
4 HERB GARDEN
5 RECEPTION TERRACE
6 REFLECTING POOL
7 CARETAKER HOUSE

7 CARETAKER HOUSE
8 PRIVATE QUARTERS AMBASSADOR
9 GUESTS
10 STAFF

Ground floor

Second floor

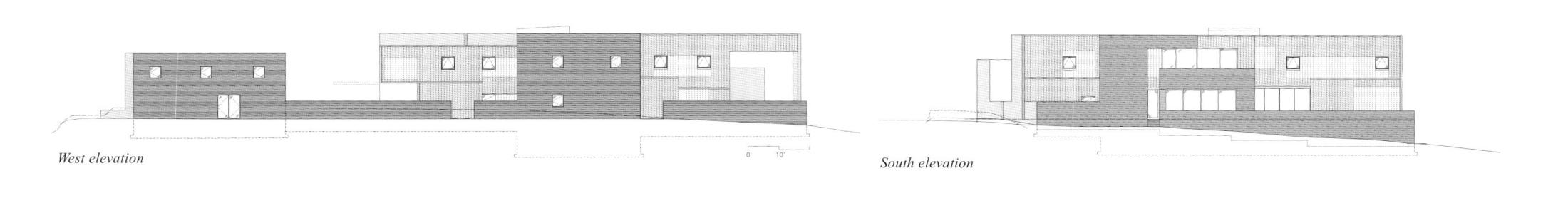

West elevation

South elevation

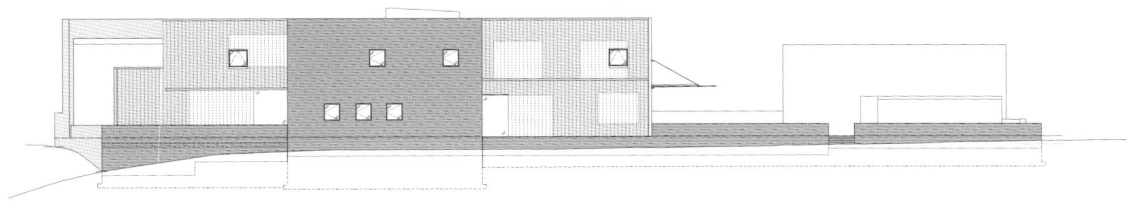

East elevation

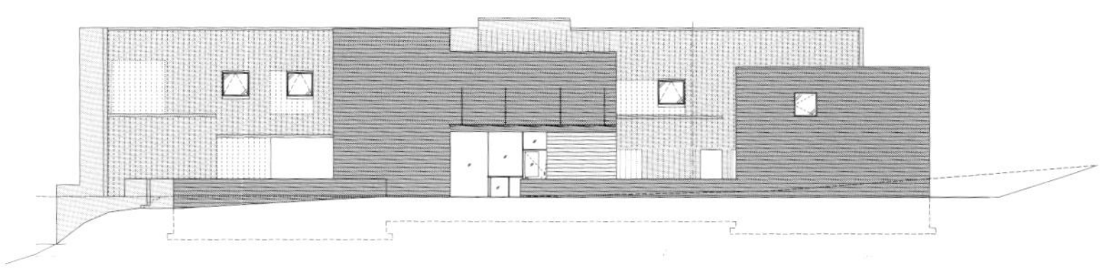

North elevation

Model: view toward entrance from north　模型：北より玄関を見る

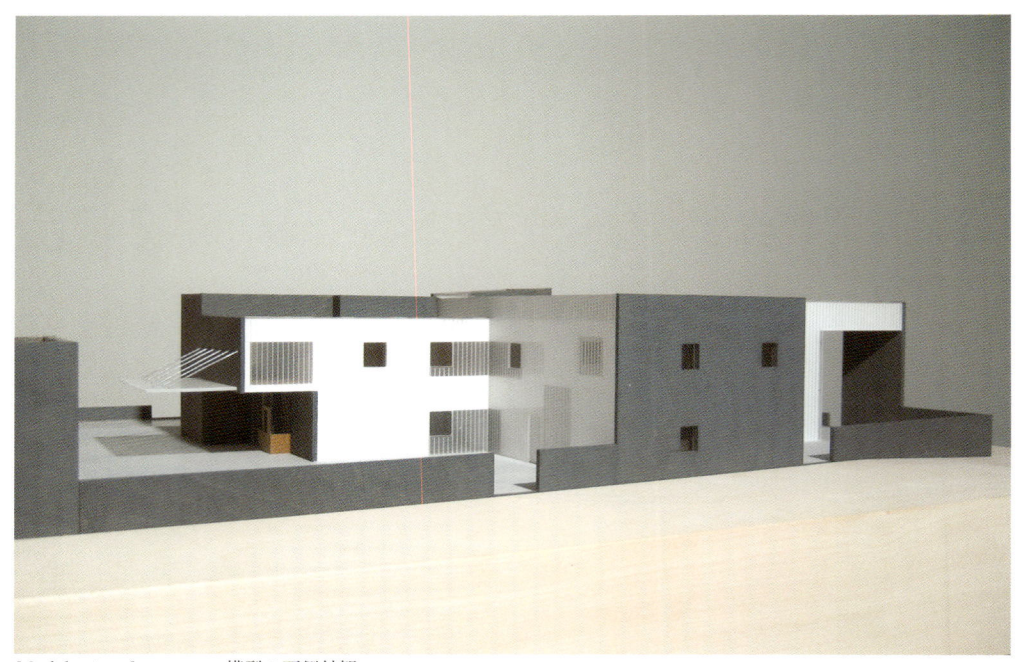

Model: view from west　模型：西側外観

South view　南側外観

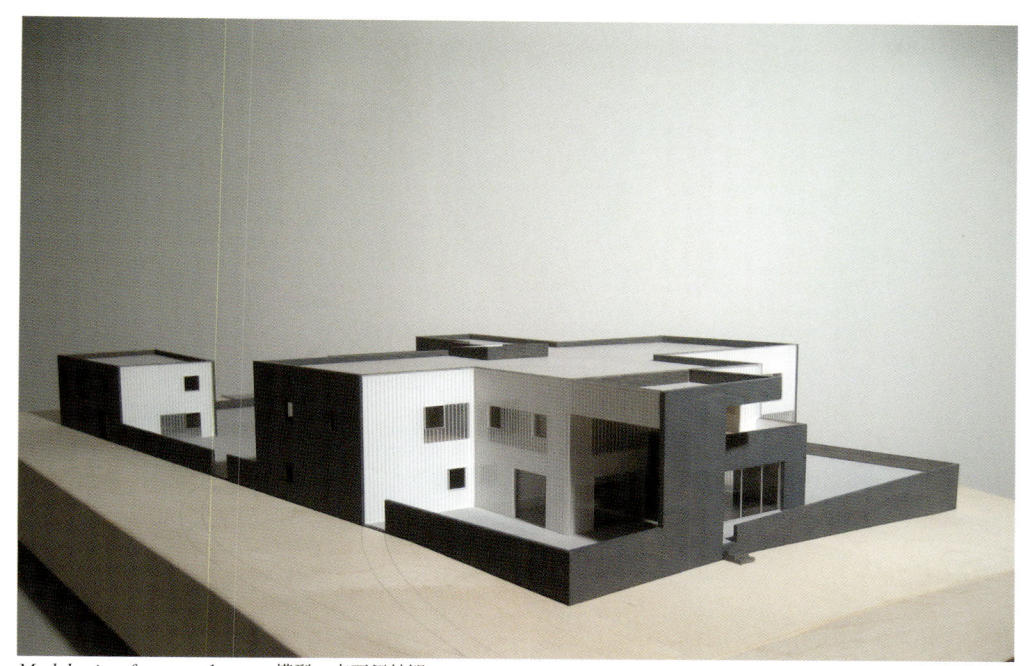

Model: view from southwest 模型：南西側外観

Model: entrance hall 模型：エントランス・ホール

Model: entrance hall 模型：エントランス・ホール

Model: entrance 模型：玄関

Model: entrance hall 模型：エントランス・ホール

Model: staircase 模型：階段

Reception area レセプション・エリア

Model: landing 模型：踊り場

Entrance hall エントランス・ホール

Reception area レセプション・エリア

Architects: Steven Holl Architects, Ruessli Architekten AG—
Steven Holl Architects:
Steven Holl, principal-in-charge; Stephen O'Dell, Tim Bade, associates-in-charge; Olaf Schmidt, project architect; Arnault Biou, Peter Englaender, Annette Goderbauer, Li Hu, Irene Vogt, project team
Ruessli Architekten AG:
Justin Ruessli, principal-in-charge; Mimi Kueh, project architect; Andreas Gervasi, Phillip Röösli, Rafael Schnyder, Urs Zuercher, project team
Client: Swiss Federal Office for Building and Logistics
Consultants: A. F. Steffen Engineers, Robert Silman Associates, P.C., structural; B + B Energietechnik AG, B2E Consulting Engineers, mechanical; ZedNetwork Hannes Wettstein, interior; Robert Gissinger, landscape
Program: living spaces of the ambassador, representational spaces, staff quarters
Structural system: concrete
Major materials: board form black concrete, translucent channel glass
Site area: 250,000 sq.ft.
Total floor area: 25,000 sq.ft.
Cost: approx. $10,000,000

NEW TOWN: GREEN URBAN LABORATORY

Liusha Peninsula, Nanning, China
Design: 2002

Site
Liusha Peninsula in Nanning was once a beautiful rolling ridge of green which was likened to the tail of a dragon whose head lay in Qingxiu Mountain Park. The green dragon was sliced by an aborted development in the early 1990s leaving a muddy flat plateau in its midst.

Program
For this new town of approximately 27,000 residence, 9,000 units of housing (of 120 square meters per unit on average) are planned. The town will also include schools, shops, hotel and recreational facilities, as well as a Beiqiu anthropology museum and the rebuilt Tianning Buddhist Temple.

Concept
The overall shape of the town results from an organic link between idea and form. A figure-8 plan takes its form from the shape of the peninsula together with the preservation of two large existing green hills. The linear city loops back over itself like nature's cycles.

Two new central parks are contained by the linear looped form. One offers recreational and athletic activities; the other has cultural elements such as modern Chinese gardens, meditation pavilions, cafes, and school playgrounds.

A new light rail line is proposed to connect to the heart of Nanning with three stops within the new town and continuing to Qingxiu Mountain Park, the great feature of the peninsula. Together the old and new form an expanded tourist destination.

Low scale (grass roofs)
The main housing aims for a maximum porosity with natural ventilation and shading.

Precast concrete sections with 50% wall and 50% window are basic structural elements forming porous architecture. Deep set operable windows allow for natural sun shading. Green roofs are hydroponic vegetable gardens accessible to the residents.

Within a strictly defined building envelope, the aim of individuation in housing is achieved through overlapping spatial configurations.

High Scale (mountains)
Hybrid buildings of multiple stories (with a defined cubic envelope of 60 m x 60 m x 60 m) yield rich urban experiences with multiple functions and views over the garden city. The master plan allows for the eventual construction of 7 mountain buildings, which could be constructed in phases.

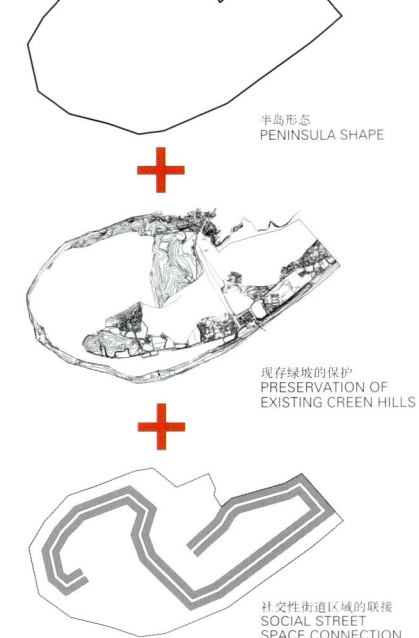

Following the proposed mountains are described in order of construction:
1. Folded street mountain
- Shops connected by a stepped ramp
- 100 room hotel
- Public observation roof with café (Tourist destination: Green Town scientific exhibition ongoing)

2. Cultural mountain
- Schools
- Bieqiu anthropology museum
- Monastic cells & Tianning Temple at top
3. Rock mountain
- Clad in local rough cut stone
- Train station
- Bike and auto garage
- Offices
- Community meeting room
- Rooftop observation deck
4. Knowledge mountain
- Schools/classrooms
- Auditoriums
- Faculty offices
- Offices/workspaces
- Rooftop library and reading rooms
5. Implosion mountain
- Media Center
- Cinemas
- Digital health club
- Parking
6. Subtraction mountain
- Train station
- Schools at ground level adjoining playground
- Offices, work and studio space
7. Gate mountain
- Schools at ground level
- Workshop/shops
- Luxury apartments
- Hotel

Green Laboratory
The new city is to be a model of the underlying principles that govern natural cycles on earth; and in the universe. The most advanced ecological/architectural systems and techniques will be explored, creating an added attraction to eco-tourists (with economic consequences).

Some aspects include:

a. Solar power by arrays of Gallium arsenide cells; 30% more efficient than current silicon cells.

b. Natural ventilation through natural passive solar shading walls boosted by solar powered fans.

c. Geothermal cooling from river

d. Recycled water system using the latest treatment technologies

e. Ecosystem standards of non-polluting transportation; light rail connection, electrical hybrid cars, bike and pedestrian paths

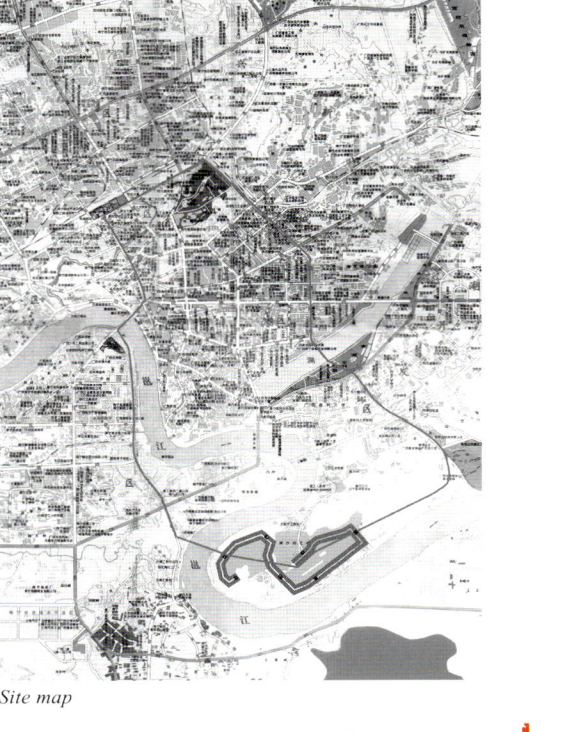

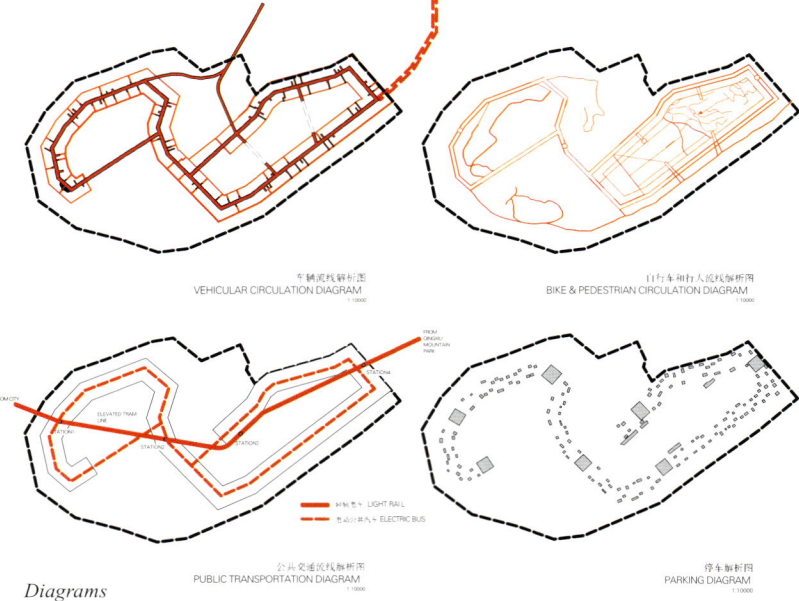

GA PROJECT

1 FOLDED STREET MOUNTAIN
2 CULTURAL MOUNTAIN
3 ROCK MOUNTAIN
4 KNOWLEDGE MOUNTAIN
5 IMPLOSION MOUNTAIN
6 SUBTRACTION MOUNTAIN
7 GATE MOUNTAIN
8 LIGHT RAIL TRAIN
9 NEW CHINESE GARDEN
10 CAFE PAVILION
11 SCHOOL PLAYGROUND
12 ATHLETIC COMPLEX
13 GYMNASIUM & POOLS
14 TENNIS COURTS
15 BASKET BALL COURTS
16 ROWING & LAP POOLS
17 ORGANIC GOLF COURSE

Site plan

〈敷地〉
南寧市の,川に突き出た柳沙半島は,かつては緑に包まれた起伏する美しい尾根を構成し,さながら,頭を青秀山公園に横たえる竜の尾のように見えた。緑の竜は,1990年代初頭の,中断されてしまった開発で切り刻まれ,その真ん中に泥土の平らな台地を残したままになっている。

〈プログラム〉
このニュータウンには,約27,000戸の低層住宅,9,000戸から成るハウジング(平均面積は120m²)が計画されている。この町には,学校,店舗,ホテル,レクリエーション施設,貝丘人類学博物館,再建された天寧寺も含まれることになるだろう。

〈コンセプト〉
町全体の形は,アイディアと形態の有機的な連携から生まれている。8の字型のプランは,半島の形と,緑に包まれた大きな2つの丘を保存することから考えられた。線形の都市は,自然の循環のように輪を描いて自らの上に戻ってくる。

輪を描くリニアーな形態によって,新しい中央公園が2つ,そのなかに納められる。一方はレクリエーションや運動の場を提供し,他方は,現代的な中国庭園,瞑想のパビリオン,カフェ,学校の運動場などの文化的な場を備える。

南寧の中心と結び,ニュータウン内で3つの駅に停まり,半島の大きな特徴である青秀山公園へ続く新しい軽鉄道が提案されている。新しいものと古いものが一つになって,大きな広がりを持つ,ツーリストの目的地を形成する。

〈低いスケール(草屋根)〉
メインのハウジングは,自然通気が可能で日除けのついた,最大限多孔性の建物を目指す。

50%が壁,50%が窓となったプレキャスト・コンクリートの部材が,多孔性建築を構成する基本的な構造要素である。深く後退させて設置した開け閉めできる窓が,自然の日差しを遮る。緑の屋根は,住民が入れる水耕法による菜園である。

厳格に既定された建物外壁のなかで,ハウジング内の独立性は,重なり合う空間配置によって達成される。

〈高いスケール(山)〉
多層階で構成されたハイブリッド・ビル(60×60×60メートルの明瞭な輪郭を持つキュービックな外壁に包まれている)は多様な機能とガーデン・シティーを見晴らす眺めによって,豊かな都市体験をもたらす。マスター・プランは,最終的には段階的に7棟のマウンテン・ビルの建設を予定する。

以下に提案しているマウンテン・ビルを建設の順に説明する。

1.折り畳まれたストリート・マウンテン
——階段を刻んだランプによってつながれた店舗
——100室のホテル
——カフェのあるパブリックな屋上展望台(ツーリストの目的地:グリーン・タウンの科学展覧会が進行中)

2.文化の山
——学校
——貝丘人類学博物館
——頂上に,僧坊と天寧寺

3.岩の山
——地元産の切石で被覆
——鉄道駅
——バイクと車のガレージ
——オフィス
——コミュニティの集会室
——屋上の展望デッキ

4.知識の山
——学校/教室
——オーディトリアム
——教職員室
——オフィス/ワークスペース
——屋上図書室と閲覧室

5.内部破裂する山
——メディア・センター
——シネマ
——デジタル・ヘルスクラブ
——パーキング

6.減法の山
——鉄道駅
——運動場に隣接して1階に学校
——オフィス,ワーク/スタジオ・スペース

7.門の山
——1階に学校
——ワークショップ/店舗
——高級アパート
——ホテル

〈グリーン・ラボラトリー〉
新しい街は,地球と宇宙の自然の循環を支配する法則を強調するモデルとなるだろう。最新のエコロジカルな建築システムと技術を探求し,エコ=ツーリスト(経済的帰結と共に)に対するさらなる魅力をつくりだす。

〈含まれるいくつかの局面〉
a.ガリウムヒ素電池の配列による太陽光発電。現在のシリコン電池より30%効率がよい
b.自然のパッシブソーラーの日除け壁を通した自然換気。太陽光発電によるファンによって効果を高める
c.川からの地熱冷房
d.最新の処理技術を使用した水の再利用システム
e.汚染のない交通によるエコシステム規格:軽鉄道による接続,ハイブリッドな電気自動車,自転車と歩行者道路

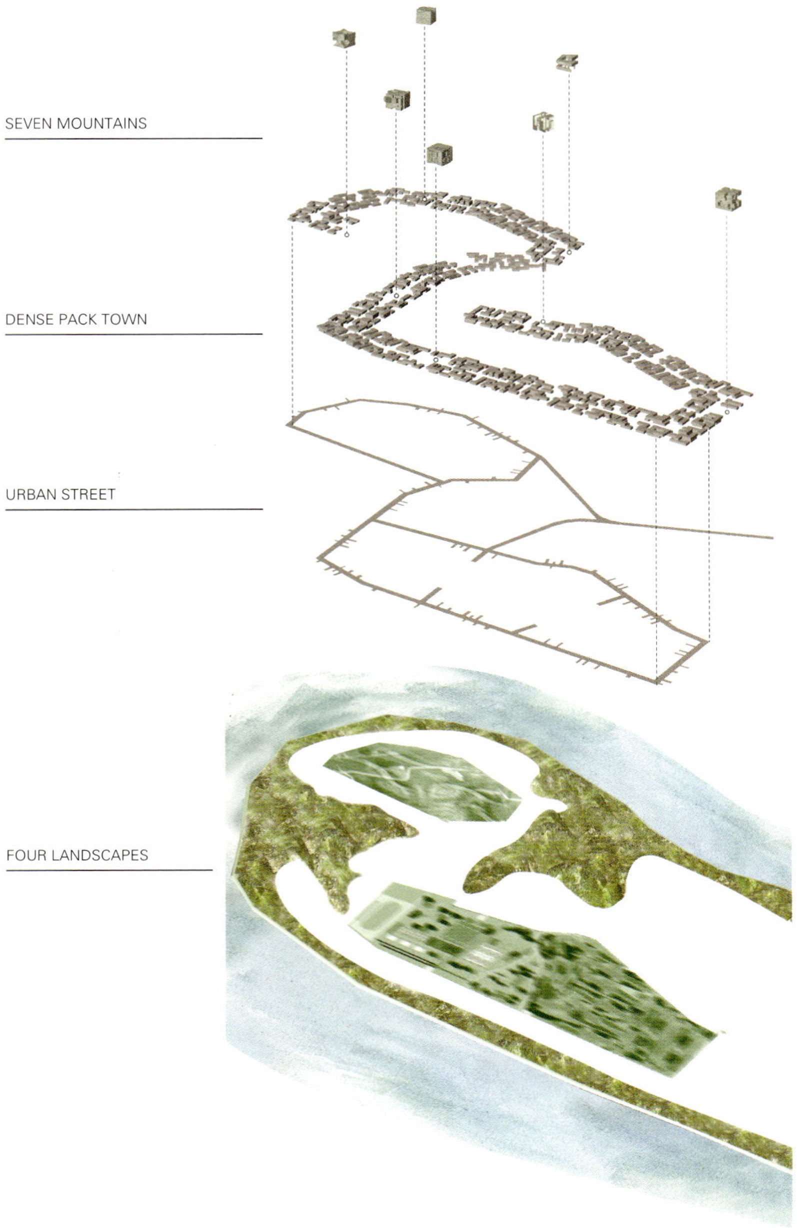

GA DOCUMENT

SEVEN MOUNTAINS

DENSE PACK TOWN

URBAN STREET

FOUR LANDSCAPES

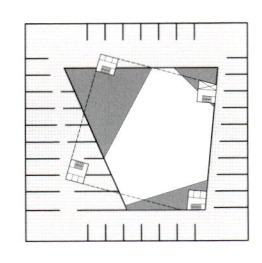

Architects: Steven Holl Architects—Steven Holl, principal-in-charge; Makram El Kadi, Anderson Lee, project architect; Li Hu, project manager; Ziad Jamaleddine, project team
Client: Guangxi Runhe Estate Development Co. Ltd.
Program: 9,000 residences, schools, shops, anthropology museum
Structural system: "Perf Con" system
Major materials: pre cast concrete
Site area: 1,865,000 m² (Liusha peninsula)
Built area: 480,000 m² (1 floor)
Total floor area: 1,350,000 m²

1. 交叠街道之山
各种商店沿缓步台阶螺旋而上，最后到达具有100个房间的宾馆，以及设有咖啡茶室的观景平台。持续的绿色城市科技展览成为旅游景点。

FOLDED STREET MOUNTAIN
- THE STEPPED RAMP SECTION SPIRALS UP WITH SHOPS OF ALL KINDS ARRIVING AT A 100 ROOM HOTEL AND OBSERVATION ROOF WITH CAF .
(TOURIST DESTINATION: GREEN TOWN SCIENTIFIC EXHIBITION ONGOING)

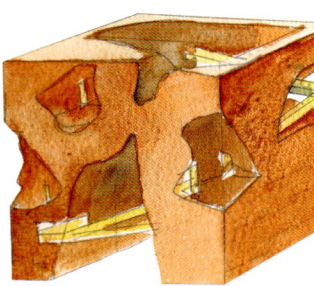

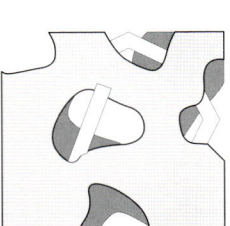

2. 文化之山
- 学校
- 贝丘人类学博物馆
- 顶部为禅房和天宁寺

CULTURAL MOUNTAIN
- SCHOOLS
- BEIQIU ANTHROPOLOGY MUSEUM
- MONASTIC CELLS & TIANNING TEMPLE AT TOP

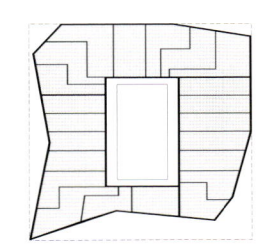

3. 岩石之山
(用当地毛坯岩石作墙面)
- 轻轨电车站、自行车停放处和停车房
- 办公室
- 社区会议室
- 楼顶观景台

ROCK MOUNTAIN
(LOCAL ROUGH CUT STONE FACED)
- RAIL STATION AND BIKE AND AUTO GARAGE
- OFFICES (TOWN OFFICIALS OFFICE)
- COMMUNITY MEETING ROOM
- ROOFTOP OBSERVATION DECK

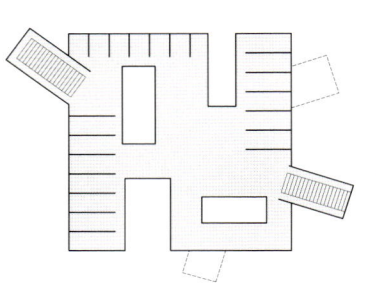

4. 知识之山
- 学校／教室
- 大礼堂
- 教师办公室
- 其它办公和工作空间

KNOWLEDGE MOUNTAIN
- SCHOOLS / CLASSROOMS
- AUDITORIUMS
- FACULTY OFFICES
- OTHER OFFICES / WORKSPACES

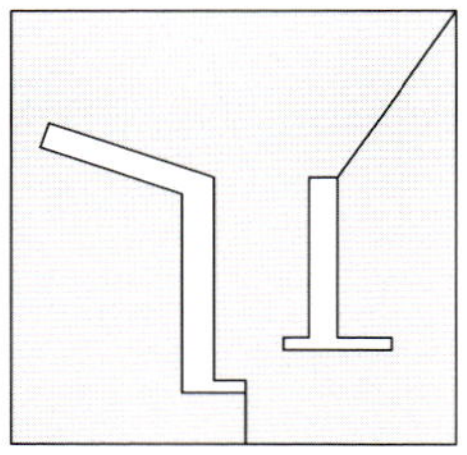

5. 内聚之山
- 媒体中心
- 影剧院
- 数码化健身房
- 地下停车房

IMPLOSION MOUNTAIN
- MEDIA CENTER
- CINEMAS
- DIGITAL HEALTH CLUB
- PARKING BELOW

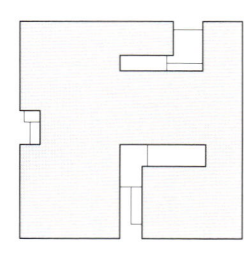

6. 减法之山
- 轻轨电车站
- 办公室、工作室和艺术创作室
- 低层为与室外活动场所邻接的学校

SUBTRACTION MOUNTAIN
- TRAIN STATION
- OFFICES, WORK AND STUDIO SPACE
- SCHOOLS AT BASE NEXT TO PLAYGROUND

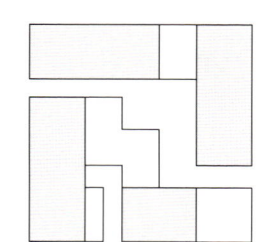

7. 城门之山
- 豪华公寓
- 宾馆
- 作坊／商店
- 低层为学校

GATE MOUNTAIN
- LUXURY APARTMENTS
- HOTEL
- WORKSHOP / SHOPS
- SCHOOLS AT BASE

GA PROJECT

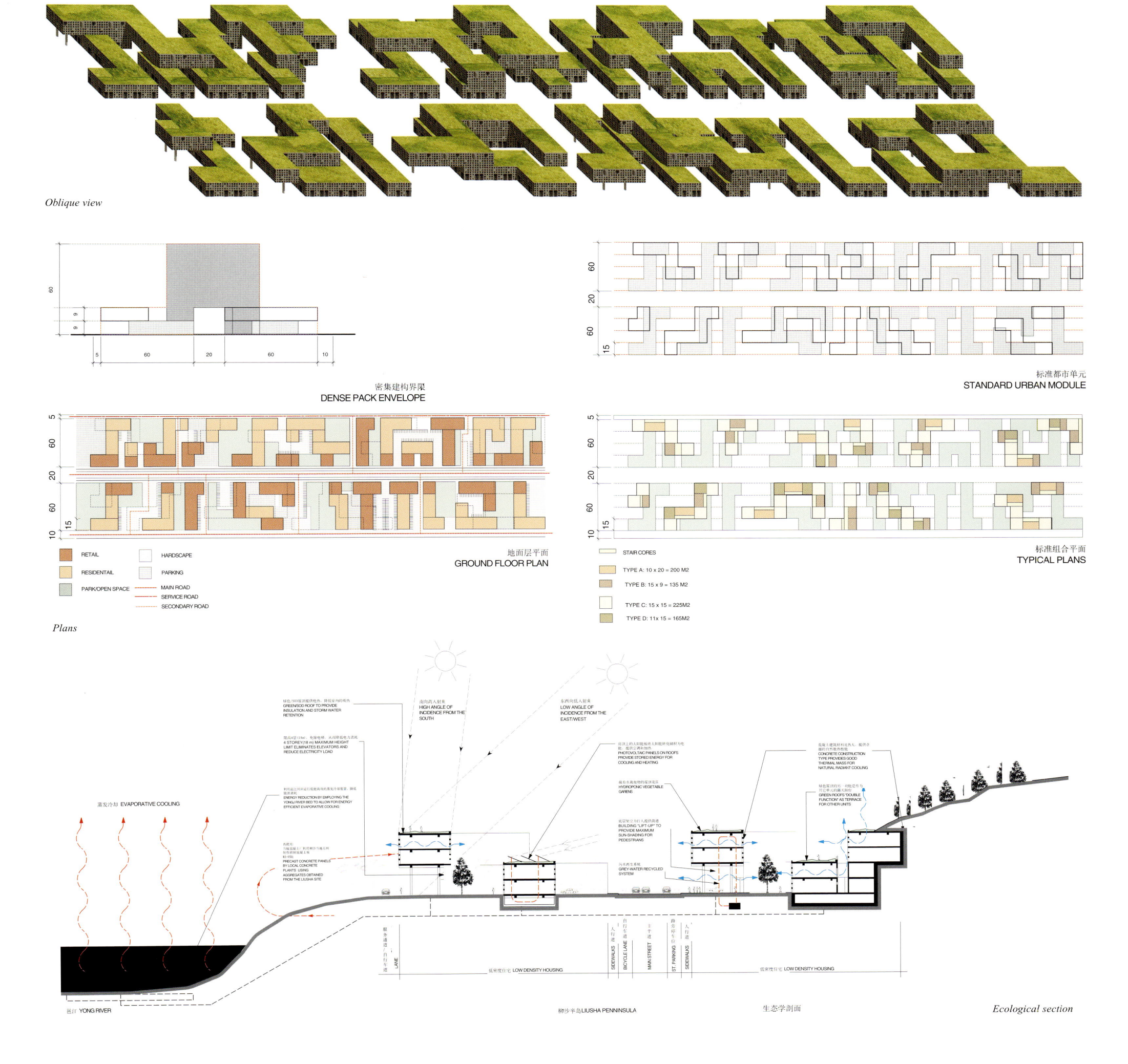

Oblique view

密集建构界限
DENSE PACK ENVELOPE

标准都市单元
STANDARD URBAN MODULE

地面层平面
GROUND FLOOR PLAN

- RETAIL
- RESIDENTAIL
- PARK/OPEN SPACE
- HARDSCAPE
- PARKING
- MAIN ROAD
- SERVICE ROAD
- SECONDARY ROAD

标准组合平面
TYPICAL PLANS

- STAIR CORES
- TYPE A: 10 x 20 = 200 M2
- TYPE B: 15 x 9 = 135 M2
- TYPE C: 15 x 15 = 225 M2
- TYPE D: 11 x 15 = 165 M2

Plans

Ecological section

- 蒸发冷却 EVAPORATIVE COOLING
- 绿化/900屋顶提供绝热、降低室内的吸热 GREEN/SOD ROOF TO PROVIDE INSULATION AND STORM WATER RETENTION
- 南向高角入射 HIGH ANGLE OF INCIDENCE FROM THE SOUTH
- 东西向低入射 LOW HIGH ANGLE OF INCIDENCE FROM THE EAST/WEST
- 最高4层(18 m)，免装电梯，从而降低电力消耗 4 STOREY (18 m) MAXIMUM HEIGHT LIMIT ELIMINATES ELEVATORS AND REDUCE ELECTRICITY LOAD
- 利用邕江河床进行低能耗的蒸发冷却措施，降低能量消耗 ENERGY REDUCTION BY EMPLOYING THE YONG RIVER BED TO ALLOW FOR ENERGY EFFICIENT EVAPORATIVE COOLING
- 屋顶上的太阳能板将太阳能转化储存为电能，提供升降和加热 PHOTOVOLTAIC PANELS ON ROOFS PROVIDE STORED ENERGY FOR COOLING AND HEATING
- 混凝土建筑材料优热入，提供非常好的自然热质量 CONCRETE CONSTRUCTION TYPE PROVIDES GOOD THERMAL MASS FOR NATURAL RADIANT COOLING
- 预制混凝土板 PRECAST CONCRETE PANELS BY LOCAL CONCRETE PLANTS USING AGGREGATES OBTAINED FROM THE LIUSHA SITE
- 无水水栽培植物的家庭花乐 HYDROPONIC VEGETABLE GARDENS
- 底层架空引入空气通道 BUILDING "LIFT-UP" TO PROVIDE MAXIMUM SUN-SHADING FOR PEDESTRIANS
- 污水再生系统 GREY-WATER RECYCLED SYSTEM
- 绿色屋顶的片、功能还是作为其它单元的露天阳台 GREEN ROOFS DOUBLE FUNCTION AS TERRACE FOR OTHER UNITS
- 邕江 YONG RIVER
- 柳沙半岛 LIUSHA PENNINSULA
- 低密度住宅 LOW DENSITY HOUSING
- SIDEWALKS
- BICYCLE LANE
- MAIN STREET
- ST. PARKING
- SIDEWALKS
- 低密度住宅 LOW DENSITY HOUSING

生态学剖面 *Ecological section*

Overall view 全景

G·A PROJECT

Precast concrete sections with 50% wall and 50% window are basic structural elements. This is "PerfCon" system used in Simmons Hall, MIT

50%が壁、50%が窓になったプレキャスト・コンクリートが、基本的な構造部材となっている。これはMITのシモンズ・ホールで使われた"パーフ・コン"システムである

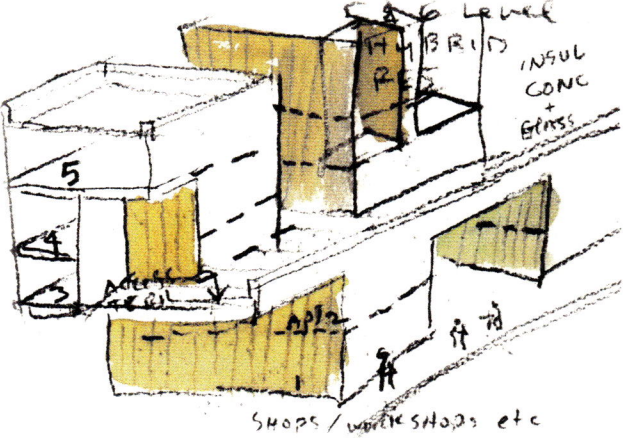

Concept sketches: Dense park town

GA DOCUMENT

Street 街路

View toward folded street 折り畳まれたストリートを見る

Interior: river view 内部：川の眺め

Elevation 立面

Athletic park 運動場

PROJECTS FOR WTC SITE

New York, New York, U.S.A.
Design: 2002

Floating Memorial/Folded Street

Steven Holl Architects' first proposal in response to the World Trade Center tragedy was exhibited at Max Protech Gallery in New York City in January 2002.

As the World Trade Center tragedy took many souls without leaving bodies to bury (no ground) this monumental space "floats" with the river water moving below. Strips of sunlight animate the floors and walls from light slots which allow oblique views of the Hudson River. In a memorial hall each person lost has a photographic portrait below a candle.

The memorial ramps up to a new bridge over west street, connected to a "folded Street" which ascends over the site. Along the ascending "street" are a number of functions: galleries, cinema spaces, cafes, restaurants, a hotel, classrooms for a branch of New York University. Sheathed in translucent glass the truss construction allows for grand public observation decks.

A new street level plan allows N-S and E-W streets to go through the site while accommodating auditorium halls with 9,000 and 6,000 capacity.

Footprints of the original towers are formed into 212′ x 212′ reflective ponds, with thousands of glass lenses allowing light to spaces below.

折り返しながら浮上する追悼の道
世界貿易センターの悲劇に対するスティーヴン・ホール・アーキテクツの最初の提案は，2002年1月，ニューヨークのマックス・プロテッチ・ギャラリーで展示された。

世界貿易センターの悲劇は，埋葬する（地面がない）身体を残さずに多くの魂を奪い去った。それゆえにこの記念碑的なスペースは下を流れる川の水から離れて"浮上"する。陽光の細い帯が，ハドソン川の眺めを斜めに切り取る細長い開口から射し込み，各フロアの床や壁を生き生きとさせる。メモリアル・ホールのなか，失われた一人一人の肖像写真が蝋燭の下に置かれる。

メモリアル・ランプが西側の道を架け渡す新しいブリッジへ上って行き，敷地の上高く上昇していく"折り返す道"につながる。上昇する"道"に沿って，ギャラリー，シネマ，カフェ，レストラン，ホテル，ニューヨーク大学分校の教室など多くの機能空間が並ぶ。半透明ガラスに包まれたトラス架構は，一般公開される広い展望デッキをつくりだす。

街路レベルの新しいプランによって，敷地内を南北，東西に通り抜ける道が生まれ，9,000から6,000人を収容できるオーディトリアム・ホールの設置も可能となる。

崩壊したタワーの跡地は，212フィート×212フィートの反射する池をかたちづくり，そこに嵌め込まれた数千枚のガラスレンズから下の空間に光が透過する。

Distant view 遠景

Mixed use building 複合施設

Site plan

Roof 屋上

"Street" "道"

Architects: Steven Holl Architects—Steven Holl, principal-in-charge; Makram el Kadi (phase 1 and phase 2), Ziad Jameleddine (phase 1), project architects
Program: galleries, cinemas, restaruants, hotel, NYU facilities, auditorium, offices

Confluence Center of World Religions

The New York Times Magazine sponsored a study, inviting leading architects to create ideas capable of bringing people together in the wake of the tragedy. Steven Holl Architects' was among six teams subsequently chosen from this group by the Lower Manhattan Development Corporation to develop further proposals in a new competition.

The Orpheum has three auditoriums: 900 seats, 600 seats and 500 seats. These are different circular shapes like the two large circular ascending public ramp spaces. Together the five different circles occupy a "formless" envelope, a scatter of thick walls covered with a paper thin fabric. The lighting is within the thick walls and glows brightly when turned up or becomes mysteriously dim. To close the different spaces, sliding glass walls are concealed in the fabric walls.

The floors of marble have a scatter of poems carved into them from poets, alive and dead, chosen for this special place.

The Confluence Center of World Religions
A public educational facility which turns in an ascending spiral up to public observation terraces and roof gardens, the Confluence Center has several 'main entrances' around the perimeter of the block. These begin in exhibitions of the history of a religion, which begot an architectural type. The Christian entry with churches and chapels, the Jewish with synagogues, the Buddhist with zendos and monasteries, the Islamic with mosques. For example, a large exhibition of the work of the great architect Sinan who built Turkey's wonderful mosques might be accompanied with large scale models.

The center contains libraries for each section which can be digitally accessed and simultaneously translated into one hundred different languages. Gradually the building ascends to a large meeting hall sculpted in washes of natural light, it opens out to public roof gardens and observation terraces.

世界の宗教が合流するセンター

ニューヨークタイムズ誌は，悲劇の跡に，人々の心を一つにまとめることのできるアイディアを創造するためのスタディを後援し，指導的建築家を招待した。スティーヴン・ホール・アーキテクツは，ロワー・マンハッタン開発公社によって，さらに提案を深めるためにあらためて行われたコンペのために，引き続いて選ばれた6つのチームの一つになった。

オルフェウムには，900席，600席，500席の3つのオーディトリアムがある。これらは，パブリックなランプ・スペースを上っていく2つの大きな円形のように見える，それぞれに径の違う円形で構成されている。5つの異なった円形はまとまって，"はっきりとした形をもたない"，紙のように薄いファブリックで覆われた厚い壁がまき散らされたエンベロップを占有する。照明は厚い壁のなかに取り付けられ，スイッチを入れると明るく輝き，あるいは神秘的なほの暗さになる。異なったスペースを閉ざすために，ガラスのスライディング・ウォールが布地の壁のなかに隠されている。

大理石の床には，この特別な場所のために故人を問わず選ばれた詩人の詩が，刻み込まれ，散りばめられる。

〈世界の宗教が合流するセンター〉
展望テラスや屋上庭園に登っていく螺旋へ転じていく，公共の教育施設であるこの"合流するセンター"には，ブロックの周縁部に幾つもの"メイン・エントランス"がある。これらは，建築の型を生み出した，宗教の歴史の展示で始まる。教会と礼拝堂の付いたキリスト教徒のエントランス，シナゴーグのあるユダヤ教徒のエントランス，禅堂と僧坊のある仏教徒のエントランス，モスクのあるイスラム教徒のエントランス。たとえば，トルコの素晴らしいモスクを建てた偉大な建築家シナンの作品の大規模な展示には大スケールの模型が添えられるだろう。

センターには各部門別に図書室があり，デジタルにアクセスして，100の言語に同時翻訳ができる。建物は徐々に広いミーティング・ホールへ登って行く。そこは自然光の奔流のなかに刻まれ，パブリックな屋上庭園と展望テラスに続く。

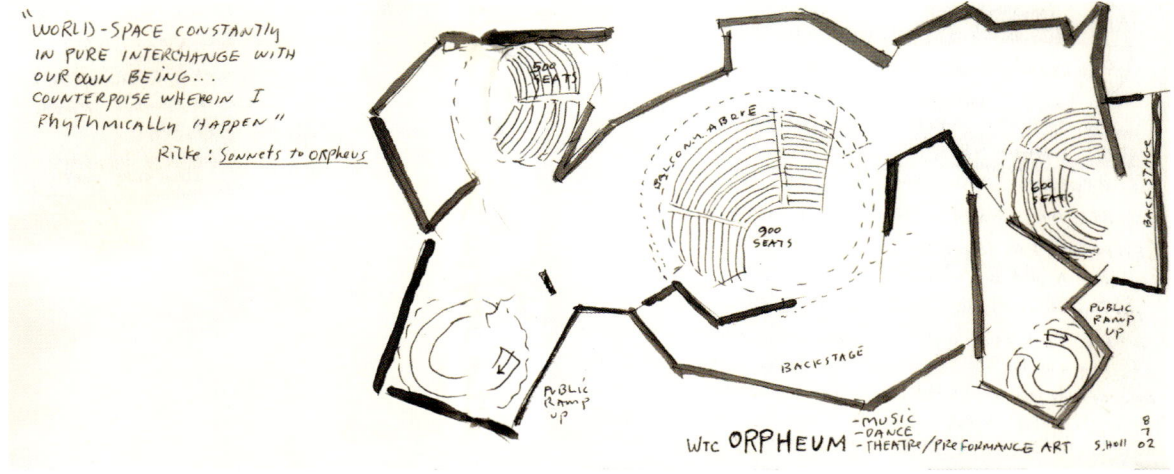

Plan

Interior 内部

Interior: skylight　内部：スカイライト

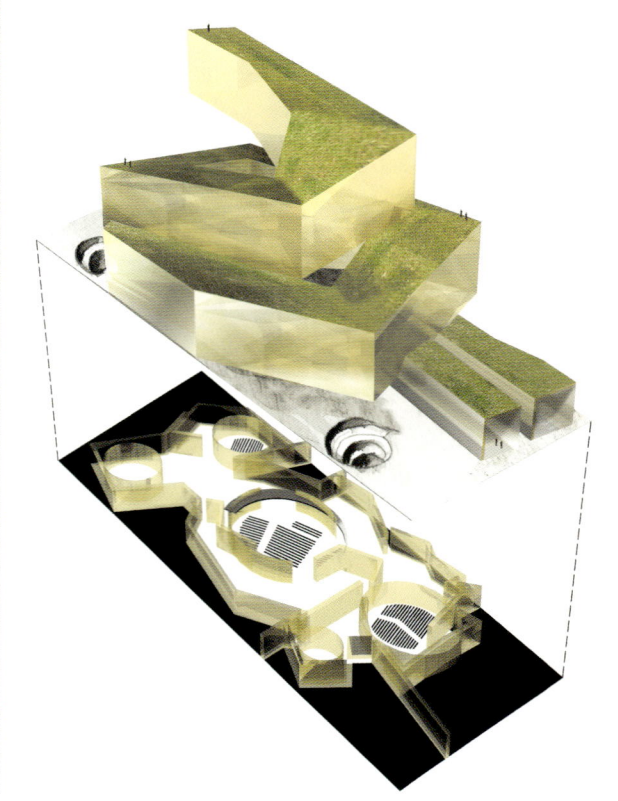

Memorial Square

Richard Meier & Partners Architects:
Richard Meier, Lisetta Koe, Alfonso D'Onofrio,
Robert Lewis, Michael Gruber, Milton Lam,
Michal Taranto, Elizabeth Lee, Esther Kim,
Tetsuhito Abe
Eisenman Architects:
Peter Eisenman, Cynthia Davidson,
Pablo Lorenzo-Eiroa, Marta Caldeira, Selim Vural,
Milisani Mniki, Larissa Babij
Gwathmey Siegel & Associates:
Charles Gwathmey, Robert Siegel, Gerald Gendreau,
Scott Skipworth, Brian Arnold, Shannon Walsh,
Laurel Kolsby, Yongseok John, Tim Butler,
Clarisse Labro, Barry Yanku
Steven Holl Architects:
Steven Holl, Makram el Kadi, Simone Giostra,
Christian Wassmann, Irene Vogt

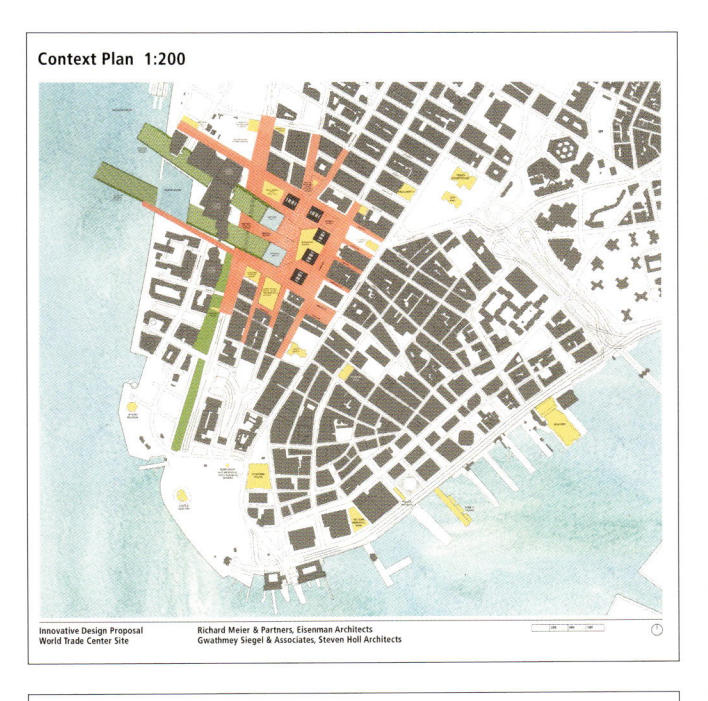

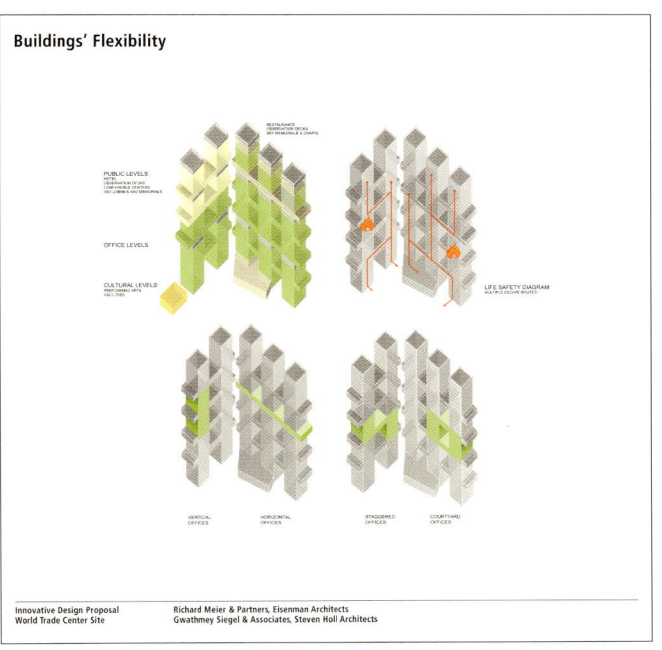

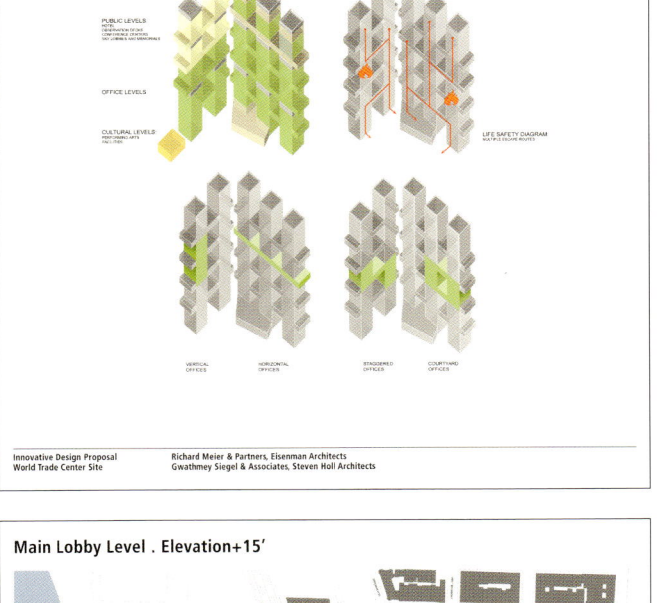

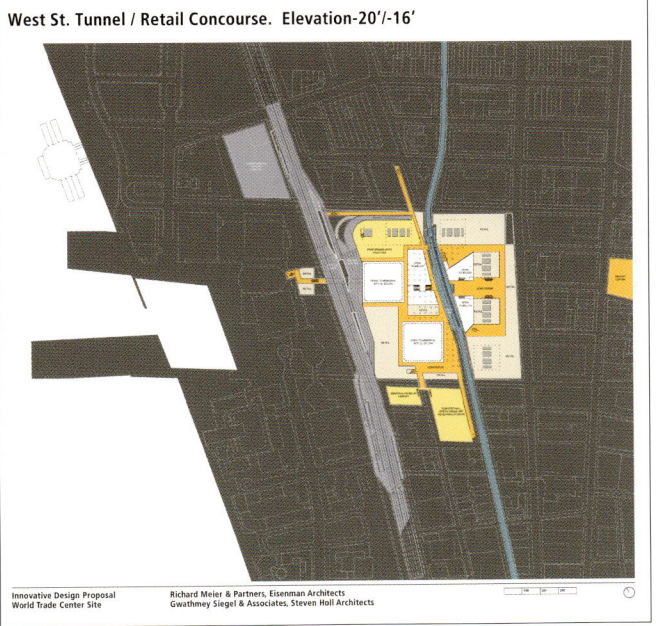

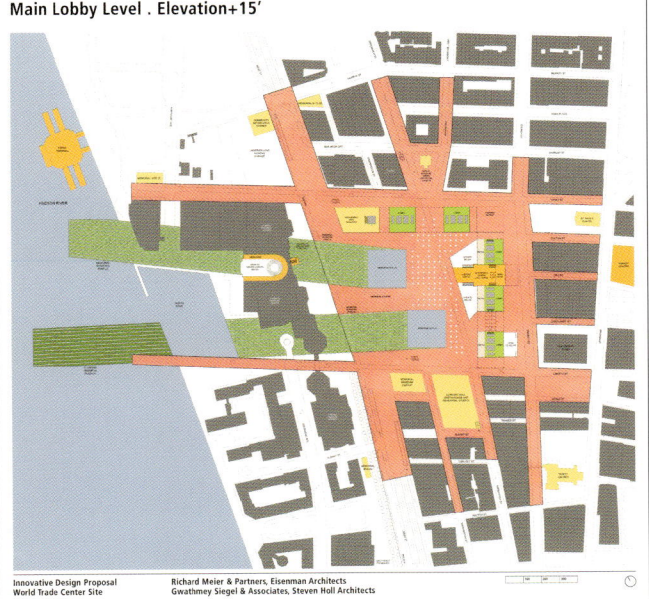

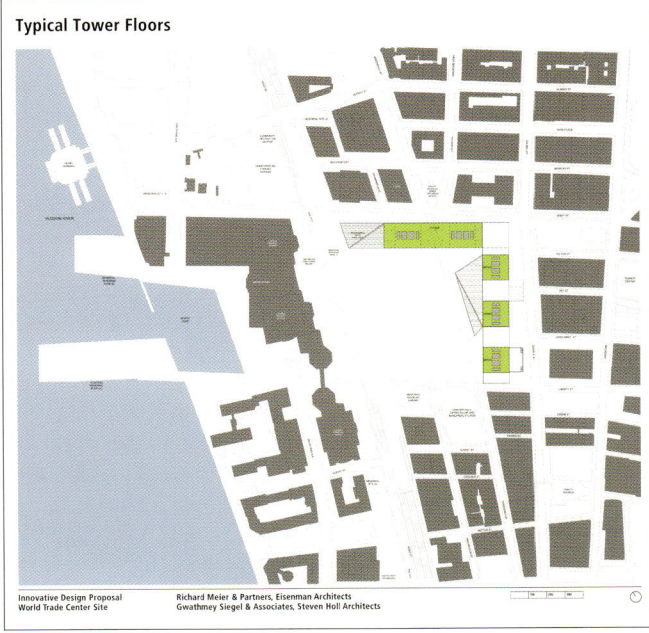

Level -20'/-16'   *Level +15'*   *Typical floor plan*

In the tradition of Rockefeller Center and Union Square, we propose to build a great public space for New York City at the World Trade Center site. We call this place Memorial Square. While the 19th and 20th century precedents for urban plazas are contained spaces, our 21st century Memorial Square is both contained and extended, symbolizing its connections to the community, the city, and the world.

The ideas of presence and absence, containment and extension, are conveyed across every element of our proposal for the design of the World Trade Center Site. We do not attempt to contain or divide the site, but rather extend it into the surrounding streets through a plan which contains series of "fingers," reminders that the magnitude of what happened here was felt far beyond the immediate site. At the same time, the fingers facilitate pedestrian connections between Memorial Square, the Hudson River, the proposed NYCT Transit Center, and greater Lower Manhattan.

The granite-paved fingers help to orient pedestrians as well as enable them to enter the site above and below grade. Pedestrians walking south on the Greenwich Street finger can continue through a ceremonial gateway into Memorial Square and enter the Intermodal Center or, alternatively, take a stairway down to the retail concourse under the square, which also leads to the PATH Station and 1/9 subway trains. Following the concourse, pedestrians return to grade via a stairway on the Greenwich Street finger south of Liberty Street, and adjacent to the new Concert Hall and Opera House.

Memorial Square will renew the spirit and the quality of life in Lower Manhattan. But the most visible sign of renewal for the city and the world will be the proposed hybrid buildings, which rise 1,111 feet to restore the Manhattan skyline with geometric clarity in glowing white glass. For all the activity that the buildings will sustain, from a hotel and conference center to offices, cultural spaces, and a memorial chapel, the image they project is one of dignity and calm. As the iconic pieces of Memorial Square, they will draw visitors from around the world, who will travel to the memorial observation terrace to once again view New York City from the top of Lower Manhattan.

Comprised of five vertical sections and interconnecting horizontal floor elements, the two buildings represent a new typology in skyscraper design. At ground level, these forms become ceremonial gateways into the site. In their quiet abstraction solids and voids, the buildings appear as screens, suggesting both presence and absence, and encouraging reflection and imagination. Their cantilevered ends extend outward, like the fingers of the ground plan, reaching toward the city and each other. Nearly touching at the northeast corner of the site, they resemble the interlaced fingers of protective hands.

As in all of the great public urban places of the world, Memorial Square is a space for pedestrians. Our proposal contains buildings on 27 percent of the site, with over 12 acres designated as open space for commuters, visitors, and residents alike. With the convenience of multiple mass transit lines on site, as well as new concerns about security, we propose to limit public automobile access to the curbsides of Church, Vesey, and Liberty streets, with off-site parking in a new underground garage at the northwest corner of Vesey and West streets. Buses and private cars can enter the site from the proposed West Street Tunnel, stop at an underground security checkpoint, and then take service roads to designated parking levels. Service trucks will use the same checkpoint, and all vehicles exit the below-grade circulation ring back into the West Street Tunnel. The separation of pedestrians and vehicular traffic allows Memorial Square to become both an active public space as well as a place that allows for moments of contemplation and silence.

Memorial Square contains multiple memorial sites. The ceremonial gateways to the east and north open onto a grand space that contains two glass-bottom reflecting pools, which demarcate the footprints of the former World Trade Center towers. Below the pools volumes extend to the main concourse level, where they become memorial rooms lit from above. The pools also overlook two memorial groves of shade trees, planted to mark the final shadows cast by the World Trade Center towers before each fell. The groves extend over the West Street Tunnel to the Winter Garden and then continue west of the World Financial Center. The peaks of the shadows are marked by piers on the Hudson River. The illuminated tip of the south shadow is a floating outdoor plaza that would accommodate 5,000 people for public events.

Memorial Square is a place of many cultural facilities, including a Memorial Museum and Freedom Library. Located at the corner of Liberty and West streets, the memorial engages the proposed Memorial Promenade, which extends from the site to Castle Clinton in Battery Park. A Concert Hall and Opera House with rehearsal studios is proposed for the Liberty Street block east of the museum. Anchoring the northwest corner of Memorial Square are Performing Arts Facilities for film, theater, dance, and music, all under one roof. Together, these programs respect the memorial sites and form an important Lower Manhattan cultural district that will attract visitors from the city and beyond, while providing meaningful nighttime activity in the local community.

The new cultural district of Memorial Square also links the World Financial Center and residents of Battery Park City to the retail shops and transit stations. Previously separated from the World Trade Center site by six lanes of traffic and an elevated plaza, the World Financial Center will now open onto and define the western edge of the square. Visitors to the Winter Garden can descend to the main concourse below Memorial Square and connect to the PATH Station, the Intermodal Center, or further east, to the proposed NYCT Transit Center at Broadway and Dey Street. The concourse is lined with shops, and connects via escalators to a second level of shopping that leads to the great hall of the Intermodal Center. Along with the cultural facilities and parks, these amenities will bring new life to the neighborhoods of Lower Manhattan.

Memorial Square is a sacred precinct where loss is remembered and renewal is celebrated. The spirit and dignity of its design are made in the belief that from a tragic occurrence can come a life-affirming opportunity.

On September 11, 2001, nearly 2,800 people lost their lives in New York City. This loss profoundly affected families, loved ones, the men and women who worked at Ground Zero, the nation, and the world. We do not think it an overstatement to say this was an attack on humanity and the principles of freedom for all. We are among those that experienced the horror of that day first-hand. As New Yorkers, as architects, and as a visionary collaborative group, we are honored to be asked to make a meaningful contribution to rebuilding our city.

追悼の広場

ロックフェラー・センターとユニオン・スクエアの伝統のなかで、私たちは世界貿易センターの跡地に広大な公共空間の建設を提案する。私たちはこの場所を追悼の広場と名付ける。都市広場の、19世紀、20世紀の先例が囲まれた空間であるのに対し、私たちの21世紀の追悼の広場は、囲まれていると同時に延び広がり、コミュニティ、都市、そして世界との結びつきを象徴する。

この案には、存在と不在、抑制と拡張という考えが、ひとつひとつのエレメントを横断しながら伝えられている。敷地を囲んだり、分割したりするのではなく、目前の敷地を越えて遥か先まで伝わるように、ここで起こったことの重大性を思い出させるための暗示である"フィンガー"が周囲へ延びて行く。同時にフィンガーは追悼の広場、ハドソン川、提案されているNYCT交通センター、グレーター・ロワー・マンハッタンの間を歩行者が楽に行き来できるようにするだろう。

花崗岩を敷き詰めたフィンガーは、歩行者の行く先を示すと同時に、敷地の上方や地下にも導く。南のグリニッチ・ストリート・フィンガーを行く歩行者は、"儀礼の門"を抜けて追悼の広場に至り、さらに進んでインターモダル・センター（2種類以上の輸送機関を利用する交通網）に入るか、あるいは、広場の下の小売店の並ぶコンコースへ階段を降りて行ってもよい。コンコースもPATH駅と地下鉄1／9線に続いている。コンコースを進むと階段を上って地上に戻り、リバティー・ストリートの南側、グリニッチ・ストリート・フィンガーに出る。ここは新しいコンサート・ホールとオペラ・ハウスにも近い。

追悼の広場はロワー・マンハッタンの生活の精神と質を一新するだろう。しかし、この都市と世界のための最も目に付く再生のサインは、提案した、輝く白いガラスで幾何学的な明晰性によってマンハッタンのスカイラインを復活させる、1,111フィートのハイブリッド・ビルになるだろう。ホテルやコンファレンス・センターから、オフィス、文化スペース、メモリアル・チャペルに至る、建物に入ることになる機能のすべてにとって、意図するイメージは、尊厳と静けさである。ハイブリッド・ビルは追悼の広場の偶像的存在として、ロワー・マンハッタンの一番高い所から、再びニューヨーク・シティーを眺めるためにメモリアル展望テラスを訪れる人々を、世界中から引き寄せるだろう。

5つの垂直部分と相互に連結された水平の床で構成された2棟の建物は、スカイスクレイパーの新しいデザイン類型を表現する。建物を組み立てているこれらの形は、地上階で敷地へ入る儀礼の門を構成する。ソリッドとヴォイドの静かな抽象のなかで、建物は、存在と不在を共に示唆し、沈黙を誘い、想像力をかりたてるスクリーンとして現れる。キャンティレヴァーで支持された端部は、地上に延びるフィンガーのように、市街やお互い向かって手を差し伸ばしながら外に広がる。敷地の北東コーナーに触れそうになるところで、身を守ろうとして組み合わされた手の指に似たかたちをとる。

世界の都市の優れた公共空間がそうであるように、追悼の広場も歩行者のためのスペースである。私たちの提案は、敷地の27%を建物が占め、12エーカー以上を、通勤者、ビジター、住民など、すべての人のためのオープン・スペースとしている。敷地の大量輸送交通の利便と、新たな安全対策のため、チャーチ、ビジー、リバティー・ストリートの縁石側への公共的な車の進入を限定し、敷地から離れたパーキングとして、ビジーとウェスト・ストリートの北西コーナーに新しい地下ガレージを提案する。バスと自家用車は、提案されているウェスト・ストリート・トンネルから敷地に入れる。車は地下のセキュリティ・チェック・ポイントで停止し、指定されたパーキング階へサービス路を通って進む。サービス・トラックも同じチェック・ポイントを使い、すべての車は地下の環状通路を出てウェスト・ストリート・トンネルに戻る。歩行者と自動車交通の分離によって、追悼の広場は、活気のある公共空間であると同時に、黙考し静かな時をすごせる場所となる。

追悼の広場には多種多様なメモリアル・サイトがある。東と北の儀礼の門を入ると、元の世界貿易センター・タワーの建物の跡をなぞって、底がガラスになった2つのリフレクティング・プールのある広い空間へ出る。プールの下には、メインのコンコース・レベルへ広がるスペースが、上から光が注ぐメモリアル・ルームを構成する。プールからはまた、日影を落とす樹木がつくる2つの小さな記念樹の木立を見渡せる。2群の木立は、世界貿易センターの2本のタワーが崩壊する前に最後の影を落とした位置に植えられる。木立はウェスト・ストリート・トンネルを越えてウィンター・ガーデンへ延び、そこから世界金融センターの西へ続く。影の頂点を、ハドソン川に面した桟橋が標す。照明された、南側の影の先端は、パブリックなイベントで5,000人を収容できる地上に浮かぶ戸外広場である。

追悼の広場は、メモリアル・ミュージアム、フリ

ーダム・ライブラリーをはじめ，様々な文化施設の場所である。リバティーとウェスト・ストリートの角に位置するメモリアル・ミュージアムは，敷地からバッテリー・パークのキャッスル・クリントンまで延びる，提案されているメモリアル・プロムナードと結ばれる。リハーサル・スタジオの付いたコンサート・ホールとオペラ・ハウスはミュージアムの東のリバティー・ストリート・ブロックに提案されている。追悼の広場の北西コーナーに，映画，演劇，ダンス，音楽のためのパフォーミング・アーツ施設が一つ屋根の下にまとめられる。これらの施設は共に追悼の広場に敬意を表し，市内や遠方からの客を惹き付ける一方で地元のコミュニティに有意義な夜の催しを提供する，ロワー・マンハッタンの重要な文化地区を形成する。

追悼の広場の新しい文化地区は世界金融センター，バッテリー・パーク・シティーの住民，小売店舗，乗り継ぎ駅へとつながる。以前は6車線の道路と高く持ち上げられた広場で，世界貿易センターの敷地から分離されていた世界金融センターは，ここで，広場に開かれ，その西端の境界線を形成するだろう。ウィンター・ガーデンを訪れる人は，メモリアル・スクエアの下にあるメイン・コンコースへ降りて行ける。コンコースはPATH駅，インターモダル交通センターへ，さらに，東へ，ブロードウェイとデイ・ストリートの提案されているNYCT交通センターへ続く。コンコースには小売店が並び，エスカレータで2階のショッピング・フロアに上がるとそこからインターモダル交通センターの大ホールへ出られる。文化施設と公園と共に，これらのアメニティはロワー・マンハッタン地区に新しい生活を運び込むだろう。

追悼の広場は，死者を記憶し，再生を祝う聖域である。そのデザインの精神と尊厳は，悲劇的な出来事は生命を強く肯定する機会とすることができる，という信念のなかでつくられた。

2001年9月11日，ニューヨーク・シティーで，2,800人近くの人がその命を失った。この喪失は，家族，恋人たち，グラウンド・ゼロで働いていた男たち，女たち，国家そして世界に深い悲しみを与えた。これは人間性に対する，自由の信条に対する攻撃であるといっても，言い過ぎではないと私たちは思っている。私たちは，この恐怖をその日に，身をもって経験した人たちの一員である。ニューヨーカーとして，建築家として，夢想的な協同グループとして，私たちの都市を再建するために，意義深い貢献を求められたことを誇りに思っている。

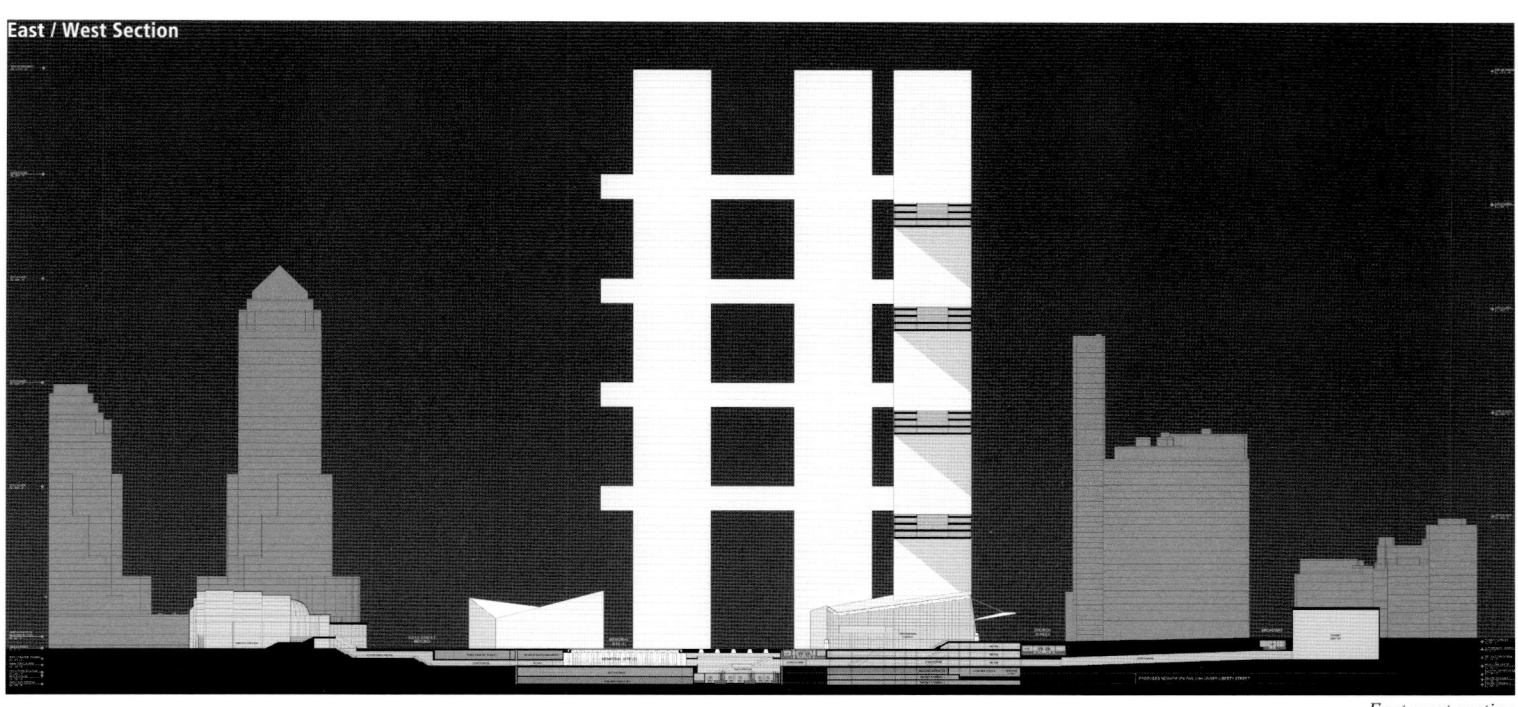

East-west section

Model

West view accross Hudson River　西側，ハドソン川越しに見る

Night view from north　北より見る

GA PROJECT

NATURAL HISTORY MUSEUM OF LOS ANGELES COUNTY

Los Angeles, California, U.S.A.
Design: 2002–   Construction: –2008

Model: view from Exposition Boulevard　模型：エクスポジション大通りより見る

GA PROJECT

Rhizome (root-like) is the basis for the new system of linkages which can be entered at any point in any order. The new building opens up the existing museum with multiple connections to the surrounding park and city.

Inscribed in a 420′ x 420′ square a "rhizomatic" architectural ordering with a topographical landscaped roof expresses an open-ended, non-linear new museum order. Research, education, and exhibition programs are located in an open envelope with multiple circulation routes and maximum flexibility. An open tower emerges from the new rhizomatic envelope symbolizing "observation of life on earth with research offices, a public observation deck/café and a special meeting room.

"Spiracle Courts" occur at node points in the building, sometimes working as outdoor gardens with micro-climate respiration benefits to the HVAC systems energy saving aspects. The museum's mission "to inspire wonder and discovery" would be uniquely embodied in a new architectural extension fusing landscape, urbanism, and architecture.

リゾーム（地下茎状）は，どの地点からも，どの配列のなかにも入ることのできる新しい結合システムのための基盤である。新しい建物は，既存博物館を，周囲の公園や市街との多種多様な接続によって開放する。

420フィート×420フィートの正方形のなかに刻み込まれた"地下茎状の"建築的配列は，地形としてランドスケーピングされた屋根と共に，オープン・エンドで非線形の，新しい博物館構成を表現する。研究，教育，展示の各プログラムは，多種多様な導線ルート，最大限の柔軟性を備えたオープン・エンベロップのなかに配置される。地下茎状のエンベロップからオープン・タワーが立ち上がり，"地球上の生命の観察"を象徴する。ここには研究オフィス，一般に開放された展望デッキとカフェ，特別な集会室が配置される。

"風穴のコート"が，建物内の結節点に生まれ，時に，微気候の屋外庭園として働き，HVACシステムの省エネルギー面に呼吸作用で貢献する。博物館の使命である，"不思議と発見の感覚を呼び起こすこと"は，ランドスケープ，アーバニズム，建築を融合させた新しい増築棟のなかに，独特なかたちで形象化されるだろう。

Architects: Steven Holl Architects—Steven Holl, principal-in-charge; Chris McVoy, partner;
Makram El Kadi, Olaf Schmidt, project architects;
Tim Bade, Noah Yaffe, Masao Akiyoshi,
Ziad Jamaleddine, project team
Client: Natural History of Los Angeles
Structural system: fabric formed concrete frame, perimeter shear wall, acousticast panels
Major materials: perforated screen walls, structural glass entry and green garden roof
Program: permanent and temporary exhibition space, research and collection, educational facilities, exhibit gardens
Total floor area: 65,000 sq.ft. (phase 1: 1913 building), 127,000 sq.ft. (phase 2: new museum), 222,000 sq.ft. (phase 3: 1920s building)

Aerial view　上空より見る

Site

Diagram

Site plan

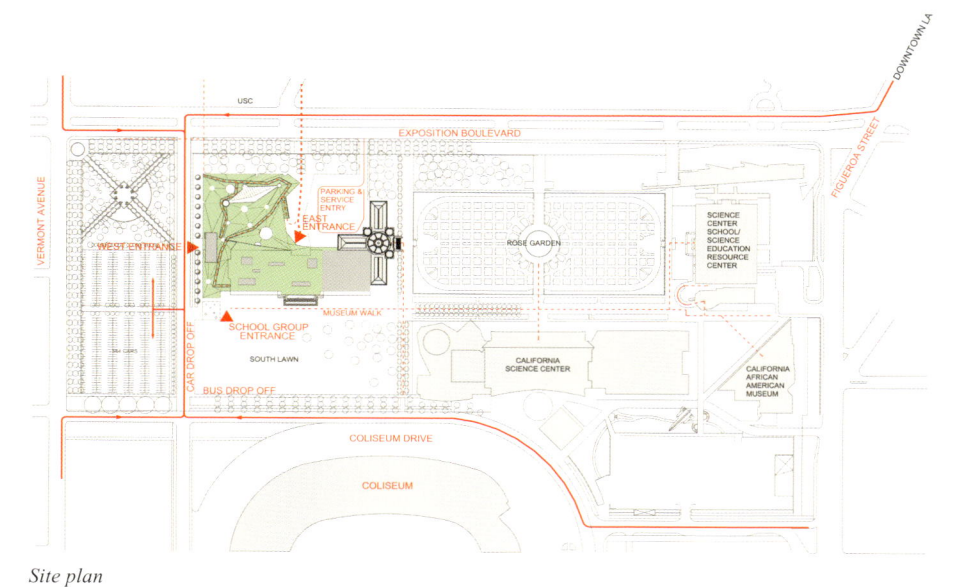

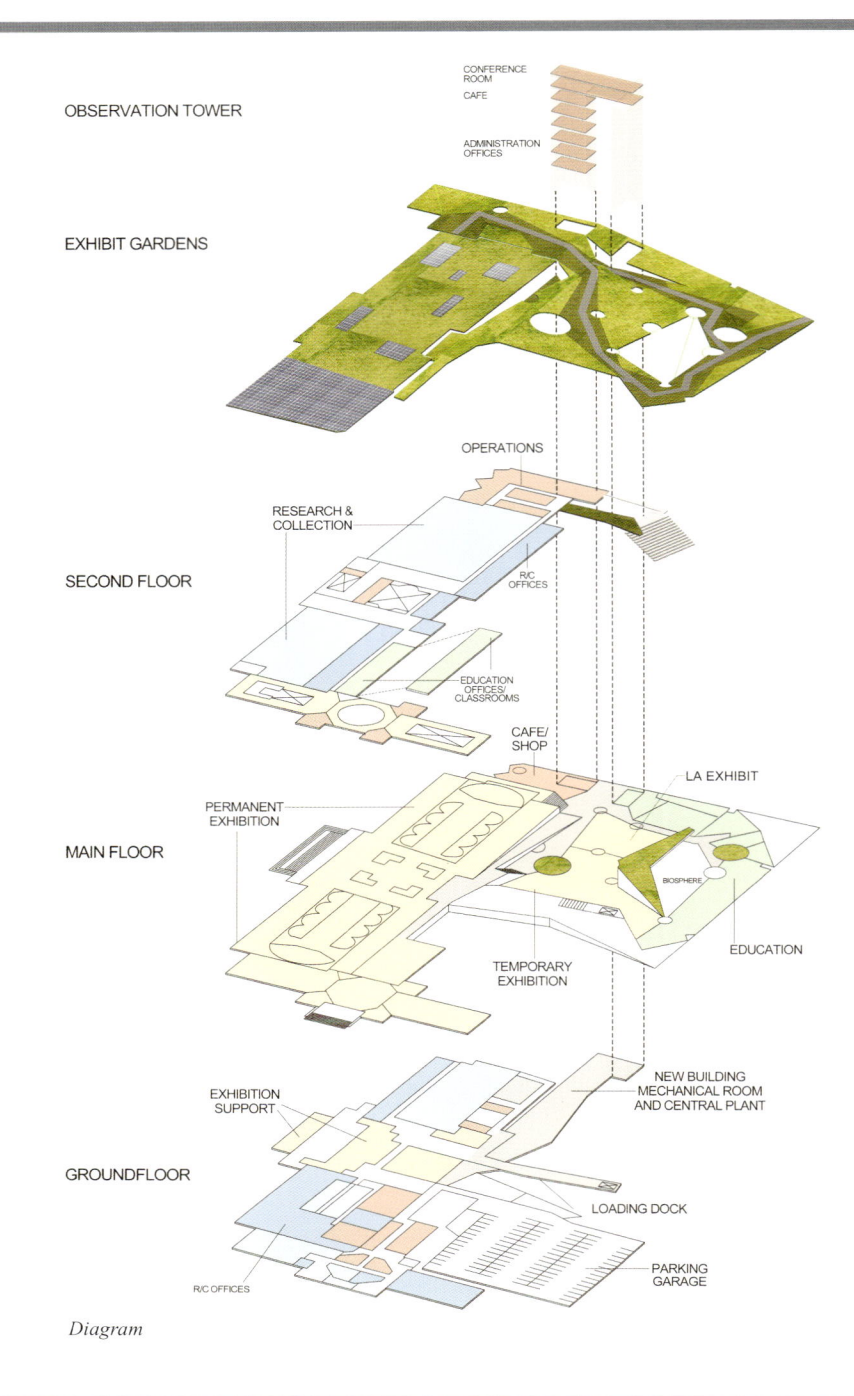

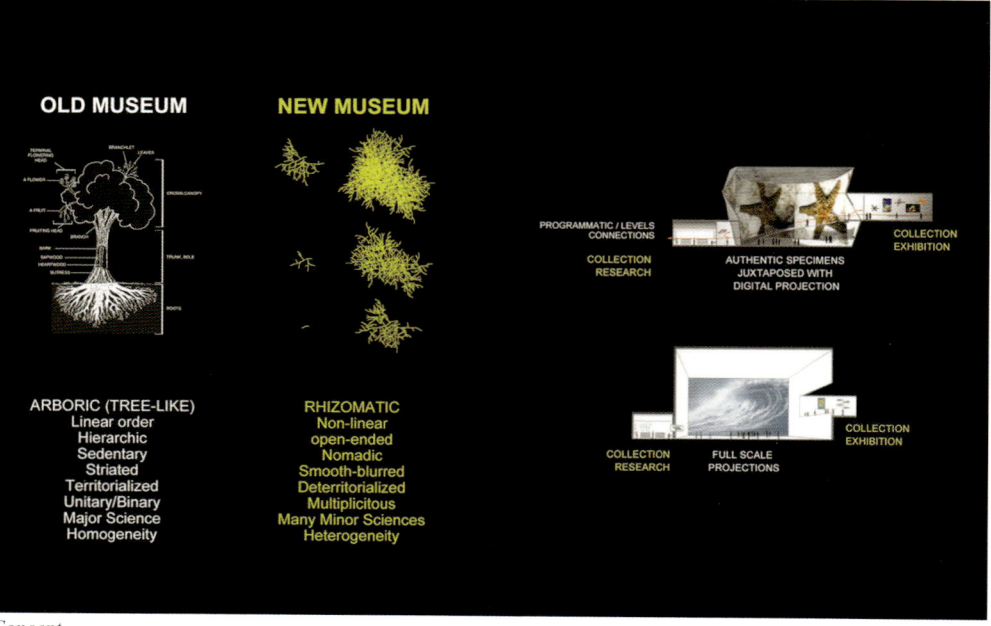

Concept

Topographical landscaped roof　地形としてつくられた屋根

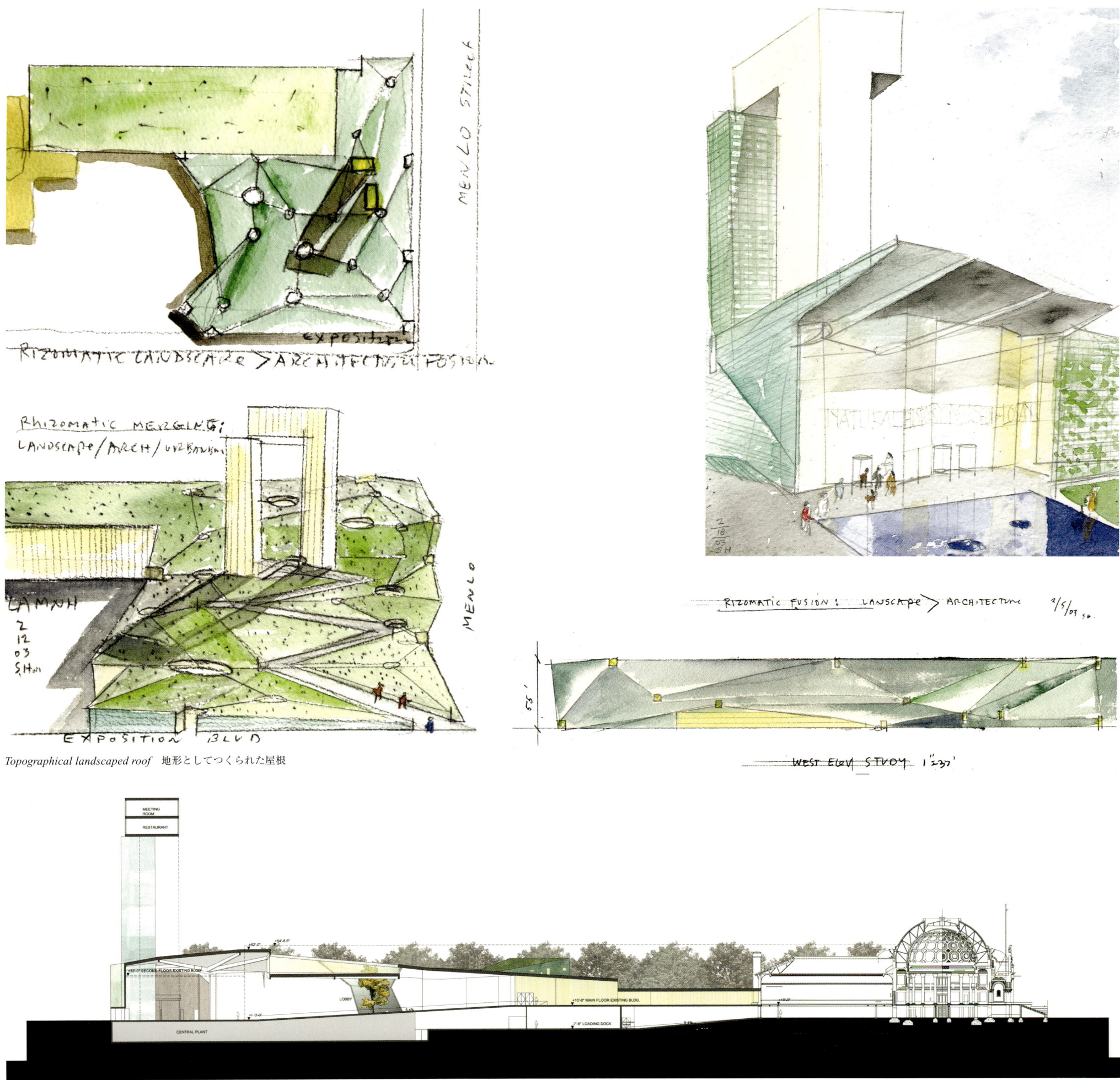

Section

GA DOCUMENT

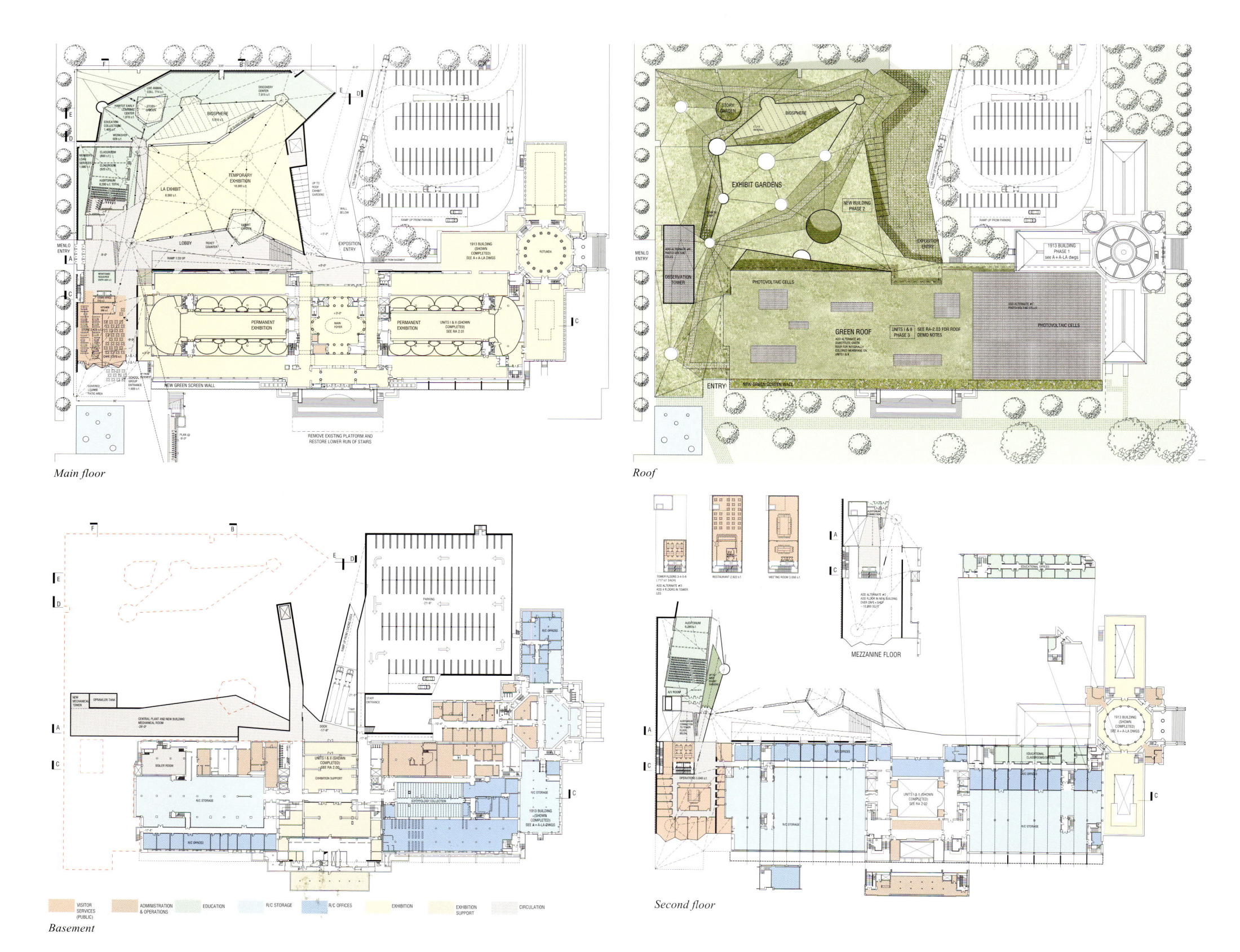

Main floor

Roof

Basement

Second floor

115

View from south lawn 南側の緑地より見る

Southwest view 南西より見る

GA DOCUMENT

116

Observation Tower 展望タワー

Exhibition space 展示スペース

Lobby ロビー

"Spiracle Courts"　"風穴のコート"

"Rhizomatic" architectural ordering expresses open-ended, non-linear new museum order
"地下茎状"の建築的配列は、オープンエンドで非線形の新しい博物館を構築する

MUSÉE DES CIVILISATIONS DE L'EUROPE ET DE LA MÉDITERRANÉE

Marseille, France
Design: 2003

119

GA DOCUMENT

Complementariness of Contrast
The structure of the new museum acts as a tool, in constant mutation, and makes a complementary contrast with Fort Saint-Jean. The museum of civilizations and the fortress together are engaged in an everlasting conversation.

コントラストの相補性
新しい博物館は、常に変化を遂げる道具として、サン=ジャン要塞とは対極的相補関係にある建物である。文明博物館と要塞は一対となり休みなく対話を続ける。

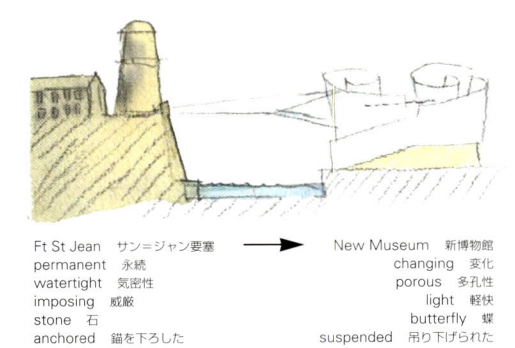

Ft St Jean サン=ジャン要塞	→	New Museum 新博物館
permanent 永続		changing 変化
watertight 気密性		porous 多孔性
imposing 威厳		light 軽快
stone 石		butterfly 蝶
anchored 錨を下ろした		suspended 吊り下げられた
historical site 史跡		instrument of change 変化の装置
closed mass 閉じたマッス		permeable vessel 浸透性のある船舶

Five Embedded Spirals
A pleasant series of five spirals pierces the square shell of the new museum: two come from the direction of Mistral, one from the Esplanade, one in relation with the fortress on the east, and a fifth one as an extension of the Seaside promenade. A malleable geometry that 'reflects time from top to bottom', these spirals characterize the interior movements of the museum and the dramatic views toward the exterior.

はめ込まれた5つのらせん
楽しげな5つらせんが新博物館の四角い外観を貫通している。2つはミストラルの方面から、1つはエスプラナードから、1つは西にある要塞との関連で、そして5つ目は海沿いの遊歩道の延長線上に。柔軟な形状を持ち「隅々まで時間を映す」5つのらせんは、博物館の内部の動きと外部へのドラマティックな眺めを特徴づける。

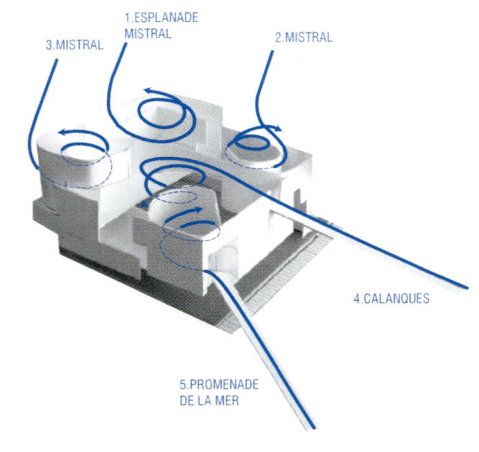

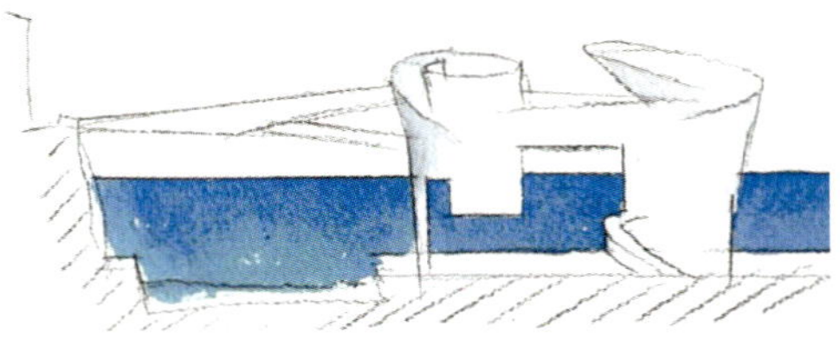

The Horizon and the Sea
"... for in the end, everything returns to the sea"—Le Corbusier
Through the building, one perceives the Mediterranean horizon: from the bright view of the entrance hall; up the ramp initiating the beginning of the spiral in a sequence of square galleries; from the overhanging terraces giving to the sea; and eventually from the rooftop garden which, as a rocky bay, is a form of space for reflection, comprising a cafe with a terrace and a view over the horizon, shaded by an undulating spiral.

水平線と海
「…そして最後には、すべてが海へと帰ってゆく」—ル・コルビュジエ
建物を通して地中海の水平線が見える。玄関ホールの明るい眺めから。四角い展示室が連なるらせんのはじまりを告げるスロープをのぼりながら。海へと張り出したテラスから。そして、切り立った岩で囲まれた入江のような屋上の庭園から。そこは沈思のための空間であり、水平線を見渡せるカフェテラスがあり、波打つらせんが陰を落としている。

"...A prolongation of spirals that reverberate up and down space and time...So it is that one ceases to consider art in terms of an 'object'. The fluctuating resonance rejects 'objective criticism' because that would stifle the generative power of both visual and auditory scale. Not to say that one resorts to subjective concepts, but rather that one apprehends what is around ones eyes and ears, no matter how unstable and fugitive. One seizes the spiral and the spiral becomes..." from Spiral Jetty, Robert Smithson

Concepts:

1) Complimentary Contrast:
The new museum structure acting as a tool and in permanent mutation is in Complimentary Contrast with the Fort St Jean. For the Museum of Civilization they work together in constant dialogue;

Changing	Permanent
Porous	Impervious
Lightweight	Heavyweight
Butterfly/sail	Stone
Suspended	Sedimented
Tool of change	Historic artifact
Open vessel	Closed mass

2) 5 Embeded Spirals:
In a welcoming outreach of extensions, five spirals pierce the square envelope of the new museum; two coming from the direction of the Mistral, one from the Esplanade, one connecting from the Fort to the east and a Fifth connecting directly along the Promenade de La Mer. As a malleable geometry that "reverberates up and down time" these spirals characterize the movement within and the dramatic views out from the new museum. (diagram)

3) The Sea Horizon:
"Everything begins and finally ends in the sea"—Le Corbusier

Through the building section the Mediterranean sea horizon is part of the experience; from the clear view though at the entrance lobby, from the ramp up that begins the upward square spiral of gallery sequence, from the special terraces thrust out to the sea, and finally from the roof garden which, like a Calanque, is a shaped space of reflection with a cafe terrace under a spiral shade with horizon views.

The Materials
In contrast to the sedimentary stone, the new museum is composed of light, ultramodern materials. The exterior white concrete mixed with agglomerated glass lets light pass through the slightest of thickness. Like scallop shell, the material becomes more opaque in the structural layers inside. The geometry of the base rests on a framework of 9 squares 20 meters by 20 meters which allows to integrate supporting structures inside the walls of exhibition rooms.

材質
堆積物である石材とは対照的に、新博物館は超現代的で軽い材質で構成されている。外面の白いコンクリートにはガラスが混ぜ込まれており、その薄い厚みを通り抜けて光が入ってくる。ホタテ貝の殻のように、その構造層は内側に行くほど不透明性をおびる。基部は、一辺が20メートルの正方形9つの上に乗るかたちで、展示室の壁に囲まれた支持構造体を一体化している。

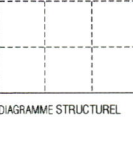

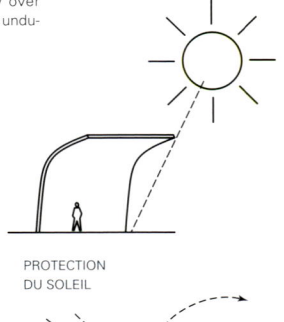

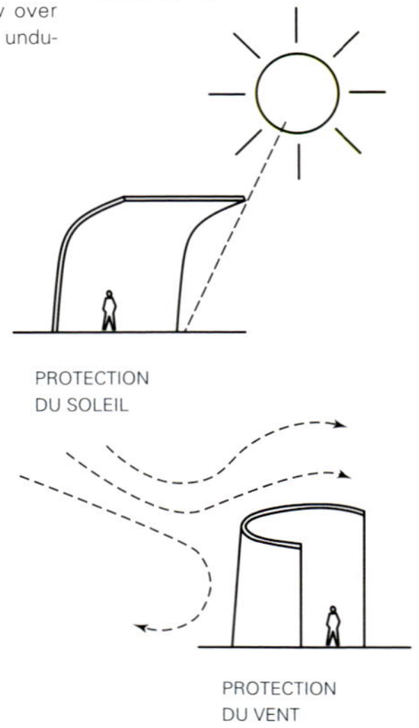

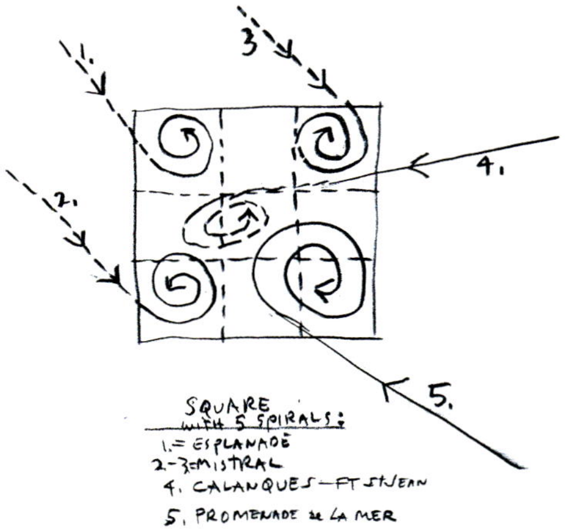

Site plan

MUCEM · LE FORT ST JEAN

GA PROJECT

「……空間と時間を上に下に反響させる螺旋の延長……そこで人は、アートを"オブジェクト"という角度から考えることをやめる。絶えず変化する反響は"客観的批評"をはねつける。なぜなら、視覚や聴覚の尺度、その両方の生成する力を抑圧してしまうからだ。主観的概念に頼るということではなく、いかに不安定で変わりやすくあろうとも、目と耳を取り巻いているものを理解するということだ。人は螺旋をはっきりと理解し、螺旋は……」

ロバート・スミッソン
「螺旋形の突堤」より

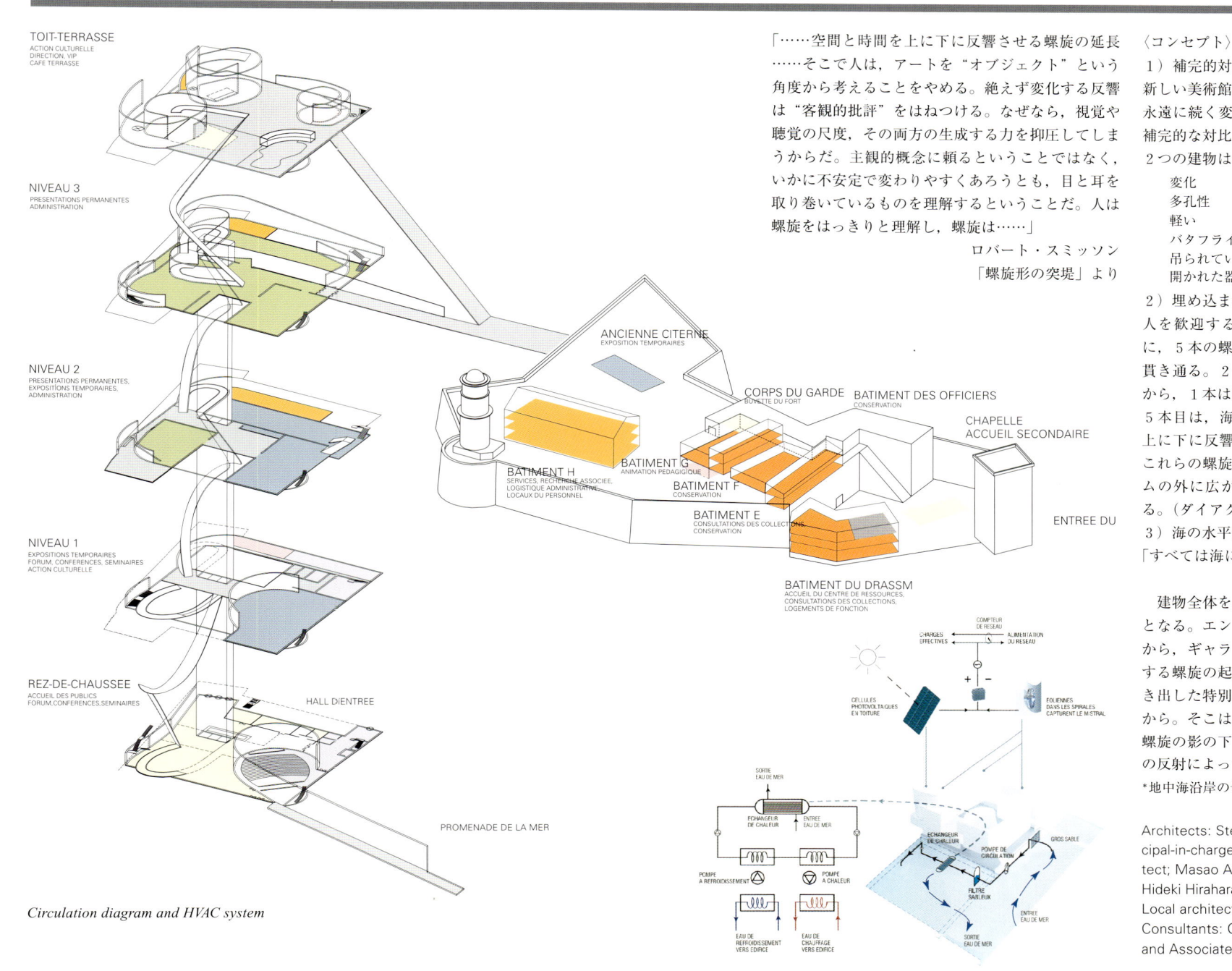

〈コンセプト〉

1) 補完的対比：
新しい美術館の建物は、一個の道具として振る舞い、永遠に続く変化のプロセスはサン・ジャン要塞との補完的な対比となる。文明のミュージアムのために、2つの建物は休み無く続く対話を共に進める。

変化	永遠
多孔性	不浸透性
軽い	重い
バタフライ/帆	石
吊られている	沈められた
開かれた器（船）	閉ざされたマス

2) 埋め込まれた5つの螺旋：
人を歓迎するように差し伸ばされた延長部のなかに、5本の螺旋が新しいミュージアムの方形の壁を貫き通る。2本はミストラルが吹き寄せてくる方向から、1本は遊歩道から、1本は要塞と東をつなぎ、5本目は、海の散歩道沿いを直接つなぐ。"時間を上に下に反響させる"従順なジオメトリーとして、これらの螺旋は、内部での動き、新しいミュージアムの外に広がるドラマティックな眺めを特徴づける。（ダイアグラム）

3) 海の水平線：
「すべては海にはじまり、海に終わる」

ル・コルビュジエ

建物全体を通して、地中海の水平線は体験の一部となる。エントランス・ロビーを通した透明な眺めから、ギャラリー・シークエンスを構成する、上昇する螺旋の起点となるスロープの昇りから、海に突き出した特別なテラスから、そして最後に屋上庭園から。そこはカランク*のような、水平線が見える、螺旋の影の下にあるカフェ・テラスのついた、光の反射によって象られたスペースである。

*地中海沿岸の切り立った岩に囲まれた入江

Architects: Steven Holl Architects—Steven Holl, principal-in-charge; Annette Goderbauer, project architect; Masao Akiyoshi, Makram El-Kadi, Hideki Hirahara, Brett Snyder, Irene Vogt, project team
Local architect: Andre Jollivet (Marseille, France)
Consultants: Ove Arup (New York), Guy Nordenson and Associates (New York), Jacobs Serete (Paris)

Circulation diagram and HVAC system

Entrance aproach エントランス・アプローチ

Site/ground floor

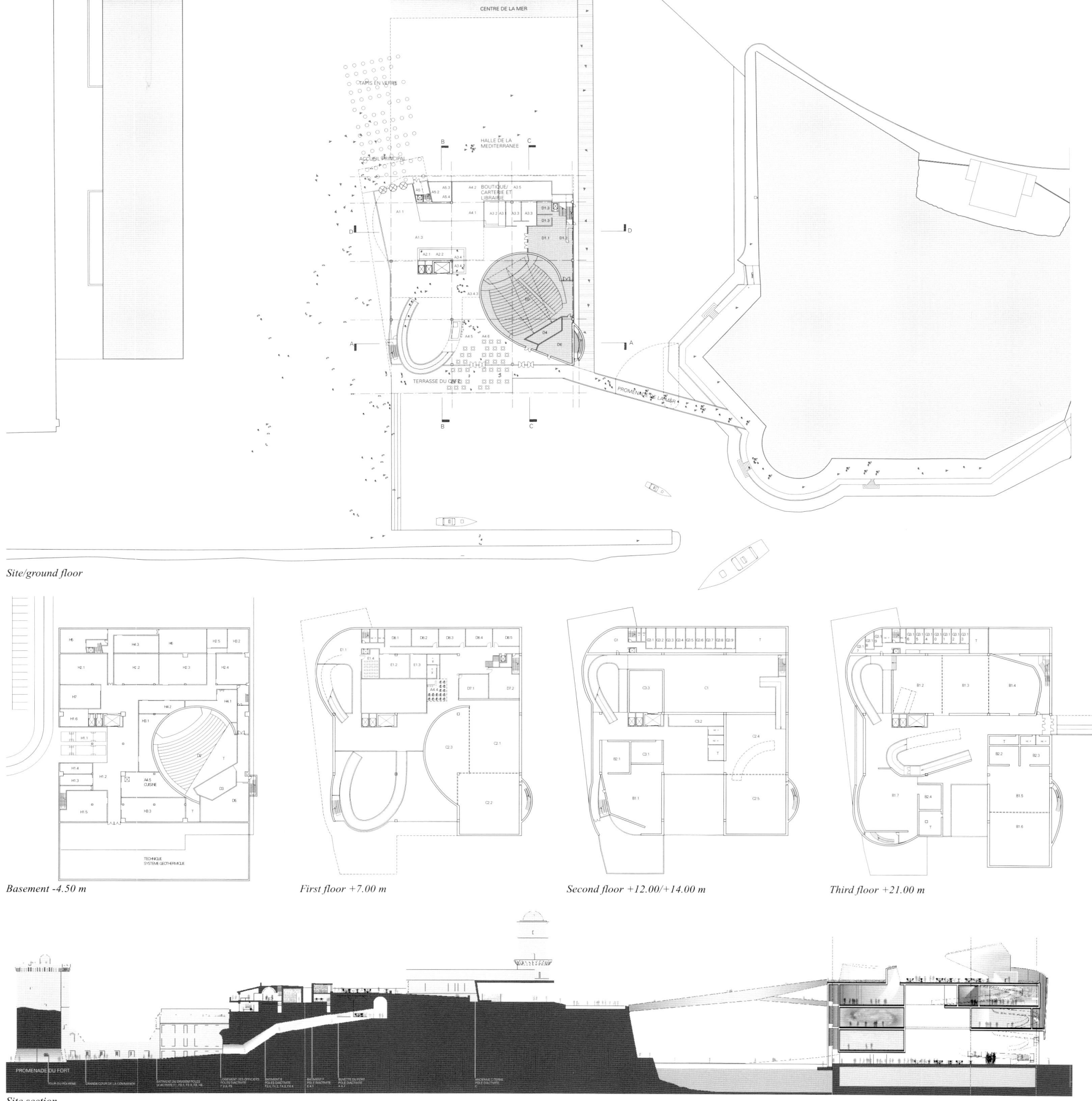

Basement −4.50 m   *First floor +7.00 m*   *Second floor +12.00/+14.00 m*   *Third floor +21.00 m*

Site section

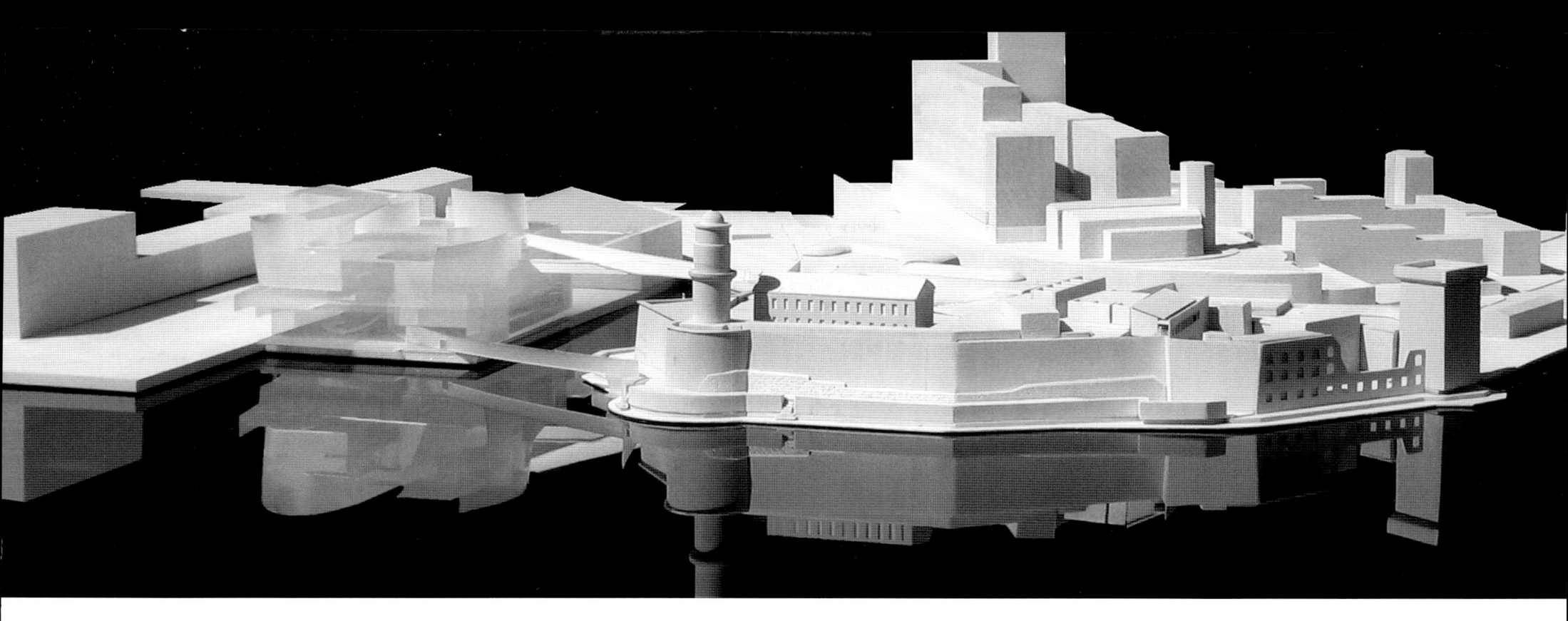

Model

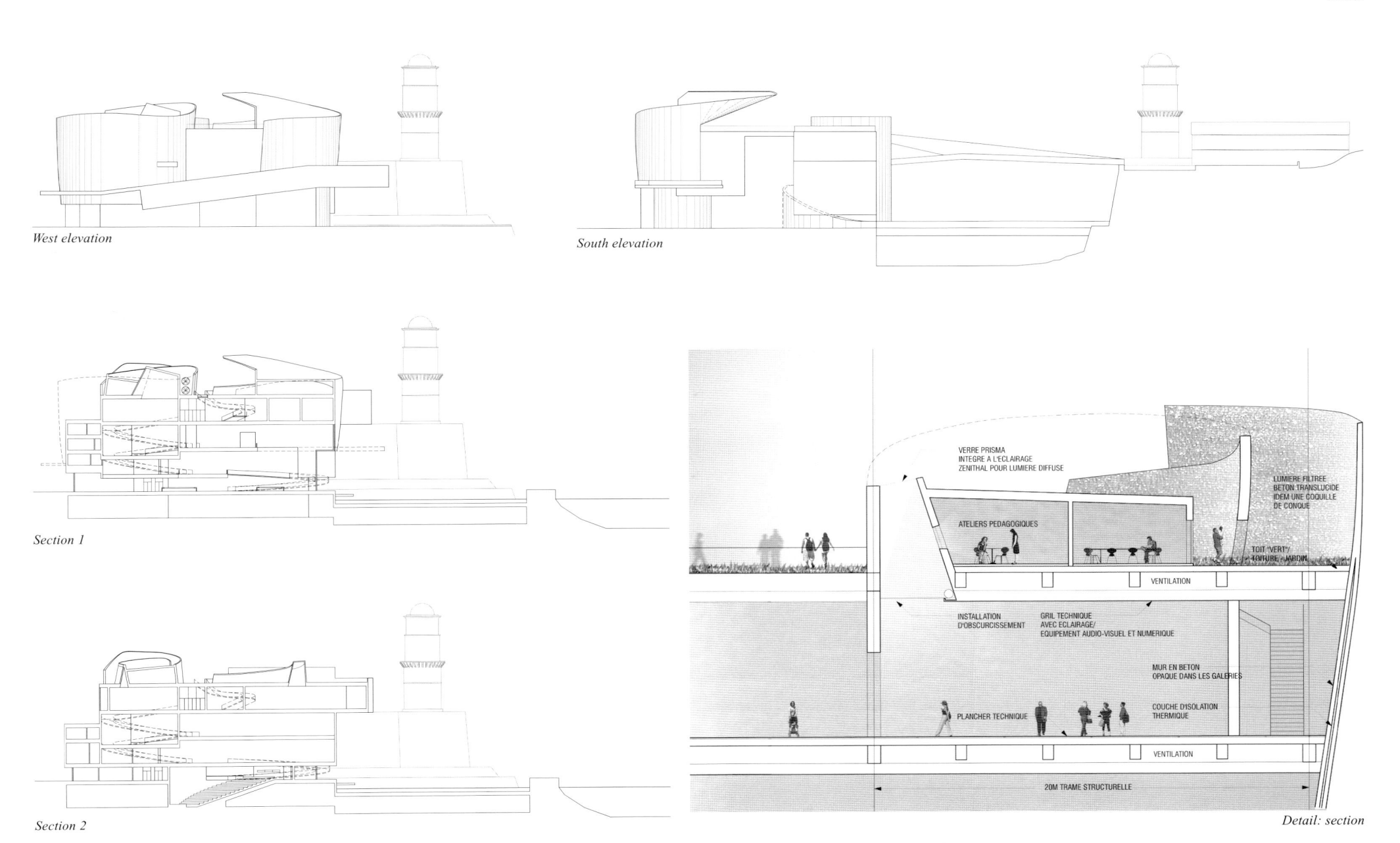

West elevation

South elevation

Section 1

Section 2

Detail: section

Bridge over "Calanques": Fort St. Jean on left and museum on right　　"カランク"（入江）に架かるブリッジ：左は要塞，右は美術館

View toward Mediterranean sea from terrace　　テラスから地中海を望む

Exhibition space 展示スペース

NEW NATIONAL LIBRARY OF LUXEMBOURG

Luxembourg
Design: 2003

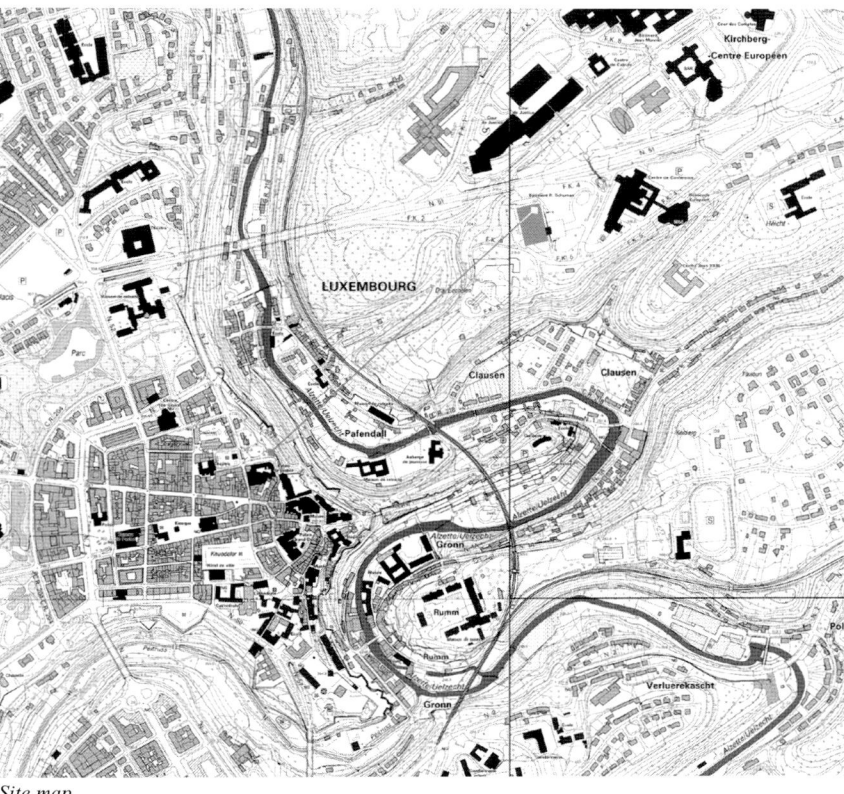

Introduction:

Poised on the edge of the Plateau Kirchberg overlooking the Old City, the site of the New National Library offers the potential to join the new European Union precinct with the old city in an exemplary international library. The existing 1970's office building, with its inadequate structural capacity and cellular spaces is unfit for the program and aspirations of the New National Library; to upgrade and expand the building would be costlier than constructing a new building.

Our proposed new building aims to tap the potential of the site and program and form a New National Library for the 21st century, a public place of knowledge contributing to the life of Luxembourg and the European Union community.

Concept:

An elevated public space of the New European Union is formed from a Plateau of Books. The largest element of the building program, 15,000 sq.m. of closed stacks, is simply formed into a trussed three-story rectangle of 80 m x 126 m. With walls of translucent, low-transmission glass, light is filtered out of this treasure of books yet the facade has its own luminous presence.

The 21st century's unprecedented compression of knowledge in many digital forms is expressed here in ongoing voids cutting through the closed stacks that form the Book Plateau. These curvilinear spaces passing through the Book Plateau have balconies lined with computers, expressing immediate open access to all. The Luxembourgensia has a unique position within the Book Plateau facing the old city.

On top of the Public Plateau, alongside the Compression Voids, various meeting rooms are shaped into the conference center, analogous to the diversity and complexity of the European Union. The large Foyer opens out to terraces overlooking the city.

Rising taller from the plateau, like the many thin spires which rise above the city of Luxembourg, a public observation room and restaurant are set within a hovering "L-shape", granting amazing views of the old and the new city. Three, simple, thin, sand-blasted, glass "spires" symbolize the new optimistic aim of the National Library, setting the night sky aglow with a pure, crystalline luminosity.

Below the Book Plateau glass walls open to the landscape while enclosing lobby, exhibition and administrative functions in transparent membranes. Passing through the site along a large reflecting pool is a wide, ramped, public passage that joins the main entry on Place de L'Europe with the plaza below. The plaza joins the Art Museum, Park and National Library with integrated public space.

Building Organization:

Plateau of Books:

In section, the compression voids open up a third of the book plateau, connecting public functions above and below with all the highest technological amenities of a modern public library. One can see the balconies of the latest computers in section and immediately spot the machines that are free. Light from the openings in the terrace level above streams down in inspiring beams to shape these public spaces and penetrate the plateau of books.

The four compression voids form the reading areas the various collections. The pair of northern voids serves the two-part non-Luxembourg collections. The southwest void combines News and Media collections. The Luxembourgesia occupies the most central void, with reading areas extending out to give views of the old city. From the street-level lobby, visitors can ascend through the base of the Luxembourgesia to reach the Plateau of Books. Luxembourg's cultural heritage is centered and joined with the international collections.

The open inaccessible stacks permit flexible allocation to each collection as needed. Support spaces surround the reading areas and enable efficient staff access to the stacks.

Plaza Levels:

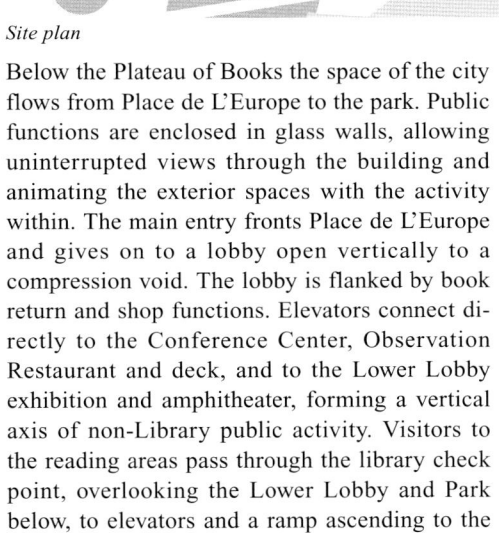

Below the Plateau of Books the space of the city flows from Place de L'Europe to the park. Public functions are enclosed in glass walls, allowing uninterrupted views through the building and animating the exterior spaces with the activity within. The main entry fronts Place de L'Europe and gives on to a lobby open vertically to a compression void. The lobby is flanked by book return and shop functions. Elevators connect directly to the Conference Center, Observation Restaurant and deck, and to the Lower Lobby exhibition and amphitheater, forming a vertical axis of non-Library public activity. Visitors to the reading areas pass through the library check point, overlooking the Lower Lobby and Park below, to elevators and a ramp ascending to the Book Plateau.

The lower plaza joins the Place de L'Europe ramp, the Lower Lobby entrance, and the kindergarden; with the Art Museum and Park. The Lower Lobby floor (Floor–2) opens out to the plaza and includes a café, exhibition, amphitheaters and administration. A mezzanine level above the administration houses the research functions.

Service functions are located along the street below the Place de L'Europe and are capped by a large reflecting pool, an urban mirror for the Place. Light filters through the compression void above to illuminate the water's surface.

Conference Terrace:

The conference center occupies the top of the Plateau of Books, elevating its standing within the city and signaling its importance as a place cultural exchange for Luxembourg and the European Union. The varied forms of the meeting rooms, clad in zinc on the exterior and wood on the interior, are brought together by the Foyer which opens out to terraces. From here one can see both the Old City and the new European Union precinct. The meeting rooms, Foyer and Terrace form an ensemble capable of hosting large international and local events and receptions.

Observation Spires:

Accessed directly from the Lobby and conference levels, the top of the spires house a restaurant, bar and meeting rooms, roofed by an observation terrace. With amazing views of the old and the new city these spaces will become destinations in their own right. Kitchen functions are connected directly via dedicated service elevators to preparation areas and delivery in the base of the building. Marking the library's cultural prominence on the city's horizon, the glass "spires" symbolize the new optimistic aim of the National Library.

Site map

Site plan

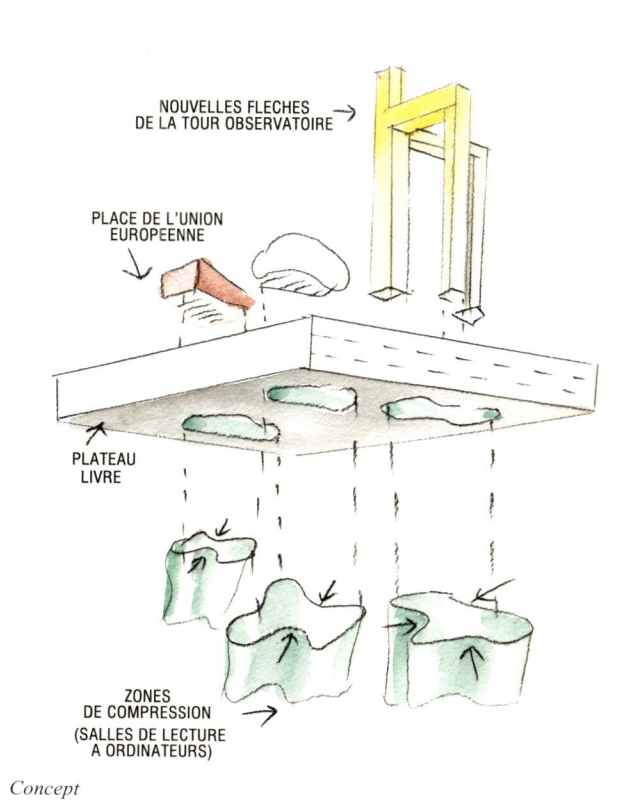

Concept

Night view from street 通りより見た夜景

Aerial view 上空より見る

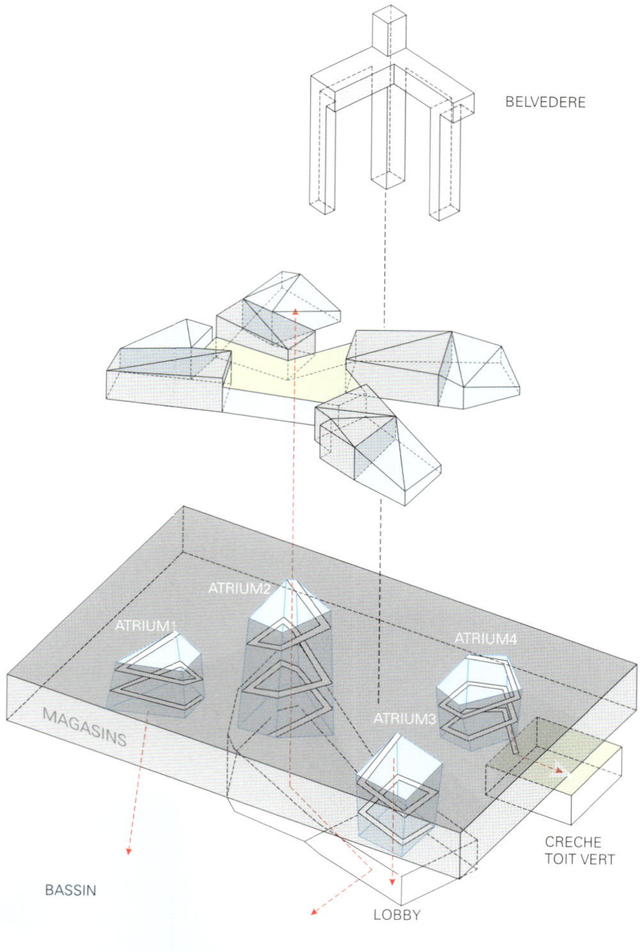

Diagram

129 GA PROJECT

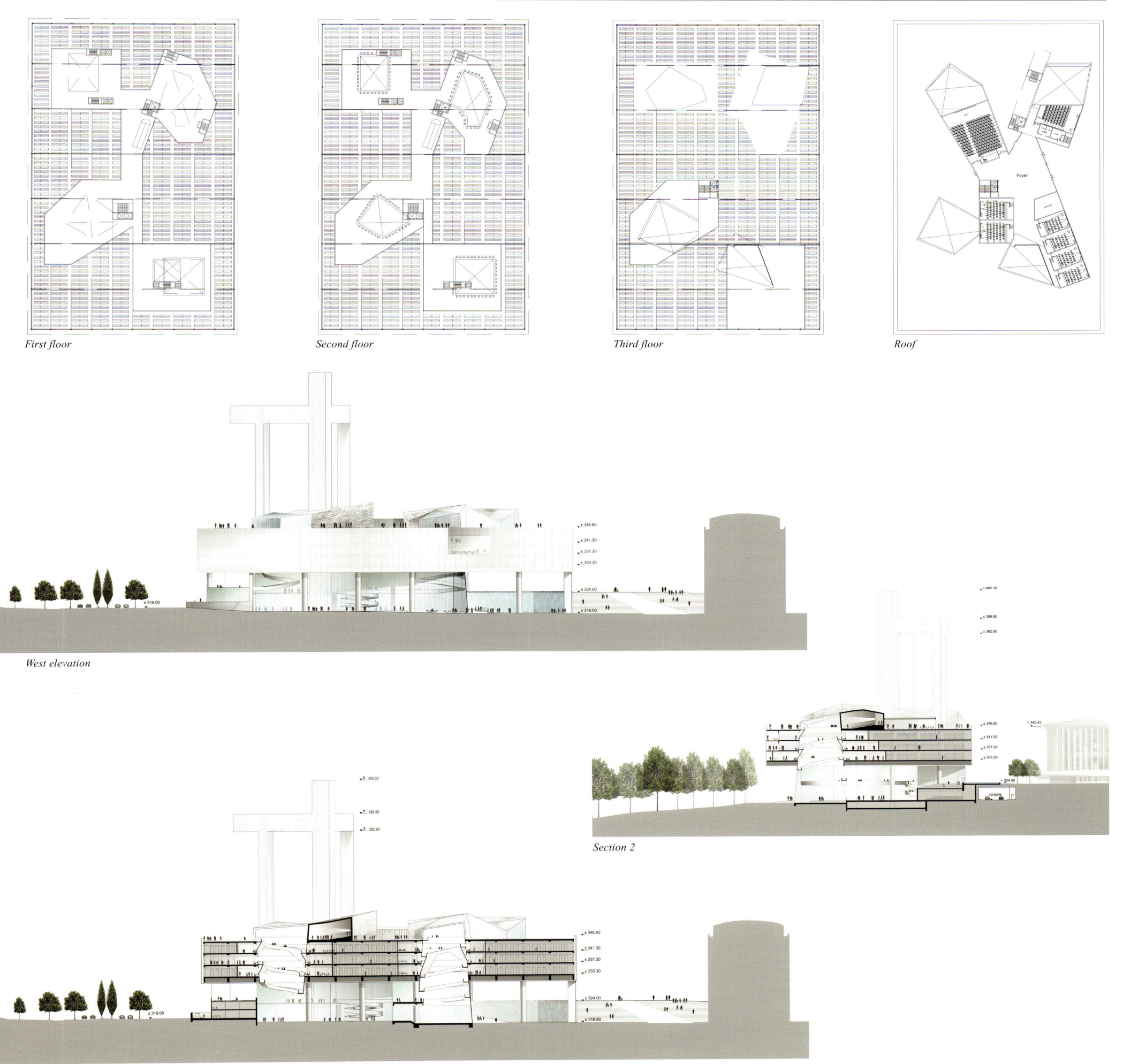

First floor

Second floor

Third floor

Roof

West elevation

Section 2

Section 1

序

旧市街を見晴らすキルヒベルク台地の先端に，浮かぶように広がる新国立図書館の敷地は，手本となるような国際図書館によって，旧市街と共に新しいEU域内に加わるに相応しい可能性を備えている。70年代に建てられたオフィス棟は，不十分な収容能力と小区画に分かれた空間が，新国立図書館のプログラムや目指しているものに適合しなくなっている。建物を改修し，拡張する方が，新しく建物を建てるより高価なものになるだろう。

新しい建築案は，敷地とプログラムに潜在する可能性を開発し，21世紀の新国立図書館，ルクセンブルクとEUコミュニティの生活に貢献する公共的な知識の場を形成することを目標としている。

コンセプト

新EUの高く持ち上げられたパブリック・スペースは"書物の台地"からかたちづくられる。15,000平方メートルの閉架式書庫は，プログラム中最大の要素で，80メートル×126メートル，3層の単純な矩形トラスを形成する。半透明の透過度の低いガラス壁によって，外光はこの書物の宝庫の外で濾過されるが，ファサードは輝きとその存在感を失うことはない。

様々なデジタル方式による，前例をみない21世紀の知の圧縮が，"書物の台地"をかたちづくる閉架書庫を切り進む，連続するコンプレッション・ヴォイドに表現されている。"書物の台地"を貫くこれらの湾曲するスペースにはコンピュータの並ぶバルコニーがあり，あらゆる情報にすぐにアクセスできる。

ルクセンブルク関連の書物は旧市街に向いた"書物の台地"のなかに特別な場所を与えられる。

パブリック・プラトーの最上部，コンプレッション・ヴォイドのそばに，EUの多様性と複雑さの類似物として，さまざまな集会室が会議センターを構成する。広いホワイエが市街を見晴らせるテラスに面している。

ルクセンブルク市街にそびえる数多くの尖塔のように，プラトーから高く立ち上がる，一般に開放された展望階とレストランが，舞い上がるような"L形"のなかに配置され，旧市街，新市街の素晴らしい眺めをほしいままにする。3本の，シンプルでほっそりした，サンドブラスト・ガラスの尖塔は，国立図書館の新たな建設的な目的を象徴し，夜空を，澄んだ透明な輝きで照らす。

"書物の台地"の下のガラス壁は風景に開く一方，ロビー，展示，管理事務などの機能空間は透明な被膜で囲まれる。大きなリフレクティングプールに沿って敷地を抜け，幅の広いスロープとなった公共通路が，下にプラザのあるヨーロッパ広場の正面入り口に続く。プラザは美術館，公園，国立図書館を，一体となった公共空間として結びつける。

建築構成

〈書物の台地〉プラトー・オブ・ブックス

断面上で，コンプレッション・ヴォイドは"書物の台地"の3分の1を切り開き，上や下に広がるパブリック・スペースを現代の公共図書館が備えるあらゆる高性能機器につなぐ。断面上で，最新のコンピュータが並ぶバルコニーが目に入り，すぐに自由に使えるマシンを見分けられる。上のテラス・レベルに開けられた開口から，心を高揚させるような光の束が流れ落ち，これらのパブリック・スペースを象り，"書物の台地"に浸透する。

4つのコンプレッション・ヴォイドは様々な蔵書の閲覧エリアを形成する。対になった北側のヴォイドは，ルクセンブルク関連以外の2部門の蔵書，南西のヴォイドはニュースとメディア関連の蔵書の閲覧エリアである。ルクセンブルク関連は，一番中央寄りのヴォイドで，閲覧エリアは旧市街を見晴らせるように外に広がっている。道路レベルにあるロビーからルクセンブルク関連エリアの基部を通って"書物の台地"まで上がれる。ルクセンブルクの文化遺産は中心に配置され，国際関連の蔵書と結ばれる。

一般の人は入れない開架式書庫は，必要に応じて，各部門の蔵書に柔軟に配分することができる。閲覧エリアを囲むサポート・スペースによって，スタッフは効率よく書庫に出入りできる。

〈広場レベル〉

"書物の台地"の下で，都市空間はヨーロッパ広場から公園へ流れて行く。パブリックな機能を納めたスペースはガラス壁で囲まれ，建物を通して遮るもののない眺めが見え，内部の活動の様子が外を活気づける。メイン・エントランスはヨーロッパ広場に面し，垂直方向にコンプレッション・ヴォイドに向けて開いたロビーに続く。ロビーは本の返却受付とショップに挟まれている。エレベータがコンファランス・センター，展望レストラン，デッキ，下のロビーの展示室とアンフィシアターを直接結び，図書館以外の公共的な活動領域の垂直導線を形成する。閲覧エリアへの来館者は図書館のチェック・ポイントを抜け，下のロビーと公園を見下ろしながら"書物の台地"へ昇るエレベータやスロープへと進む。

ロワー・プラザはヨーロッパ広場のスロープ，ロワー・ロビー・エントランス，幼稚園を美術館や公園と結んでいる。ロワー・ロビー階（フロア2）はプラザに面し，カフェ，展示場，アンフィシアター，

Distant view 遠景

管理事務室がある。管理事務室の上のメザニン階には研究調査部門が置かれる。

　サービス機能は，ヨーロッパ広場の下の道路に沿って配置され，広場にある"都市の鏡"，大きなリフレクティング・プールがその上に被さる。光は上のコンプレッション・ヴォイドを抜けて濾過され，水面を照らす。

〈コンファレンス・テラス〉
コンファレンス・センターは"書物の台地"の頂部を占め，この都市におけるその地位を高め，ルクセンブルクとEUの文化交流の場所の重要性を伝える。外側は亜鉛，内側は木で仕上げられた様々なかたちの集会室は，テラスに開いたホワイエで一つにつながれる。このテラスから，旧市街と新しいEU地区の両方が見える。集会室，ホワイエ，テラスは，まとまって国際的な，あるいは地元の大きなイベントやレセプションを主催できる場となる。

〈展望尖塔〉
ロビーや大会議場のある階から直接行ける尖塔の頂部には，レストラン，バー，集会室があり，展望テラスがその屋根となる。新旧両市街の素晴らしい眺めと共に，これらのスペースはそれだけで人が訪れる場所となるだろう。厨房設備は，建物の基部にある下準備とデリバリーのためのエリアと専用エレベータで直接つながれる。ガラスの"尖塔"は，都市の地平線上に図書館の文化的重要性を標しながら，国立図書館の新しい建設的な目標を象徴する。

View from southwest 南西より見る

Roof terrace ルーフ・テラス

Entrance エントランス

Atrium アトリウム

Architects: Steven Holl Architects—Steven Holl, principal-in-charge; Arnault Biou, project architect; Chris McVoy, Jongseo Lee, Makram El-Kadi, Christiane Deptolla, Irene Vogt, Urs Vogt, Annette Goderbauer, Peter Englaender, Ziad Jamaleddine, project team
Program: university and national library, offices, conference center, cafe
Total floor area: 400,000 sq.ft.

Panorama view from observation tower 展望タワーからのパノラマ

LOMBARDIA REGIONAL GOVERNMENT CENTER

Milan, Italy
Design: 2004

View from Pirelli tower ピレッリ・タワーより見る

The Lombardia Regional Government Center forms a new Civic Piazza for Milan: a 21st Century urban space of inspiring proportions. As opposed to conventional practice, which tends to restrict public space to ground level, a new public openness on the part of the regional administration will be expressed by placing major public spaces in an upper frame with magnificent views encompassing the city and the Alps.

While the new Piazza has public functions and cafes activating the ground level, ceremonial functions such as press conferences, exhibitions and debates etc. will take place on the upper level with a regional rather than a local backdrop.

The dual condition of the local (urban) and regional (landscape) aspects of the Lombardia center will be emphasized by in the new Civic Piazza and the upper level alpine views.

Offices in the supporting towers maximize functions in their openness to air and light. Circulation is facilitated by horizontal connections between verticals at grade, midpoint and upper levels.

Democracy and openness are thematized by the sophisticated technology of the glass facades. Operable windows to the offices located for views are bracketed by sunlight controlled translucent cavity walls, circulating filtered air.

The piazza paved in red porfido Lombardian stone has arcades with shops and cafes with entrances on the street side as well as the piazza side. Water from the Martesana canal is filtered and utilized in three "Canals of Milan" fountains, located centrally in the piazza with glass lenses on their bottoms, bringing light to the parking below.

The highest levels of the complex are crowned by a public observation deck and the president's offices. These mark the "prow" of the new urban composition, aligned urbanistically and geometrically with the Pirelli tower.

At night the special glowing walls of the complex radiate the sunlight captured that day from the roof's photovoltaic cells, yielding different qualities of light by night depending on the previous day's sun.

ロンバルディア地方行政府センターはミラノの新しい市民広場をかたちづくる。それは，人を活気づけるような均衡を備えた，21世紀の都市空間である。公共空間を1階に限定しがちな従来の方法とは異なり，地方行政府センターでは，主要な公共空間を，市街からアルプスまでを見渡せる素晴らしい眺望を望める上階に配置することで，公共に対する新しい開放性が表現されるだろう。

新しい広場はパブリックな機能とカフェによって1階を活気づけ，記者会見や展覧会や討論会などの儀式的なイベントは，都市風景ではなく，地方の景色を背景にした上階で行われる。

ロンバルディア・センターの地元（都市）と地方（風景）の両側面を持つ二元的状況は，新しい市民広場と上階のアルプスの眺めによって強調されるだろう。

サポート・タワー内のオフィスは，外気や陽光へ開放され，機能性が最大限に高められる。水平導線が，1階，中間階，上階で垂直導線と連結することで移動はスムースである。

民主主義と開放性が，ガラス・ファサードの洗練された技術によって，主題化されている。見晴らしのあるオフィスの開閉窓は，陽光を制御する半透明の中空壁で挟まれる。壁の中空は濾過された空気を循環させる。

ロンバルディアの赤い斑岩を敷き詰めた広場には，広場側と道路側に入り口のあるショップやカフェの並ぶアーケードがある。マルテサーナ運河から曳いた水は濾過されて，広場中央にある3つの"ミラノの運河"噴水で利用される。噴水の底にはガラスレンズが填り，地下の駐車場へ光を送る。

コンプレックスの最上階には一般の人に開放された展望デッキと長官室が帽子のようにかぶさり，新しい都市構成の"舳先"となり，都市的にも幾何学的にもピレッリ・タワーと整列する。

夜には，建物を包む特殊な輝く壁が，その日に，屋根の光電池が捕獲した陽光を放射させる。毎晩の光の質は，前日の陽射しの如何によって変わる。

Aerial view 上空より見る

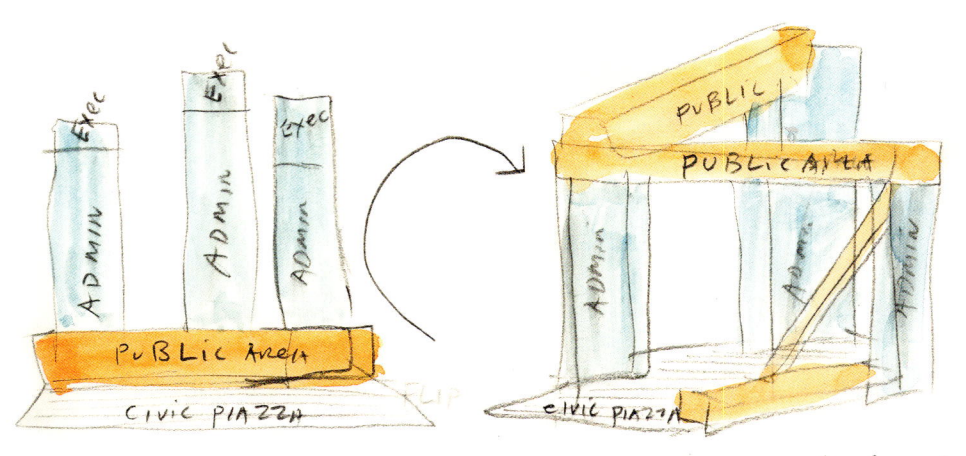

Site plan

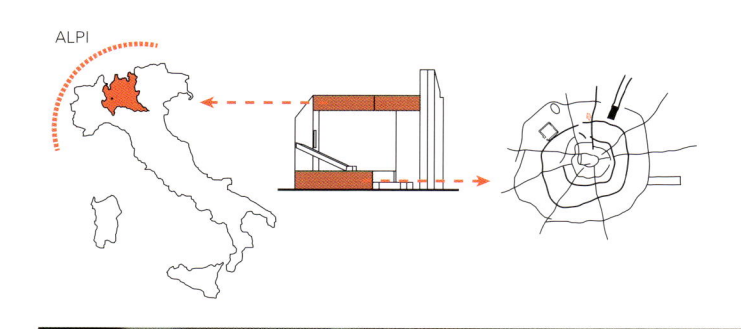

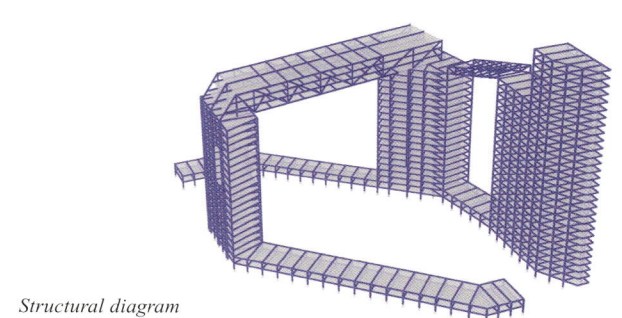

Structural diagram

Urban visual relationship

Network of urban nature

Ped access publ transport

Vehicular traffic

Monuments of Milan

137 | G A PROJECT

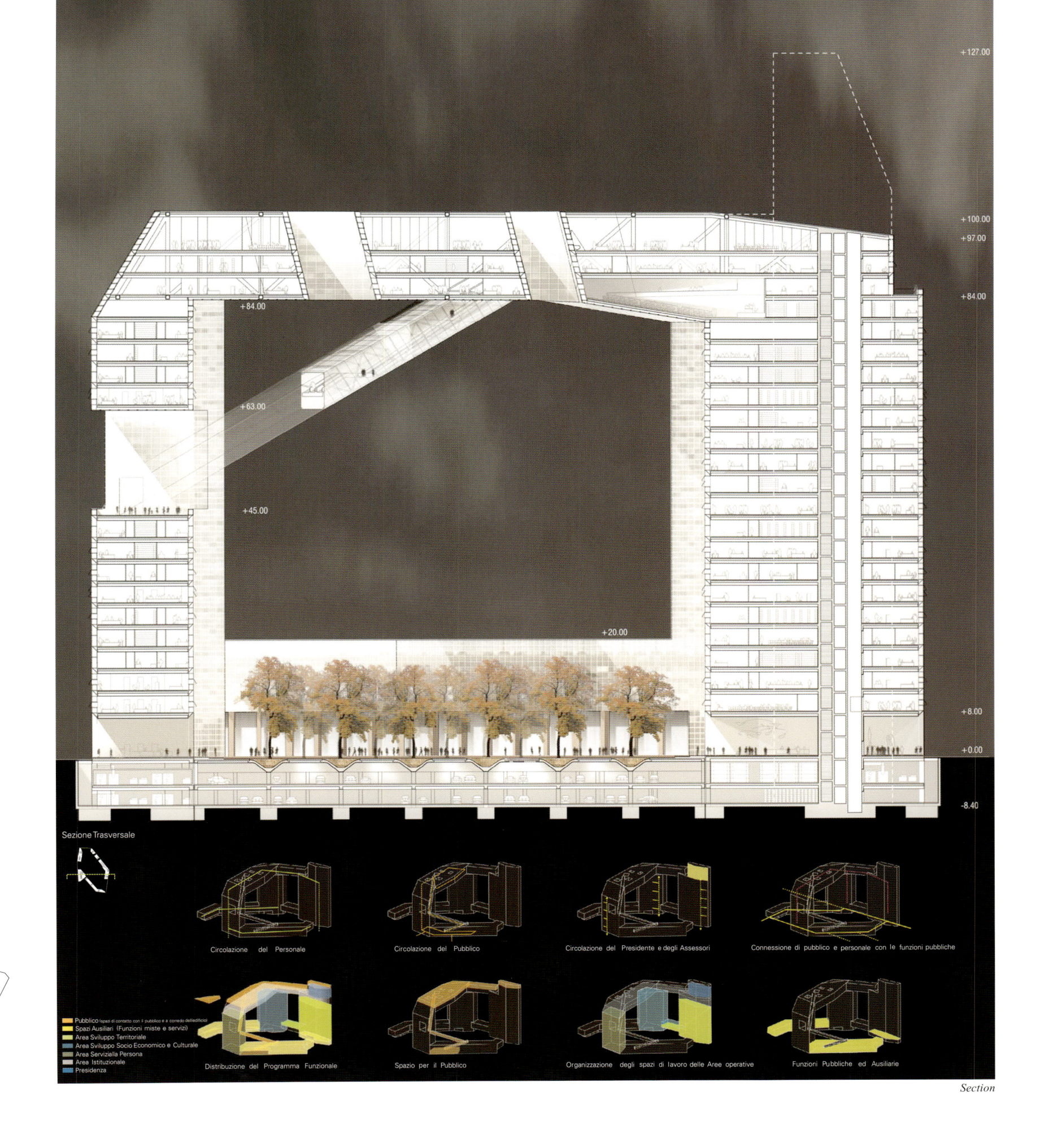

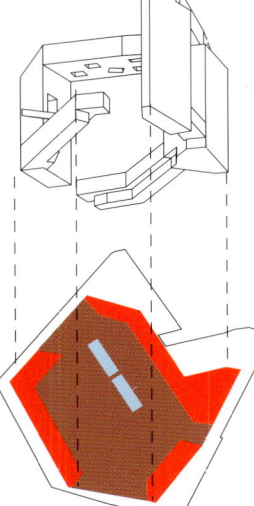

Axonometric

Section

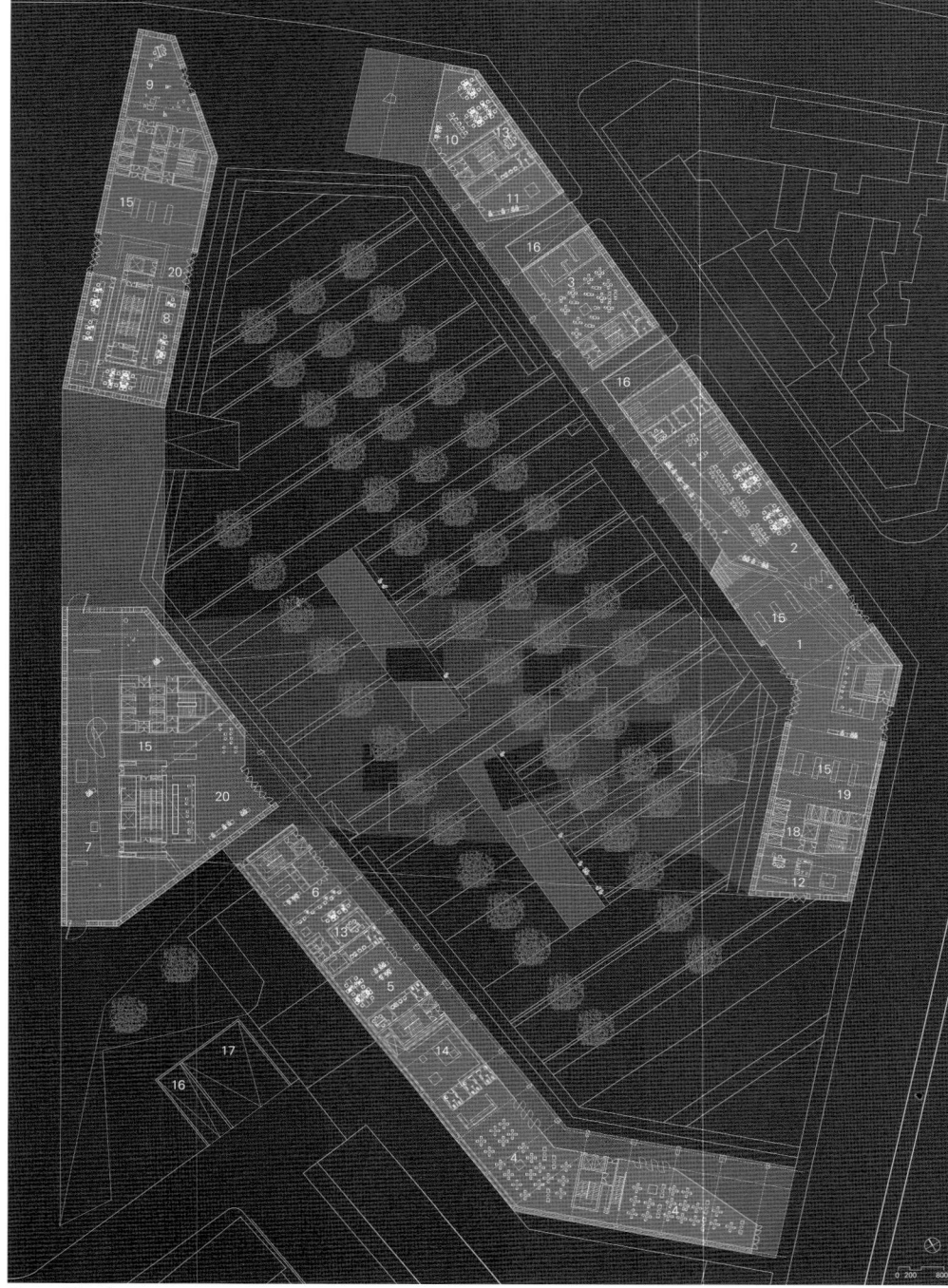

Ground level

1. MAIN PUBLIC ENTRANCE
2. REGIONAL ROOM
3. BAR
4. RESTAURANT
5. POST OFFICE
6. BANK
7. DISPLAY ROOM
8. CALL CENTER
9. INFORMATION CENTER
10. POLICE STATION
11. TOURIST OFFICE
12. REGIONAL BOOK STORE
13. OFFICE
14. KITCHEN
15. SECURITY
16. CAR ENTRANCE
17. CARGO
18. ELEVATOR TO THE PUBLIC
19. ELEVATOR TO THE PERSONAL
20. AUDITORIUM

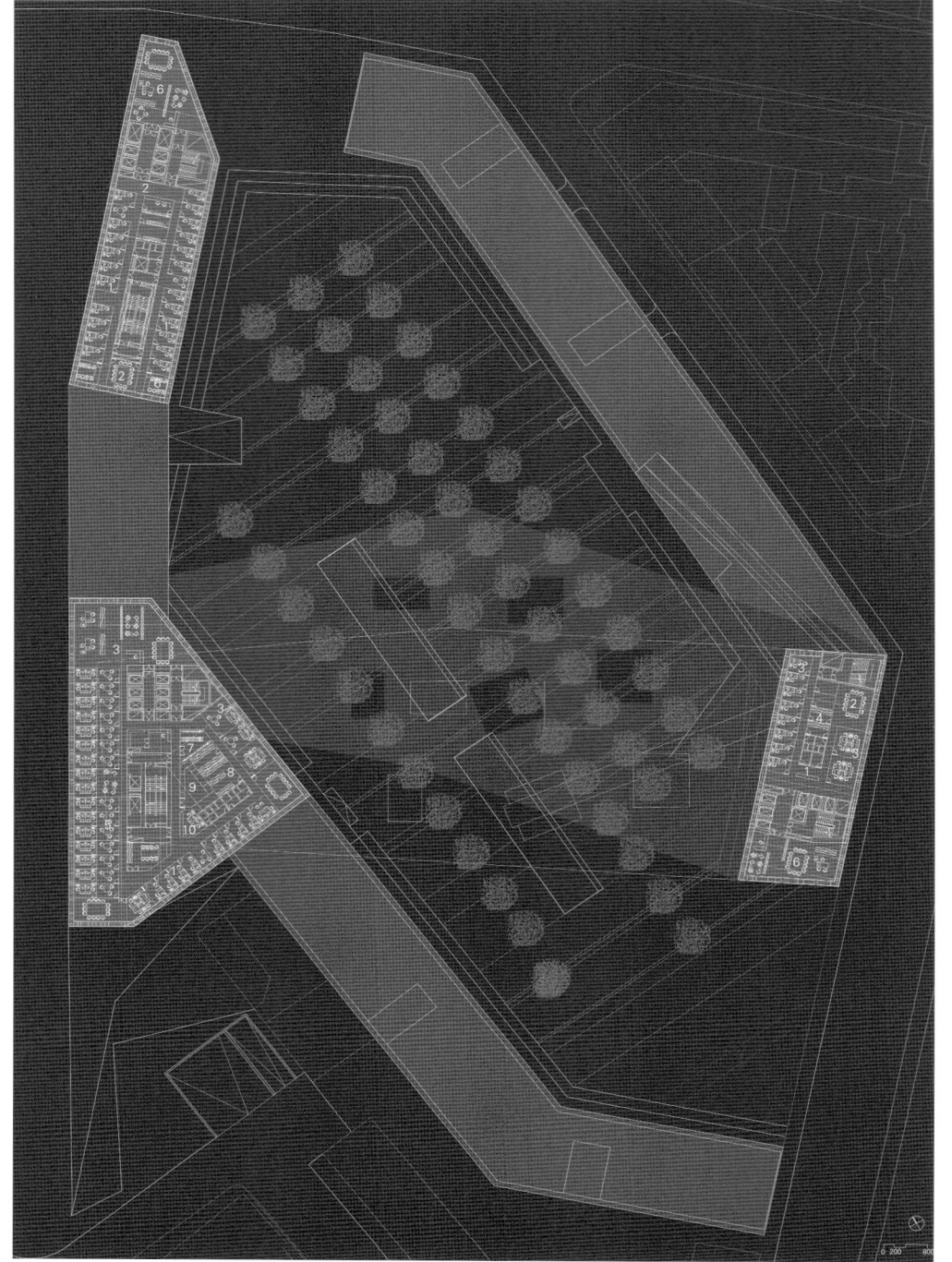

Office level

OPERATIVE SPACE
1. RECEPTION
2. MEETING ROOM
3. OFFICE
4. SPACE FOR EMPLOYEE
5. SPACE FOR EMPLOYEE AND WAITING ROOM
6. MUNICIPAL ROOM

SUPPORT SPACE
7. CLOAK ROOM
8. ARCHIVE
9. REST ROOM
10. COPY

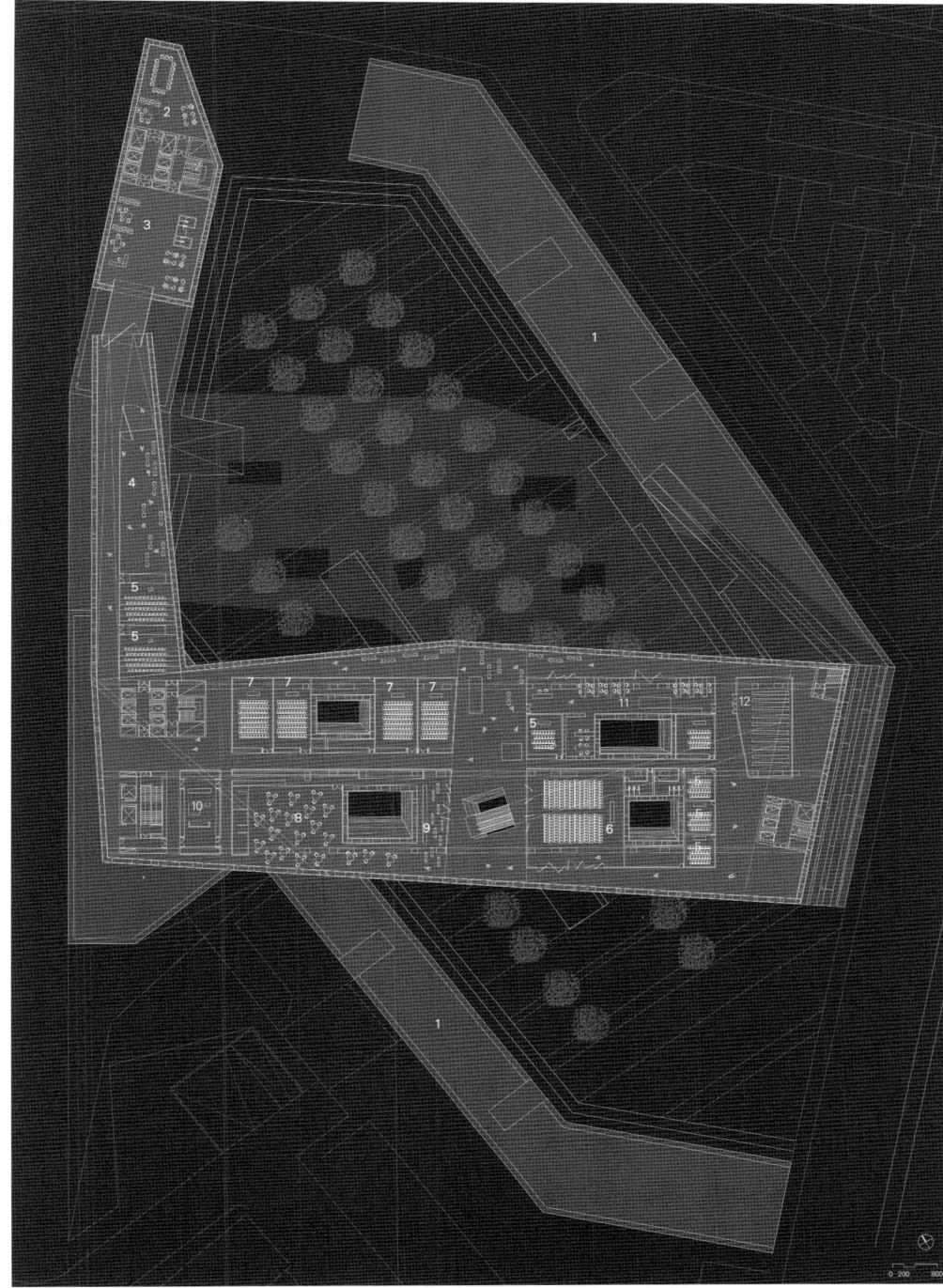

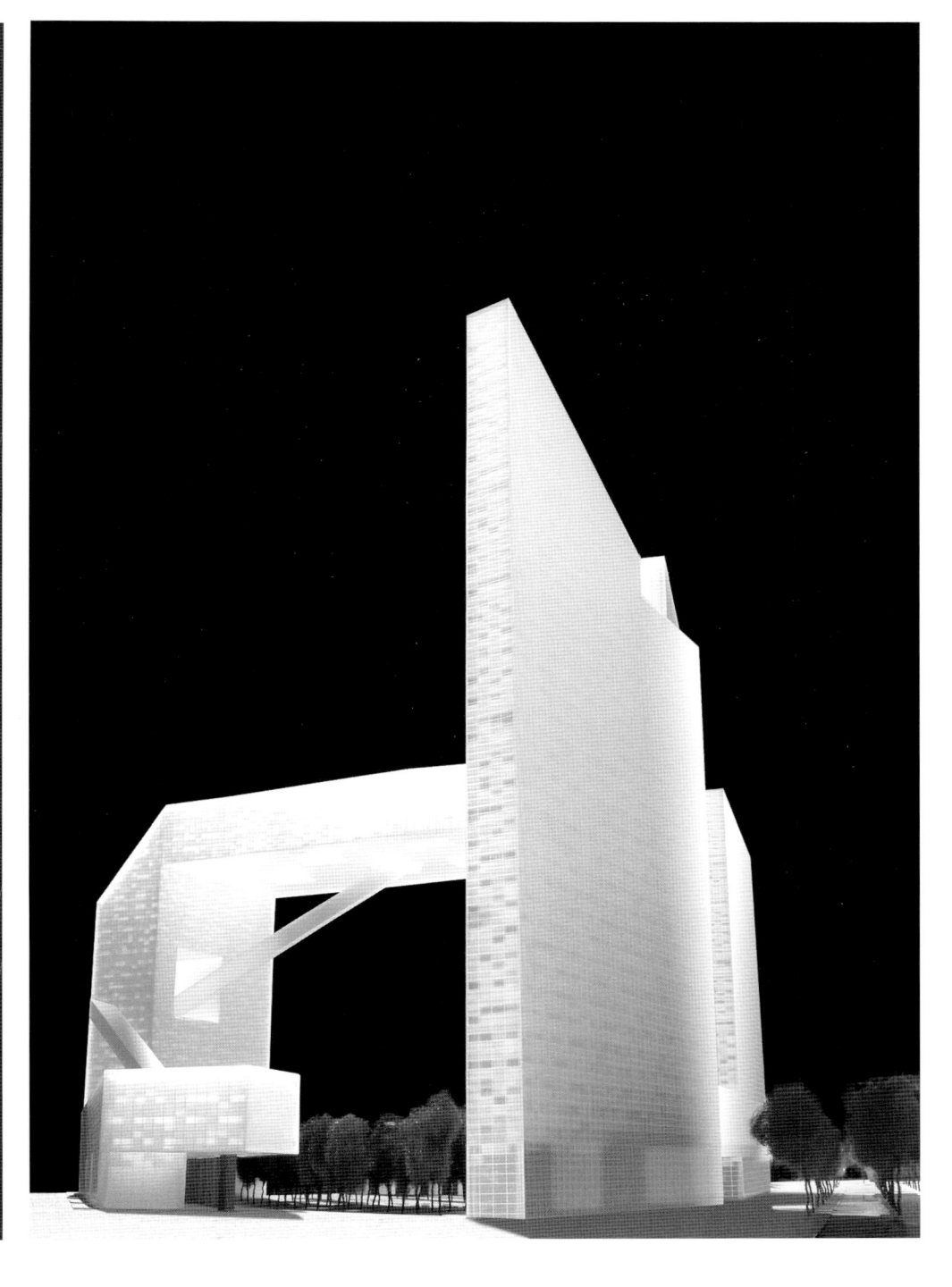

Deck level

1. ROOF GARDEN
2. MEETING ROOM
3. PRESIDENT ROOM
4. PRESENTATION ROOM
5. MEETING HALL
6. PRESS CONFERENCE ROOM
7. CREATION ROOM
8. RESTAURANT
9. BAR
10. KITCHEN
11. LIBRARY
12. ARCHIVE

Architects: Steven Holl Architects—Steven Holl, Martin Cox, principals-in-charge; Garrick Ambrose, Guido Cuscianna, Makram El-Kadi, Gian Carlo Floridi, Simone Giostra, Young Jang, Ariane Weigner, project team
Associate architects: OdA Associati—Remo Dorigati, principal
Consultants: Politecnico di Milano—Matteo Gatto, Prof. Maurizio Vogliazzo, urban planning law; Prof. Claudio Bernuzzi, structural engineering chair; Prof. Pietro Manazza, constructive and general design law; Chiara Dorigati, building design law expert; SERING SRL—Lettorio Piraino, Fausto Pella, engineer building economy expert
Client: Lombardia Regional Government
Program: president's and government officials' offices, public piazza, press conference and exhibition and debate facilities, cafés, public observation deck

140

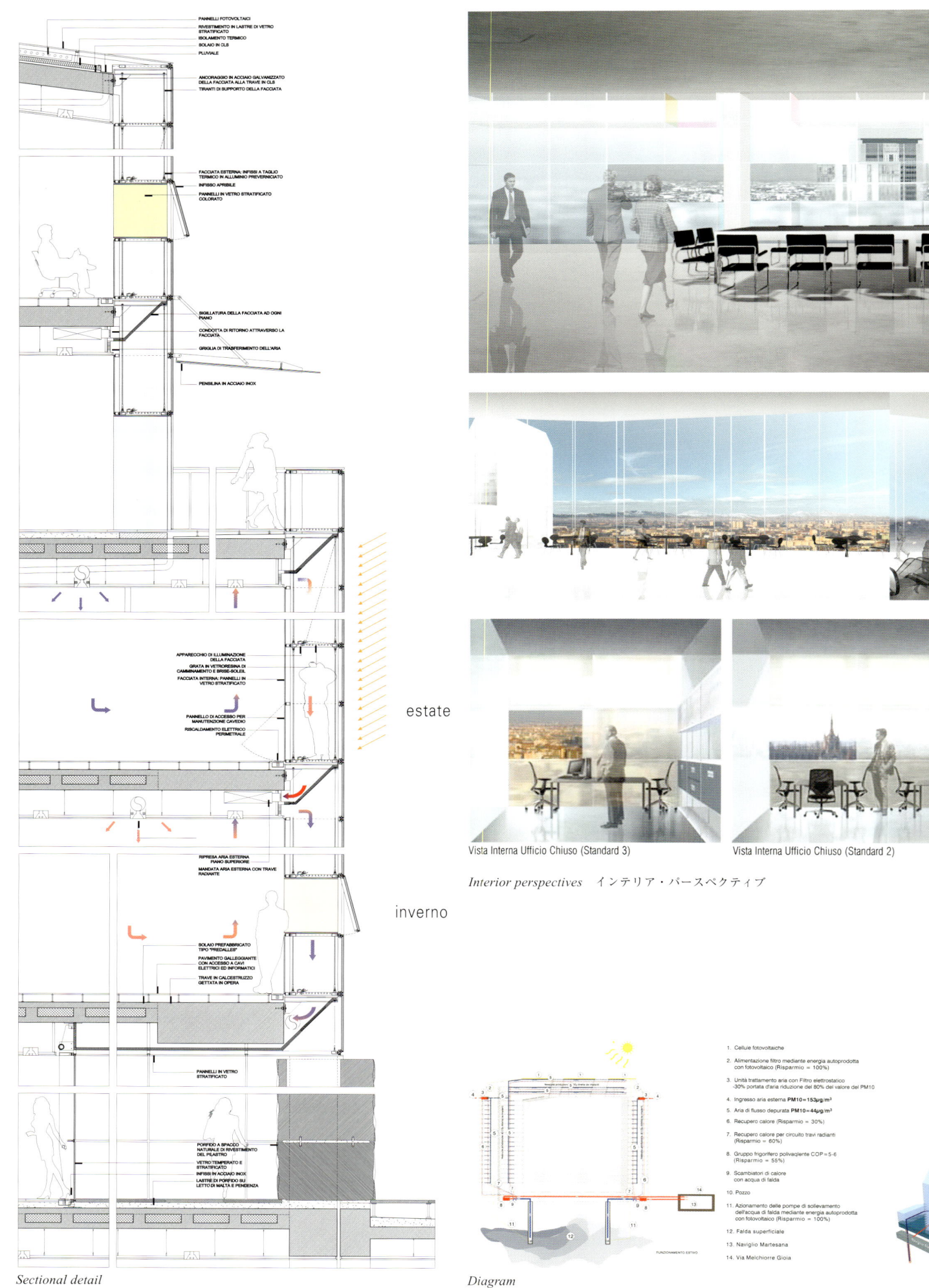

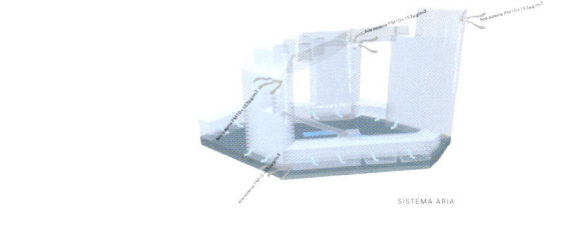

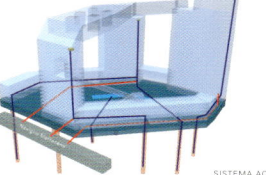

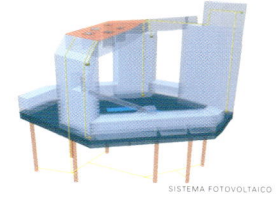

Sectional detail

Interior perspectives インテリア・パースペクティブ

Diagram

141 | GA PROJECT

Horizontal and sloped public area connects administration buildings
水平な，あるいはスロープ状のパブリック・エリアがオフィス棟をつなぐ

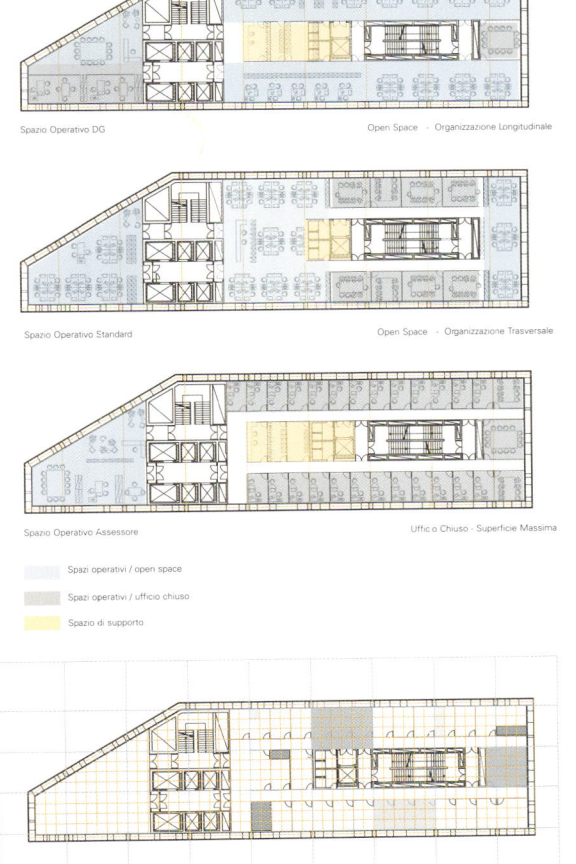

Flexibility of planning

Piazza 広場

GA
Global Architecture

English and Japanese texts
Size: 364 × 257 mm
48 total pages, 8〜20 in color

An Encyclopedia of Modern Architecture

Apart from those seminal works of architecture which imply new directions, those columns also introduce some of the classic work by such masters of modern architecture. They will become an encyclopedia of modern architecture.
現代建築の名作をじっくり見ていただくために企画された大型サイズのシリーズ。現代建築の歴史に残る名作を，1軒ないし2軒，総48頁で構成。回を重ねるごとに現代の名建築の百科事典となるでしょう。

GA6 ¥2,400
Eero Saarinen *Bell Telephone Corporation Research Laboratorys, Deere & Company*

GA17 (Revised Edition) ¥2,800
Antonio Gaudí *Casa Batlló, Casa Milà*

GA45 ¥2,400
Carlo Aymonino/Aldo Rossi *Housing Complex at the Gallaratese Quarter*

GA48 (Revised Edition) ¥2,800
Luis Barragán *Barragán House, Los Clubes, San Cristobal*

GA61 ¥2,400
Jørn Utzon *Church at Bagsvaerd*

GA64 ¥2,400
Manteola, S. Gomez, Santos, Solsona/Viñoly *Banco de la Ciudad de Buenos Aires*

GA65 ¥2,400
Sepra & Clorindo Testa *Banco de Londres y América del Sud*

GA67 ¥2,400
Alvar Aalto *Villa Mairea*

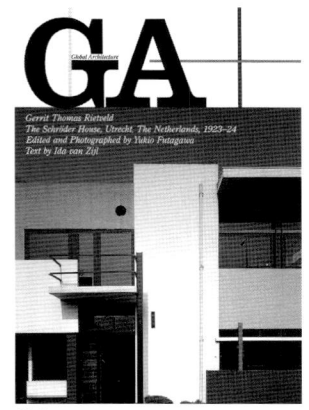

GA68 ¥2,806
Gerrit Thomas Rietveld *The Schröder House*

GA69 ¥2,806
Arata Isozaki & Associates *Tsukuba Center Building*

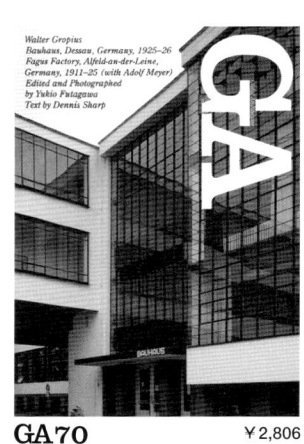

GA70 ¥2,806
Walter Gropius *Bauhaus, Fagus Factory*

GA72 ¥2,806
Louis I. Kahn *National Capital of Bangladesh*

GA73 ¥2,806
J. A. Brinkman & L. C. van der Vlugt *Van Nelle Factory*

GA74 ¥2,806
Giuseppe Terragni *Casa del Fascio, Asilo Infantile Antonio Sant'Elia*

GA77 ¥2,800
Rudolph M. Schindler *R.M. Schindler House & James E. How House*

GA DETAIL

GA Detail is a series of publications introducing masterpieces of modern/contemporary architecture by detail drawings in large format. GA Detail is to be continued to pick up masterpieces of architecture, our age's as well.

克明なワーキング・ディテールにより現代建築の名作を解析する図面集。第1巻は1976年初版の，大好評を得たディテール集の改訂版，ミース・ファン・デル・ローエの名作，ファンズワース邸。このシリーズは再び現代建築の名作をピックアップして順次出版いたします。

Japanese and English texts, Size: 364 × 257 mm

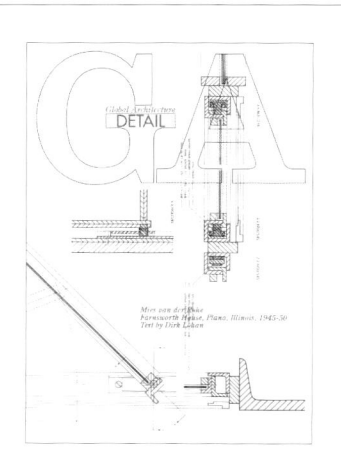

1
Mies van der Rohe
Farnsworth House
Plano, Illinois, 1945-50
Text by Dirk Lohan
ミース・ファン・デル・ローエ
ファンズワース邸
文：ダーク・ローハン／製図：北村修一
64 total pages
¥2,476

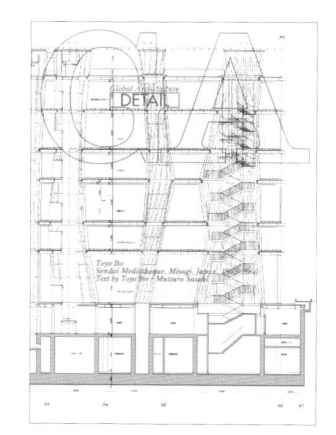

2
Toyo Ito
Sendai Mediatheque
Miyagi, Japan, 1995-2000
Text by Toyo Ito/Mutsuro Sasaki
伊東豊雄
せんだいメディアテーク
文：伊東豊雄／佐々木睦朗
64 total pages
¥2,476

表記価格に消費税は含まれておりません。

LIGHT & SPACE
MODERN ARCHITECTURE

光の空間

Edited and Photographed by Yukio Futagawa
Introduction by Paolo Portoghesi Text by Riichi Miyake

企画・撮影＝二川幸夫
序文＝パオロ・ポルトゲジ
文＝三宅理一

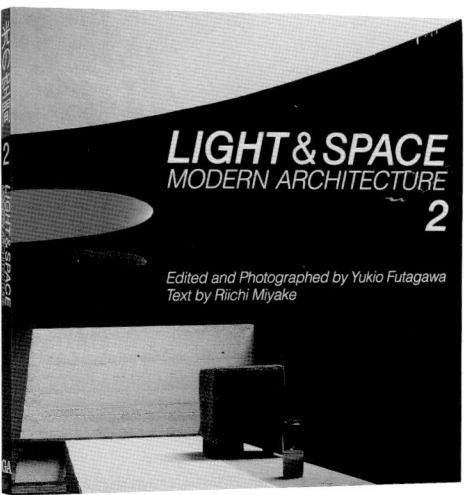

*Light is a fundamental element of architecture.
Through the finest examples
from the beginning of Modernism to the present,
this compendium examines
the way natural light is captured,
altered, and shaped in
architectural space.*

空間を構成する根源的な要素である光。
あふれる自然の光をとらえ，
絞り込み，屈折させ，
形を与えて内部に導き入れる。
近代建築の黎明期から現代にいたる，
光と影を主役として織りなされてきた
建築空間の集大成。

Vol. 1
光と近代建築―パオロ・ポルトゲジ
Light and Modern Architecture *by Paolo Portoghesi*
鉄とガラスの神話　The Myth of Iron and Glass
空の簒奪　Usurpation of the Sky
樹木のアレゴリー　Allegory of Trees
世紀末の光と影　Light and Shadow in the Fin-de-Siècle
胎内への窓　Window to the Womb
透明な質感　The Texture of Transparency
形而上学的な光　Metaphysical Light

216 pages, 30 in color ￥5,806

Vol. 2
輝く額　The Shining Brow
建築の快楽　The Pleasure of Architecture
東方への旅　Travel to the Orient
ガラス箱の神話　The Myth of the Glazed Box
透視できる建築　See-Through Architecture
影のない光　Light without Shadow
始原の光　Primitive Light
ねばっこい空間　Sticky Space
メカニカルな空　The Mechanical Sky
被膜の建築　Architecture of Membrane

216 pages, 24 in color ￥5,806

COMBINED ISSUE 合本
(*HARD COVER* 上製)

426 pages, 54 in color ￥14,369

Japanese and Enaglish texts, Size: 364×257 mm

La Maison de Verre

Pierre Chareau EDITED & PHOTOGRAPHED by Yukio Futagawa TEXT & DRAWINGS by Bernard Bauchet TEXT by Marc Vellay

ガラスの家：
ダルザス邸

企画・撮影＝二川幸夫　　文・図面＝ベルナール・ボシェ／翻訳：三宅理一

Built in the center of Paris, La Maison de Verre is neither a work which can be overlooked for it avant-garde qualities, nor as a landmark in the history of Modern Architecture. This volume attempts to give an overall picture of this major work with photographs and survey drawings.

1932年，パリのサンジェルマン大通りに近い，古いアパートの1，2階に嵌め込まれた＜ガラスの家＞は，スチールとガラスブロックの大胆な構成で，近代建築史上，その前衛性からも注目すべき建築である。光の浸透というテーマがどのような構成の原理と空間構成のテクニックのうえに成立しているのか。特別撮影の写真と実測図面により解明する。

English/Japanese texts
Size: 300×307 mm ／180 total pages, 42 in color ￥5,806

表記価格に消費税は含まれておりません。

GA HOUSES

GA HOUSES documents outstanding new residential architecture from all over the world. Included in each issue also are retrospective looks at residential works of the past which are now considered epoch-making. This magazine is essential not only for architects and architectural students but for those who wish to master the art of living.

世界各国の住宅を現地取材により次々に紹介してゆくシリーズ。最近の作品はもちろん、近代住宅の古典の再検討、現代建築家の方法論、集合住宅のリポートなど、住宅に関わる問題点を広い範囲にわたってとりあげてゆく。

Vols. 1–16, 18–24, 28, 31, 34, 52, 55 are out of print.
1–16、18–24、28、31、34、52、55号は絶版。
(17, 25, 37, 48, 49, 53, 56, 59, 60, 63号は在庫僅少)
Size: 300×228mm

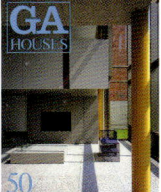

---

50 作品：イスラエル／ノタ／ホルバーグ／クルック＆セクストン／ヴァレリオ／セイトヴィッツ／ベルケル／坂本他
Israel; Nota; Hallberg; Krueck & Sexton; Valerio; Saitowitz; Berkel; Sakamoto; and others
160 pages, 72 in color　￥2,903

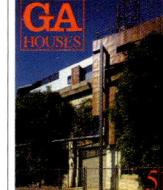

51 作品：ロト・アーキテクツ／マイヤー／ウォルドマン／ヒルドナー／マック／テン・アルキテクトス／ジョイ
Roto Architects; Meier; Waldman; Hildner; Mack; Ten Arquitectos; Joy
160 pages, 72 in color　￥2,903

53 連載：世界の村と街―西アフリカ・セネガル／巨匠の住宅―R・M・シンドラー 作品：モーフォシス／ナイルズ／他
Villages & Towns—Senegal; Essays on Residential Masterpieces—R. M. Schindler; Morphosis; Niles; and others
158 pages, 64 in color　￥2,903

54 連載：世界の村と街―イエメン 作品：コーニッグ／キャピー／ロックフェラー／フリカク／マック／齋藤／妹島他
Villages & Towns—Yemen; Koenig; Kappe; Rockefeller/Hricak; Mack; Saito; Sejima; and others
160 pages, 72 in color　￥2,848

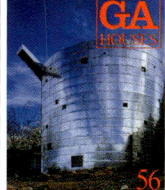

56 連載：世界の村と街―西アフリカ、ガーナ 作品：ブルーダー／アーリック／スコーギン／イーラム／ブレイ／マイヤー／ザパタ他
Villages & Towns—West Africa; Bruder; Ehrlich; Scogin/Elam/Bray; Meier; Zapata; and others
160 pages, 72 in color　￥2,848

57 連載：世界の村と街―インドネシア 作品：安藤忠雄／コールハース／ペリアン／カラチ＆アルヴァレス／レゴレッタ／他
Villages & Towns—Indonesia; Ando; Koolhaas; Perriand; Kalach & Alvarez; Legorreta; and others
160 pages, 72 in color　￥2,848

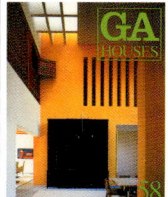

58 作品：レゴレッタ／原広司／スコーギン／イーラム／ブレイ／村上徹／岸和郎／中東壽一／マック／他
Works: Legorreta; Hara; Scogin/Elam/Bray; Murakami; Kishi; Nakahigashi; Mack; and others
160 pages, 72 in color　￥2,848

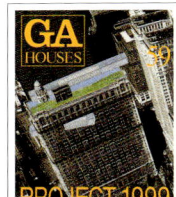

59 特集号：プロジェクト1999
Special Issue: Project 1999
176 pages, 32 in color　￥2,848

60 住宅デザインのコツ―安藤忠雄 作品：マイヤー／入江経一／ブルーダー／ジョイ／伊東豊雄／ナイルズ／八木敦司他
Tips on House Design: Tadao Ando Works: Meier; Irie; Bruder; Joy; Ito; Niles; Yagi; and others
160 pages, 72 in color　￥2,848

61 住宅デザインのコツ：スコーギン／イーラム／ブレイ 作品：マイヤーズ／ミラージェス／ソウ・デ・モウラ／レゴレッタ／他
Tips on House Design: Scogin/Elam/Bray Works: Myers; Miralles; Legorreta; Aoki; and others
160 pages, 72 in color　￥2,848

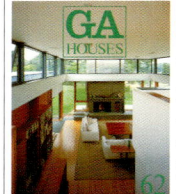

62 住宅デザインのコツ：トッド・ウィリアムズ ビリー・ツィン 作品：カラチ／テン・アルキテクトス／ノタ／マック／他
Tips on House Design: Williams/Tsien Works: Kalach; Ten Arquitectos; Nota; Mack; Ehrlich; and others
160 pages, 72 in color　￥2,848

63 特集号：プロジェクト2000
Special Issue: Project 2000
176 pages, 40 in color　￥2,848

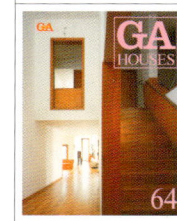

64 住宅デザインのコツ：ファーナウ＆ハートマン 作品：シザ／ホール／スミス＝ミラー＋ホーキンソン／レゴレッタ／他
Tips on House Design: Fernau & Hartman Works: Siza; Holl; Smith-Miller+Hawkinson; and others
160 pages, 72 in color　￥2,848

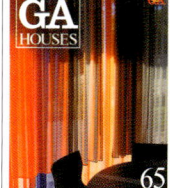

65 巨匠の住宅：リナー・ボー・バルディ 作品：ブルーダー／セイトヴィッツ／妹島和世／キャピー／岸和郎／他
Residential Masterpieces: Rina Bo & P.M. Bardi Works: Bruder; Saitowitz; Sejima; Kappe; and others
144 pages, 72 in color　￥2,848

66 特集号：プロジェクト2001
Special Issue: Project 2001
176 pages, 48 in color　￥2,848

67 編集長インタヴュー：岸和郎 作品：岸和郎／D・ノタ／北川原温／竹山聖／鈴木了二／R・ジョイ／青木淳／高松伸他
A Dialogue with Editor: Waro Kishi Works: Kishi; Nota; Kitagawara; Hertz; Takeyama; and others
160 pages, 64 in color　￥2,848

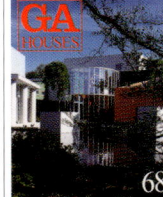

68 編集長インタヴュー：エットーレ・ソットサス 連載：巨匠の住宅―B・ガフ 作品：ソットサス／パトカウ／石山修武／他
A Dialogue with Editor: E. Sottsass Residential Masterpieces: B. Goff Sottsass; Patkau; and others
152 pages, 72 in color　￥2,848

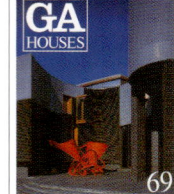

69 編集長インタヴュー：ハリー・サイドラー 作品：スコーギン・イーラム＆ブレイ／サイドラー／エンゲレン／ムーア／他
A Dialogue with Editor: H. Seidler Works: Scogin Elam&Bray; H. Seidler; Engelen Moore; and others
160 pages, 72 in color　￥2,848

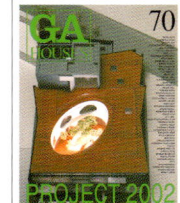

70 特集号：プロジェクト2002
Special Issue: Project 2002
160 pages, 56 in color　￥2,848

71 巨匠の住宅：ピエール・コーニッグ 作品：遠藤政樹＋池田昌弘／小野正弘／三分一博志／他
Residential Masterpieces: Pierre Koenig Works: Meier; Smith-Miller + Hawkinson; Saitowitz; and others
152 pages, 76 in color　￥2,848

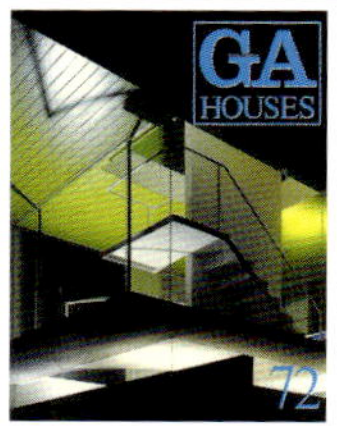

72 編集長インタヴュー：マティアス・クロッツ 作品：クロッツ／岸和郎／米田明＋池田昌弘／遠藤政樹＋池田昌弘／アレッツ
A Dialogue with Editor: M. Klotz Works: Klotz; Kishi; Yoneda + Ikeda; Endo + Ikeda; Arets
160 pages, 72 in color　￥2,848

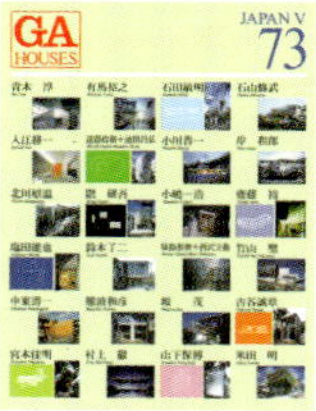

73 特別号：日本の現代住宅 第5集
Special Issue: JAPAN V
224 pages, 96 in color　￥3,200

74 特集号：プロジェクト2003
Special Issue: Project 2003
168 pages, 56 in color　￥2,848

75 編集長インタヴュー：グレン・マーカット 作品：マーカット／ゴッドセル／スタッチベリー／高松伸／アトリエ・ワン／他
A Dialogue with Editor: G. Murcutt Works: Murcutt; Godsell; Stutchbury; Atelier Bow-Wow; and others
160 pages, 80 in color　￥2,848

76 作品：エブナー＋ウルマン／ブルーダー／ドリエンデル／伊東豊雄／塩田能也／サイトヴィッツ／小嶋一浩／他
Works: Ebner+Ullmann; Bruder; Driendl; Ito; Endo+Ikeda; Shiota; Saitowitz; Kojima; and others
160 pages, 80 in color　￥2,848

77 巨匠の住宅：ル・コルビュジエ 作品：スコーギン＋エラム／宮本佳明／ニール／石山修武／アトリエ・ワン／他
Residential Masterpieces: Le Corbusier Works: Scogin Elam; Arima; Neal; Sambuichi; and others
152 pages, 96 in color　￥2,848

78 作品：ドリエンデル／レゴレッタ＋レゴレッタ／クヴェルクラフト／大堀伸／ジェネラルデザイン／長田直之／他
Works: Driendl; Legorreta+Legorreta; Querkraft; Ohori/General Design; Nagata; and others
160 pages, 88 in color　￥2,848

79 連載：家具デザイナー①ロン・アラッド／世界の村と街―中国、烏鎮 作品：クロッツ／ドゥケ・モタ／坂茂／有馬裕之／他
Furniture Designers ①Ron Arad; Villages & Towns—China Works: Klotz; Duque Motta; Ban; Arima; and others
152 pages, 88 in color　￥2,848

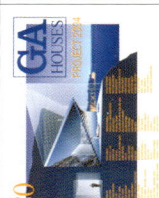

80 特集号：プロジェクト2004
Special Issue: Project 2004
176 pages, 84 in color　￥2,848

81 ミラノ・サローネ・レポート2004 連載：家具デザイナー②ロス・ラブグローブ 作品：キャピー／ハーツ／オハーリヒー／他
Milano Salone Report 2004; Furniture Designers ②Ross Lovegrove; Works: Sejima, Hayakusa, Sander; and others
160 pages, 88 in color　￥2,848

82 連載：家具デザイナー③コンスタンティン・グルチッチ 作品：ドリエンドル／ロイキンド／テン・アルキテクトス／他
Furniture Designers ③Konstantin Grcic; Works: Arima, Davids Killory, Abe, Fujimori, Swatt; and others
160 pages, 88 in color　￥2,848

83 新刊 連載：家具デザイナー④ジャスパー・モリソン／世界の村と街―イタリア、プロチダ島 作品：スタッチベリー／青木／都留／他
Furniture Designers ④Jasper Morrison; Villages & Towns—Procida; Works: Ando, Lanzinger, and others
160 pages, 96 in color　￥2,848

表記価格には消費税は含まれておりません。